CHINA AND OTHER MATTERS

China and Other Matters

BENJAMIN I. SCHWARTZ

Harvard University Press
Cambridge, Massachusetts
London, England
1996

Library of Congress Cataloging-in-Publication Data
Schwartz, Benjamin Isadore, 1916–
China and other matters / Benjamin I. Schwartz.
p.   cm.
Includes bibliographical references and index.
ISBN 0-674-11751-4 (cloth).—ISBN 0-674-11752-2 (pbk.)
1. China—Politics and government—1976– 2. Communism—China.
3. China—History. I. Title.
DS779.26.S32   1996
951—dc20
95-50479

To my beloved grandsons
Nitai, Adam, and Daniel

Contents

CHINA AND OTHER MATTERS

Introduction

*I*n re-examining these writings written over a period of some thirty years, I am as struck as others may be by their diversity, though they are all focused on that vast area of collective human experience known as China. I shall not claim that taken together they represent a tightly coherent system of thought or an equally unimpeachable expertise. I would simply suggest that at least in my own retrospective perception they do reflect certain underlying persistent preoccupations as well as more immediate responses to the shifting intellectual trends of American and general western thought during the years since the end of World War II. For better or worse, they represent an attitude which is now fashionably called "self-referential"— not in the sense that it is concerned with one's own individual subjectivity but in that it assumes that it is impossible to achieve an understanding of the cultural "Other" without a constant awareness of one's involvement with one's own culture, society, and historic location. I would hasten to add, however, that since these writings do aspire to an understanding of various aspects of China past and present, it is clear that I do not accept the view that such "self-referentiality" necessarily involves either dogmatic cultural relativism or the view that the otherness of China past or present is either inherently incommensurable or incommunicable.[1]

The range and diversity of topics discussed transgress the accepted boundaries among different fields of knowledge as these have emerged in the human sciences in the post-war years. They cut across the boundary between the modern and the traditional and assume an ongoing interplay between the two. They do not accept the boundary between the notion of "area studies" as a totally empirical fact-gathering enterprise and the notion of pure social scientific theory. They are also inclined to find the rigid boundaries among such disciplines as history, political science, economics, and anthropology to be highly problematic. While disciplinary analysis no doubt sheds light on the study of other cultures, the study of other cultures will also raise questions about the boundaries and causal claims of the disciplines themselves.

Instead of providing an apologia, however, I shall here venture to present a personal account of my own encounter with the study of China during the post-war years. While some of my attitudes were undoubtedly pre-formed, the experience of my fellow graduate students (many of them war veterans) and myself in the China program, organized by Professor John Fairbank at Harvard in the early post-war years, was to have a crucial impact on our subsequent development. While the China of this period still may have been the exotic Other, it was no longer the remote Other. During World War II we had become deeply enmeshed in the internal politics of China, and after the war we were deeply involved in the crisis which was to lead to the Chinese Communist victory of 1949. China, in fact, had become deeply enmeshed in American domestic politics.

The otherness of China was also now deeply entangled with that looming formidable Other known as World Communism. Soviet communism was thought of as alien, yet like Nazism before it, it appeared to be a transmutation of many aspects of modern Western history and exercised an enormous attraction for many in the West who still regarded it as the global "wave of the future." What then was the relationship of China to Communism and of both to us?

John Fairbank, who had recently returned from his position as an OSS officer in China, had been thoroughly caught up in the agonizing conditions of China during the last days of the Nationalist government and on the eve of the ascendancy of the Chinese Communist movement. As a "China scholar-specialist" he was convinced that the new China would play a significant role in the future history of mankind and was thus thoroughly dismayed by the prospect of a total rupture of relations between China and the USA. He most successfully conveyed his sense of urgency even to those of his students who were less policy-oriented than he. Our thorough absorption in contemporary China was not, however, simply another manifestation of American presentism and practicality. China connected to some of the most absorbing intellectual problems of the time: What was Soviet Communism and why its appeal? How did it relate to Chinese society? What accounted for the weak appeal of American liberal democracy in China and the rest of the world? While we now remember the 1950s as a period of enormous confidence, China forcefully turned our attentions to those aspects of the era which paradoxically earned it the designation "age of anxiety."

Nevertheless, one of the more buoyant manifestations of the era was the surge of confidence in the claims of the post-war social sciences, which at the time tended to bold all-embracing theories, models, and paradigms. Among these were totalistic theories of Communism as well as all-embracing explanations of "backward" (later often referred to as "developing") societies. John Fairbank was determined to expose us to these theories and models which might provide us with the keys to an understanding of contemporary China.

The theories and models were laden with potential explanatory power. Thus Karl August Wittfogel's theory of "Oriental Despotism" seemed to explain the entire nature of past Chinese society and culture as well as the modern totalitarian projection of despotism in both China and the Soviet Union, while other theories of totalitarianism such as those of Professor Karl Friedrich tended to explain totalitarianism as a thoroughly modern phenomenon which presupposed modern material and social technology. Yet whatever the differences between the Wittfogelian and what might be called the "modern" theory of totalitarianism, in projecting the future both theories assumed a watertight system immune to any fundamental change from within.

There were other paradigms and models to which we were exposed, including the particular mode of Marxism projected by Stalinist Communism itself, which assumed the universality of the unilinear progressive movement of history through slave society, feudal society, and capitalist society to the ultimate Communist society. This unilinear scheme was now enshrined as official doctrine in both Moscow and Peking. In contrast to the totalistic otherness of "Oriental Despotism," here we find a dissolution of all significant differences between the trajectory of Western and Chinese social and cultural evolution except for the awkward fact that the "feudal stage" of Chinese development seems to have maintained its tenacious hold until the very brink of the Communist revolution.

Later in the 1950s, there was the gradual emergence (or re-emergence) in the West of a third social scientific paradigm: modernization theory. Like Soviet Marxist theory, it posits a universal line of social evolution from "traditional" to "modern society." It shares with the Communist theory the notion that the basic moving forces are economic. The ultimate telos, however, is a mature, industrialized market economy plus liberal democracy. This view of development both challenged Communism and also seemed to challenge the notion of an immobile totalitarianism. The death of Stalin, the rise of Khrushchev, and the retreat of state terrorism in the Soviet Union helped foster the view among some development theorists that Soviet and even Chinese Communism represented not so much a frozen unchangeable totalitarian system as a stage in late-developing traditional societies. Others, however, believed that totalitarian systems might actually prove compatible with technical and economic growth, or that fundamental features of totalitarian systems could remain intact at the heart of what might be an alternative version of modernity itself.

In addition to these more dominant paradigms, we also became familiarized with other theories drawn from the disciplines of cultural anthropology, social psychology, and even linguistics which emphasized not so much theories of social evolution as particular salient features of Chinese culture or even the structures of language as determinative in maintaining an unbridgeable cognitive and cultural gulf between China and the West.

Without denying the possible heuristic value of these and other hypotheses, I must confess that from the outset I found myself enormously resistant to the "scientistic" pretensions which underlay them. Having barely stuck our toes into the vast sea of human experience known as China we were being invited to assume the posture of the unconditioned scientist as the "transcendent subject" who scrutinizes China as the object of his theories.

This sense of resistance was actually encouraged by the fact that while Professor Fairbank was indeed most anxious that we should explore the latest systematic social scientific theories, he himself was a China scholar who had been trained in an older historical methodology. This methodology stressed intensive language study and the ability to handle secondary and primary sources in the Chinese language, particularly sources relating to the nineteenth and twentieth centuries. While this school of history writing may have its own "scientistic" pretensions, the concept of science involved was the Baconian inductionist view. The scientist approaches the world of facts not so much with a comprehensive model as with a totally unconditioned "tabula rasa." Whatever the limitations of this positivist model, it had the immense merit of bringing us into contact through the study of documents with the voices of actual Chinese human beings, living and dead. Such documents, it is often asserted, reflect only the outlooks of the small political and intellectual elite. While this may indeed be true and while efforts have been made and must be made to understand all segments of a population, the absence of actual living human beings, whether elite or masses, seemed to be a staggering omission in all the models we had been asked to examine. For better or worse, both the utterances and the deeds of the elite had an enormous relevance to the confirmation or rejection of the available paradigms.

What is involved here is not simply the contest between the mindless accumulation of atomic facts and the application of "theory." It may be true that most observations of fact (which presuppose the question of which facts we choose to observe) are "theory-laden" as Popper maintains, although one cannot absolutize even this generalization. There are times when simple facts may kill a theory. Yet China is not a mass of self-enclosed atomic facts but vast regions and networks of human experience. If the word "empirical" refers to vast collective experiences such as the "Opium War" or "the Taiping Rebellion," we soon find that it is impossible to discuss the "empirical" without the presence of implicit or explicit theoretical assumptions. The universalistic claims of externally imposed paradigms must be constantly and mercilessly exposed to the complexity of concrete experience, which may challenge the paradigms themselves. Thus, one of the more interesting projects undertaken by John Fairbank during this period was the compilation and translation, with Professor Teng Ssu-yü, of a collection of Chinese diplomatic documents from the Opium War. I found these documents more exciting and revelatory than the large theoretical models we were hastily being invited to impose on this vast collective experience of China.

However exotic the categories used in these documents, they nevertheless introduced us to an age-long Chinese discourse in the realm of what we call "foreign affairs." They also called our attention to the complexity of the internal politics of China in the early nineteenth century and to the influences of individual personalities. If there were attitudes which reflected an all-enveloping "oriental despotic" orientation, there were other attitudes and policies to which the whole concept seemed irrelevant.

As we sporadically and painfully acquired the ability to read Chinese texts, we had the sense of entering a new, complex, and multidimensional world. It was, to be sure, the world of the politically and intellectually articulate. Much of what we read was in the "colloquial" Chinese of the post–May 4th period, a language laden with Sino-Japanese neologisms designed to translate Western ideas. Despite the fact that this was "modern Chinese," a language responding to the West, the question of whether we could really understand remained. Was the meaning of terms really communicated through the Chinese neologisms? Indeed, now one might add Derrida's cogitations about the profound difference occasioned by the role of writing as such in China's non-phonetic writing system. Nevertheless, whatever the difficulties, and whatever the errors made, one had the perhaps presumptuous feeling that the range of indeterminacy in interpretation may not have been radically different from the range within western culture. Despite their individual biases, these texts remain one of our main sources of access to the political, intellectual, and even social history of twentieth-century China.[2]

Fairbank's approach encouraged us to study not only the modern colloquial Chinese of post–May 4th China but also the forbidding classical Chinese of late Ch'ing China. In order to understand the transitional China of the twentieth century it would be crucial to understand the process of internal decay in the late traditional culture. While his own interest lay in the study of the late Ch'ing imperial state and its foreign relations, he did not object to the interest which some of us had in its intellectual history. In dealing with traditional China, Fairbank was himself drawn to systemic theories which emphasized the constants of the society and the culture. In dealing with decay, however, one had to deal not only with enduring social structures and institutions but with the much disdained history of events. Decay is a process which unfolds in time. Here one must perforce be interested not only in institutionalized blueprints but in the play of policy and of interests. Here individual agents, personality, and even the shifting winds of ideas may decisively effect reality. With all their built-in limits, documents and texts become indispensable.

In coping with traditional documents, we were confronting a language and world much less accessible than the language and world of twentieth-century "colloquial Chinese" texts. Both the language of state documents and the intellectual discourse of the literati were soaked in the idiom of a different world. The discourse of the documents was full of terms referring to age-long debates; everywhere one was confronted with allusions and tropes for which the available dictionaries were an unreliable guide. On the side of intellectual history, while it was generally agreed that Confucianism was the dominant current of eighteenth- and nineteenth-century thought, much of what we knew about Confucianism was based on a few presumably unproblematic quotations or misquotations from texts such as the Analects. In fact, the texts which we read were encrusted with the hermeneutical efforts of centuries. However limited our understanding, it was quite obvious that these literati often vehemently disagreed, with each other reacting against what they regarded as the false interpretations of preceding centuries. Reading or misreading the Analects would not suffice in reading these literati much more than the reading of the gospel of St. Luke would make us completely capable of understanding the quarrels between the Thomists and the Occamists, or how those quarrels related to the entire political, social, and cultural situation of late medieval Europe. Even if terms such as "Oriental Despotism" or "Traditional Society" may have thrown some light on certain enduring aspects of the society, they shed little light on synchronic and diachronic differences and tensions, on intergeneration strife, or on current affairs.

Even though this study of the texts raised grave questions about the validity of the simple social science models, other questions remained concerning the incommunicable nature of other cultures, based at first on linguistic determinism and cultural relativism and then on certain tendencies of post-modern thought. Did we really understand what we were reading? Despite the indeterminacy of translation[3] and the real problems of "culture-boundedness," many have emerged with the conviction that it is possible to grasp the concerns which lie behind the discourse of other cultures. Difference is ever present but it is not ultimately inaccessible.

This preoccupation with the consciousness and actions of actual human beings was of burning relevance both to our concerns with the contemporary history of China, including the evolution of the People's Republic, and to the understanding of its cultural past. It was, however, an orientation which seemed to run counter both to the dominant social scientific theoretical claims of the 1950s, and to the post-modern deconstructionist negation of any trans-cultural "humanism."

Without attempting any deep philosophic analysis, I should like to clarify what I refer to as the role of human consciousness in the study of cultures. By consciousness I refer not only to the language of cognition, but also to the language of willing, feeling, and intentional acts. The human consciousness involved is the fallible consciousness of individuals and not the march of ideas in the Hegelian sense. It assumes that consciousness may serve interests and rationalize interests. It may also make truth claims. Ideas may transcend interest and may come to serve interests. It may remain unreflectively within the boundaries of certain persistent cultural orientations as "collective mentalities" or it may deal with these orientations in a reflective-hermeneutic manner. It may even reject cultural orientations and accept tendencies introduced from foreign cultures. It is, of course, in constant interaction with a world of external "forces" both natural and socio-political, and with completely contingent situations. Finally, the realm of conscious life, far from being exclusively the abode of ideality and luminous reason, is also an area in which human uncertainty, fallibility, alienation, and moral conflict are most plainly evident. The riddle of how the same human beings who are bound to their culture, to their historic locus, to their class, status, and psychological temperaments aspire to make truth claims and to act on the bases of these claims is a riddle for us as much as it is for Chinese ancient and modern. To the extent that we must wrestle with the question of how much the intentions of human agents affect the outcomes of events, it is a question for us as well as for them. There is no privileged vantage point. While I found myself equally concerned with these questions as they applied to China past and present, for various reasons, including the sense of urgency and excitement aroused by the rise of the Communists to power, I soon found that my first research efforts focused on twentieth-century history and on the rise of Chinese Communism.

In dealing with the contemporary scene we did have access to an impressive corpus of reportage by journalists and government personnel who provided us with extensive information on political developments in the China of the late 1940s. Some of the more intrepid journalists even provided us with vivid, grim depictions of the sufferings of urban and rural masses during the same period of turmoil. Yet any sustained effort to explore in depth the conscious attitudes of the Chinese actors involved in these events was absent, with notable exceptions such as Edgar Snow's *Red Star over China,* which devoted considerable space to interviews with Mao Tse-tung and other Communist leaders. His interviews with Mao put a face on this remarkable political figure who was to play such a crucial role in the subsequent history of Chinese Communism. Yet Mao's own account, which seems to be accepted by Snow as a kind of official, authorized interpretation of the previous history of the Chinese Communist movement, is full of allusions and references to an entire complex world of political and intellectual discourse. It is impossible to reconstruct an accurate story of Mao's position without reference to the vast literature of books, periodicals, and political documents relating the entire political, social, and intellectual history of twentieth-century China. This literature reflects not only the world of ideas in the heads of the actors but also how such ideas interacted with group and individual interests and passions, and clashed with recalcitrant external realities and unforeseen contingencies.

Within the literature of reportage which emerged from China on the eve of the Communist victory, one of the main issues was that of whether the Chinese Communists were essentially "Marxist-Leninist" Communists who derived their strategies and authority from Moscow or whether they were the representatives of a Chinese revolution which might eventually move in a somewhat more "liberal" or social democratic direction rather than in a Stalinist Communist direction. The partisans of the monolithic "World Communism" school pointed to the obvious Marxist-Leninist vocabulary of the Chinese Communists and to their obvious acknowledgment of Stalin's spiritual authority. Those who stressed the unique Chineseness of the Yenan strategies of the CCP, often on the basis of their own observations, pointed to all of those features of the Yenan experience which seemed to mark an obvious departure from the image of Stalin's communism. Many features of the Yenan strategy were also favorably contrasted to the policies and politics of a demoralized Nationalist government. Many American liberal observers discerned and exaggerated the significance of what they regarded as evidence of the beginnings of "liberal" democratic institutions. By relying, as realistic journalists, on what they regarded as the concrete, empirical behavior of the Chinese Communists rather than on the gray abstraction of their Marxist-Leninist texts, they were hopeful that a Chinese revolution would move in what they regarded as a more benign and independent direction.

My own early efforts to cope with some of the texts of the Chinese Communist movement led me to believe that only a study of the inner history of the Chinese Communist movement based on a study of the texts of the movement in their relationship to the concrete historic circumstances of the early decades of the twentieth century and to the personalities and groups which constituted the movement could provide us with any true evidence of how ideological doctrine actually related to behavior. The interpretation of the texts was itself a hazardous and limited enterprise. As a study of the "elite vanguard," it certainly did not explain the "mentalities" of those who came to provide the "mass-basis" of the Communist movement. It nevertheless provided a strong sense both of the degree to which the mental world of the leadership had come to be influenced by the categories of Marxism-Leninism and of the degree to which these categories came to be "molded and twisted by living men operating in concrete situations and animated by a variety of motives."[4]

By the time I had completed my thesis on the Chinese Communist movement, the Chinese Communists had come to power, Chairman Mao had clearly enunciated his "lean to one side policy," and internal Chinese developments of the next few years seemed to vindicate the views of those who stressed the relentless power of the Soviet system to impose itself on others. Mao's "lean to one side" policy, when reinforced by the growing tendency in the early 1950s to internalize Soviet models in every sphere of life, seemed to reconfirm the power of World Communism and the strategic sagacity of the Soviet leadership which had shaped and controlled the system.

To many cold war revisionists, it often appears as obvious that a Soviet Union enormously enfeebled by the wholesale destructiveness of World War II could hardly turn its attention to the conquest of the world. Yet what actually mesmerized the post-war world was not the material power of the Soviet Union but the moral and "scientific" power of the "system," or its ideology. To many ardent western anti-Communists of a religious orientation, it was the ideas themselves which had a kind of dark Satanic power. To many secular social and political scientists, however, the potency lay not so much in the surface ideology as in the deep underlying "operational code" which endowed those who controlled the system with insights into what might be called the science of power.

To what extent did I share the cold war anxieties? While I had never been attracted to either the moral or scientific claims of Marxism-Leninism and found the Stalinist development of Soviet Communism abhorrent, it nevertheless seemed entirely understandable that many of the themes and claims of Soviet Communism would continue to make a powerful appeal to many elements in the non–western world and even in the West itself. Thus, the very Leninist conception of the Communist party as a kind of transcendental body which embodied all those infallible moral and intellectual capacities which Marx had attributed to the world proletariat continued to exercise a potent appeal particularly after the heroic Soviet victories in World War II. I did share anxieties about the ongoing powerful appeal of many Soviet Communist themes and claims. I soon found, however, that I did not share the belief in the "scientific" bases of the ideology as an "operational code."

In many ways the Chinese Communist victory of 1949 and the course of policy pursued by the People's Republic during the early 1950s seemed to vindicate and reinforce the notion of a fundamentally monolithic world Communism centered in Moscow not only for true believers but also for some of the most vehement theorists of anti-Communism. As already stated, Mao's clear adoption of the "lean to one side" policy as well as the increasing tendency until the mid-1950s to internalize Stalinist social and economic models seemed to push well into the background the significance of the Titoist challenge to Moscow's authority and effectively to refute the claims that Maoist strategies and claims to ideological authority had played any significant role in the Chinese Communist victory. Whether one spoke of Communism as an impersonal system or as a kind of infernal manipulative science of power created by an elite of social engineers who understood the evolving machinery of the contemporary world, it was clear that the true architects and masters of the "operational code" resided in Moscow. In Eastern Europe, it was clear that Moscow's authority reigned supreme. Yet despite the Titoist defection in Yugoslavia, it was assumed that even Communist parties which had seemingly come to power through their own efforts would remain subject to the controlling spiritual authority of Moscow. Indeed, despite the Tito challenge, the concept of the power of the integrated system of world Communism as it applied to China maintained its ascendancy among experts who studied Communism until the mid-1950s. All signs pointed to a growing "Sovietization" of China.

In the mid-1950s, however, China's course became erratic. From the Hundred Flowers Campaign of 1956 to the Cultural Revolution, the attention of "China watchers" was now forcibly drawn to the twists and turns of the history of events and also to the person of Mao Tse-tung, who seemed to play such a crucial role in all these events. To make a crude generalization, what we find during these decades is a growing divergence between the image of the "Soviet expert" and the "China watcher." On the one hand one finds among the Soviet experts a growing tendency to focus on what they regarded as the constant, invariant features of what appeared to be a stable Soviet "system" or model, at least as far as the internal organization of the Soviet Union was concerned. While Soviet experts in the early years of the Soviet regime had been acutely aware of the enormous role of Stalin in creating the Stalinist model of socialism, once established the model remained largely intact for the rest of his life. It had, as it were, assumed a life of its own apart from the Leader. After Stalin's death there was some discussion of whether mass terror was an organic feature of the system, and during the Khrushchev period, there was even some speculation concerning the possibility of fundamental change. After Khrushchev's departure from power, however, the view prevailed that not only were the fundamental elements of the system in place, but that it was a system which could probably not be "deconstructed" from within. This was a view which could be easily harmonized with the kind of model or paradigm so dominant in the academic social and political sciences of the West. While many "China watchers" were quite as anxious as the Soviet experts to reveal the "model" of the Chinese system and while there was much academic pressure on them to do so, in the period after 1955 it became glaringly apparent that Chairman Mao's relationship to this model of socialism was by no means the same as that of Stalin to his own creation. When confronted with vast new problems and new historic contingencies after the death of Stalin, Mao was now only too willing to draw on his own "Marxist-Leninist" interpretations of the pre-war experience of the CCP *as well as* on the wisdom of Stalin, whose status as apostolic predecessor he never totally rejected. The abrupt shifts from the "liberalism" of the Hundred Flowers movement to the "ultra-collectivism" of the Great Leap Forward and to the Cultural Revolution forced all of us to focus our attention on the shifting episodes of the post-1956 period and on the role of Mao Tse-tung in all these shifts rather than on social scientific analyses of the "Chinese system." The blunt fact was that if the new policy directions envisioned in such movements as the Hundred Flowers Campaign of 1956–57 and the Great Leap Forward had been carried forward without obstruction they would probably have led to fundamental change in the entire model established in the 1952–1955 period. The Cultural Revolution, despite its spectacular destructive activities, provided no discernible blueprint of a new order. In times of extraordinary flux it thus becomes enormously difficult to separate the history of the "underlying forces" from the history of events. In the case of China during these years it also became very difficult to consider the shifting events of the period from the mid-1950s to the death of Chairman Mao without reference to the conscious attitudes of the "leader." Whatever the nature of Mao's later interpretations of Marxism-Leninism, they had certainly ceased to be tied to any specific socio-political model.

However numerous the strictures and objections one may raise against the "great man theory of history," one can hardly understand the episodes in the history of the People's Republic after 1955 without reference to the conscious initiatives of the Chairman. The "theory" is certainly subject to a host of qualifications, yet the fact remains that his role was inescapable.

It can be argued that in many ways the entire previous history of Marxism-Leninism from Lenin to Mao had somehow demanded the creation of a space for the notion of the transcendent leader and for the "cult of personality." As suggested in later chapters, in China this may have also resonated with traditions deriving from Chinese themes of the sage-king. It also is quite clear that Mao's own erratic individual evolution cannot be comprehended apart from the entire social, intellectual, and political evolution of twentieth-century China. It can clearly be shown that he by no means foresaw the unintended consequences of his own initiatives and that he even participated in the abortion of these initiatives when their consequences became apparent. It is also quite clear that his shifting attitudes and actions were greatly influenced by his relationships to various groups and individuals within the ruling group. In dealing with his legacy one can see that in the short run his own interventions in the "system" of the 1950s which affected almost every part of it from agriculture to the concept and practice of the party indirectly prepared the ground for the bold initiatives and continuing flux of the Deng Xiaoping era. Yet as time recedes it becomes ever more doubtful that the Chinese Revolution of 1949 created a millennial "new order," and the question of the long-term legacy of Mao becomes ever less clear. To the extent that it is legitimate to speak in historical theory of "periods of transition" one might say that the "Communist" phase of the twentieth century of China still belongs to China's period of transition—a period in which mainland China's relations to its cultural past, to the outer world with which it is ever more involved and to that whole unresolved complexity which we call modernity remains, for better or worse, open and unresolved. When viewed in this historic framework, Mao's role may shrink to more modest proportions.

Yet in dealing with the recent past of China—with what might be called the "short-durational" or the generational history of the Communist period, I do not feel that the pieces in this collection which deal with the contemporary scene exaggerate the significance of the figure of Mao Tse-tung. In dealing with the history of the emerging present in Communist China, one now finds that one cannot make judgments about the durability of structures or the depth of underlying long-term trends without focusing on the actual attitudes and praxis of individuals and small groups and in the Chinese case particularly the attitude of the helmsman himself. Without making any case whatsoever for Mao as a great philosopher one can say that his shifting attitudes and projects relate to some of the most complex and deep-laid problems of a Chinese society in flux as well as to the relationship between China's cultural past and the entire complex of modernity. Even the Chairman's frustrations and disappointments throw light directly on the massive resistance he encountered in attempting to realize his projects and on the strains and tensions which existed within the society. As long as he lived, his sacred power to intervene in every sector of the society, whether wielded by himself or others, continued to inhibit all possibilities of "model-building."

While the efforts to achieve some grasp of the contemporary scene in China were, to be sure, subject to severe constraints, it will be noted that most of the writings in this collection are concerned with aspects of China's past—both the twentieth-century pre-Communist past and the past of the traditional culture, as well as on reflections concerning the relation of the past to the present. The question of how contemporary China related to the cultural past could not be ignored, even by the most present-minded "China watchers." Did Chinese Communism and the "Thought of Chairman Mao" represent a continuity with the past or a fundamental break with that past? Not only was the debate continuous, but it took on a different coloration with every shift in current policy. Since many of those who participated were primarily concerned with the present, they were eager to find a simple model of the past which would allow them to provide a formulaic account of the "traditional setting" in all their books and essays.

In dealing with the history of the Communist party before 1949 one soon found that one could not treat the ideas of the Communist leadership apart from the general intellectual and political history of early twentieth-century China. To a greater or lesser degree most of these people were in touch with the general intellectual discourse of the time. To the extent that they were associated with the "iconoclastic" wing of the so-called May 4th intelligentsia, the leaders of the CCP were part of a much broader group bent on grasping what they regarded as the heart of western modernity at a time when that modernity was itself undergoing the traumas of World War I and the convulsions which followed that war. Where was the heart of modernity and how could it be made to apply to China's contemporary conditions? Even those intellectuals who opted for the Soviet Marxist version of modernity soon became involved in intricate debates on how Marxism could be used to explicate both the chaotic society of contemporary China and the "old society" which had led to these conditions. (See Chapter 1). To the extent that Mao Tsetung claimed to be a "Marxist theorist," his ideas could only make sense within the context of this larger discussion. These Chinese perspectives on the meaning of modernity simply highlighted and threw into bold relief unresolved western dilemmas concerning the nature of modernity.

Although the May 4th iconoclasts were committed to their own versions of modernization, they also felt obliged to base their analyses of China's present condition on some particular interpretation of the old society or the old culture. There were also "neo-traditionalists" who were prepared to defend what they regarded as perennial values and orientations of the past. Like the iconoclasts, however, they differed markedly from each other in their interpretations of the essential core of the traditional. Even those who called themselves Confucianists differed vehemently on whether the essential core of Confucianism lay in the Sung synthesis of Chu Hsi, in the thought of Wang Yang-ming, or in the "empiricist" scholastic thinking of Ch'ing Confucianism. Others even sought inspiration in some of the counter-Confucian tendencies of traditional thought such as Buddhism or in "popular culture." The complexity of this discussion simply confirmed early suspicions that the simplistic models and paradigms of "traditional China" then available to us could not possibly encompass the millennial political, social, and cultural history of China and that there was no substitute for plunging into the vast sea of this collective human experience.

My own growing interest in the culture of the past was by no means fueled simply by the question of how "tradition" related to Communism or to modernization. Since I have never believed that either Communism or some final state of affairs called "modernity" have provided solutions to all the mysteries of human existence, I continue to believe that the entire experience of the human race in all its cultural and historic mutations remains relevant to both the wretchedness and grandeur of the human condition. Attention to this experience may never resolve the entire mystery, but it will certainly enrich our conceptions of the range of indeterminacy in human responses to certain persistent and—dare I say it?—universal human concerns.

In recoil from formulaic and holistic models of the Chinese integrated culture of the past, my bias has been very much toward an emphasis on difference within that culture. It is an ironic fact that the cultural relativism of postmodernism in the West tends to absolutize and totalize the concept of culture itself. The very notions that the western past has been dominated by "logocentrism" and other cultures have lacked logocentrism is a paradox which even Derrida acknowledges. The references to foreign cultures as the "Other" seem to imply that the otherness of foreign cultures is all-embracing, irreducible, and pervasive.

As I have indicated, my interest in the conscious life of the past made me particularly concerned with both the synchronic and diachronic range of difference, tension, and conflict within Chinese culture and of the relations of the cultural to the social and political history of China. It was in dealing with the variety and particularity of the various "parts" of Chinese culture that the sense of the irreducible Other recedes and the problematics of the culture become eminently comparable to the problematics of other cultures. Thus my book *The World of Thought in Ancient China,* which dealt with the ancient intellectual sources of later elite culture, was very much concerned with the range of difference, variety, and tension within that culture.

Nevertheless, the writings contained in this collection describe what seem to be certain dominant cultural and socio-political orientations of Chinese culture. In accounting for this seeming contradiction, I would simply point out that the insistence on the study of difference, variety, and tension was never intended as a total attack on the idea of persistent and shared cultural orientations. To the extent that there are "holistic" aspects to this culture, however, the whole may be a weak and precarious one which cannot preclude profound tensions and even the falling away of old parts and the acquisition of new. Also, it implies that the only honest way of studying even enduring ideas, relationships, and long-term trends is by plunging into the empirical study of how such constancies of behavior and attitudes are concretized in the contingencies and complexities of "short-durational," even "generational," history and in the lives of individuals.

1

Some Stereotypes in the Periodization of Chinese History

Any discussion of historic periodization might well be prefaced by the question: Why periodize history? To some this question may seem frivolous but actually it is entirely in order. When one considers the semantic abuses, the scholastic sophistries, and the sterility which have attended the periodizing enterprise, one may well wonder whether the undertaking is at all worthwhile.

To mention merely one or two of the more obvious abuses, there is the delusion that if one has applied some categorical name to whole centuries of historic experience one has somehow grasped that period by the backbone and revealed all its innermost secrets. Having applied a word like "feudalism" derived from a relatively narrow area of experience to a cultural epoch, one has somehow "understood" that epoch without any immersion in a concrete study of the period in question. There is the mischievous tendency to assume that the historian is more properly concerned with those periods in which the categories of his scheme are realized than with the merely "transitional" periods when all is in flux. Thus according to one scheme of periodization the whole period in European history between the fifteenth and nineteenth century is a period of transition from feudalism to capitalism. Such highly crystallized products as Newton's physics, Racine's plays, and the absolute states are transitional.[1] Not only are we here faced with the problem of how a substructure which is in flux can be accompanied by such highly crystallized forms in the superstructure but we are encouraged to slur over all the economic and social developments of these centuries as being merely transitional rather than as objects of study in their own right.

One could continue to enumerate the abuses attendant upon the periodizing enterprise. In the end, however, it must be admitted that, to a degree, all historians must periodize. In dealing with long stretches of time one must divide off certain segments of time on the basis of certain notable features characterizing the segment in question. If one then chooses to designate the whole period by a name derived from these limited features of the period—using the rhetorical device of having the part stand for the whole—this is a justifiable device so long as one is constantly aware of what one is doing.

It seems to this writer that the dangers involved in periodization might be mitigated if the following three assumptions were continually kept in mind:

1. The setting up of a periodic scheme (whether on the basis of economic, political, or intellectual categories) is not the ultimate grand goal of the historian. On the contrary, periodization is itself only one means to historic understanding alongside many others. The study of how a given generation responds to the challenge of its own situation (even though the generation in question may belong to a period spanning many generations), the study of individual biography, etc., are all approaches which may be as fruitful as the periodization schemes which span vast epochs.

2. In characterizing a whole period on the basis of a concept derived from some single sector of experience, one must avoid the illusion that one has fully explained the complex totality of a period. Medieval Europe and Namakura-Muromachi Japan may both be feudal in the sense that they share certain common patterns of political and social relations. The differences between them remain enormous and should be quite as interesting to the historian as the identities.

3. From the point of view of understanding human destiny, the so-called periods of transitions may be quite as interesting as the period in which the system is realized.

Given this more complex and accurate conception of the aims and scope of the periodization enterprise, periodization becomes a useful tool alongside many others. It is in terms of these assumptions that we shall now proceed to consider two stereotypic notions which have come to dominate and paralyze thinking on the question of the periodization of Chinese history.

The two notions—considered most broadly—are 1) the notion of
China's non-development, stagnation and "changelessness" after a
given point in time; 2) the notion that China's periodic evolution
has been precisely the same as that of the West. It is well that both
these notions be treated together since they are often presented by
their proponents as terms of a necessary antithesis barring any third
possibility.

Actually these notions cut across differences in the philosophy of
history. The notion of "changeless Asia" is, of course, to be found in
Hegel and in the writings of many of his predecessors. The notion of
identical development has been propounded by both Marxists and
non-Marxists. Naitō Torajirō's ancient-medieval and modern scheme
is a notable example of a non-Marxist concept of duplicate development. For various reasons, however, much of the discussion concerning these notions has been carried on within a Marxist or quasi-
Marxist framework, and it is to this discussion that we shall here
turn our attention. It is not our intention to raise questions concerning ultimate philosophic assumptions but rather to examine the clarity, cogency, and applicability of certain specific Marxist interpretations—interpretations which embody the stereotype notions referred
to above.

Within the Marxist framework, the notion of China's non-development takes the form of the theory of oriental or Asiatic society.
We shall not here enter into the discussion of whether the latter-day
proponents of this theory—particularly Professor Wittfogel—are or
are not good Marxists. They may or may not have strayed from
Marx's own conceptions. There can be no doubt that many of the
earlier proponents of the theory, such as Madyar, considered themselves genuine Marxists and could indeed find excellent textual support in Marx and Engels for their views. Nor shall we take up once
more the question of the empirical evidence for the theory that Asiatic society has its material basis in "Water Control" for it is entirely
possible to accept a description of Chinese society as a going concern
without accepting theories concerning its origins. The question
which we shall raise here is: how much of Chinese history does the
theory of Asiatic society explain even if its basic assumptions are
true? If all that it purports to point out is that certain relations of social power have shown a tendency to persist (or rather to recur again
and again since they are constantly breaking down) over enormous

periods of time in China—that is one thing. If the theory still presupposes the Marxist assumption that in explaining the substructure one is simultaneously explaining the superstructure, its pretensions must be rejected. The fact that changes have occurred in China's culture, that novelties have emerged, is an irrefutable fact. One needs but point to such obvious facts as the emergence of neo-Confucian philosophy, Sung painting, T'ang poetry, and Sung technological developments. From the point of view of the theory of Asiatic society, Wang Yang-ming and Juan Yuan may be dismissed as two functionaries within a bureaucratic system sharing a Confucian ideology. From the point of view of intellectual history they inhabit quite different mental universes. One may safely presume that the more familiar we become with China's cultural history, the more sensitive we will become to differences in the cultural atmosphere from generation to generation. In appreciating these differences, the theory of Asiatic society will be of little help.

Even if we turn to the sphere of economic, social, and political institutions—the sphere with which the theory is eminently concerned—we know that constant changes occur from dynasty to dynasty in political institutions, in land tenure systems, and even in the size and make-up of the ruling class. The ruling classes of early T'ang and of the Sung dynasties may both fulfill the function of a "managerial bureaucracy." Yet if the work of such men as Naitō, Kracke, and others is to be believed, the period in question is marked by a breakdown in the monopoly of bureaucratic power, an extension in the size of the bureaucratic class, and an influx of new men.

To proponents of the Asiatic society theory all these changes are superficial compared with the basic facts with which they are concerned. It is highly doubtful whether they were superficial to those whose existences they affected or whether they should be to the historians who are concerned with these existences. Whether superficial or not, there are vast areas of change to which the theory is quite irrelevant.

Furthermore, if the theory's relevance is limited even when applied to those periods when centralized bureaucracy flourished, it has little to tell us about those interdynastic periods—or periods like that of the Southern dynasties when the system was not in full operation. There is no reason why the historian should not be as vitally interested in these periods as in those which obligingly fit the norm.

In sum, then, even if one is inclined to accept that side of the Asiatic theory which stresses the tough persistence of certain social and political patterns in Chinese society, the theory still remains something far less than a universal key of explanation. Nor does it debar the possibility of historic change and development in the culture as a whole.

The rival notion to the theory of oriental society within the Marxist framework is the notion that all human cultures have traversed certain universally necessary stages of social history—primitive communism, slave society, feudalism, capitalism, and socialism. (In China, of course, the path is presumed to have diverged at the latter end.) Leaving aside the question of the adequacy of this scheme as an explanation of the social history of the West, one might simply point out in passing that there is no statement anywhere in the writings of Marx and Engels which suggests that they believed in a single uniform path of social evolution for the whole human race. On the contrary, there is considerable evidence in their scattered remarks on Asia and Russia that they, like Hegel, probably held precisely the opposite view. It is thus not surprising that many of their followers have also not accepted this notion. In the "Controversy on the Social History of China" which raged in China during the early thirties—a controversy in which all the participants regarded themselves as Marxists—there emerged a bewildering plethora of schemes of periodization for Chinese history, all of them based on Marxist assumptions. As we know, however, the theory of unilinear evolution has won official support and a consequent position of supremacy in both the Soviet Union and China. It is appropriate therefore that we consider some of the problems involved in applying this particular Marxist scheme of periodization to the explanation of China's history.

During a visit to Japan in 1956, a Chinese historian stated with regard to the question of slave society that "There can be no question whether this or that historic formation or historic stage existed in Chinese history. There can only be a question of when these formations existed."[2] It might be suggested in passing that the difficulty of discovering when slave society existed in China may not be unrelated to the question of whether it existed at all.

A textbook on Chinese history[3] recently published in Peking gives the following grounds for assuming that Shang society was a slave society.[4] The high development of technical skill achieved in the production of bronze vessels presupposes the existence of a state bureau of works and of a large force of servile skilled labor. Furthermore, in addition to the nobility, we know that there existed a large unproductive class of diviners and shamans. This large class of persons isolated from production presupposes the existence of a much larger class of producers in agriculture and the raising of livestock. Furthermore, recent archaeological excavations have revealed that often more than two hundred servants were entombed with their lords. It is safe to assume that these servants were slaves.

Now remaining strictly within the bounds of Marxist assumptions we find that these grounds are no grounds at all. In the Marxist view, the existence of non-productive classes—classes isolated from production—which are supported by the surplus appropriated from a productive class is a characteristic of all exploitative societies and not a peculiar feature of slavery. In order to determine the nature of Shang society in Marxist terms one would have to know something about the nature of the relations of the agricultural population to their "means of production," about their legal status, and about the form in which their surplus was appropriated. As for the burial of servants along with their lords, we have no reason whatever for assuming that these slaves were involved in basic production. A far more sensible assumption from any point of view is that the Shang nobility maintained immense retinues of household slaves. Large households with considerable numbers of slaves have, of course, not been unknown in later periods of Chinese history.

Another non-empirical argument often put forth to support the view that China traversed a stage of slave society is based on a text in a rather rare work of Marx entitled *Grundrisse der Kritik der politischen Oekonomie.*[5] In a chapter entitled "Epochs of Social Formation" Marx discusses in detail the whole notion of oriental society. The proponents of the theory of oriental society have rested their case very heavily on this book. At one point Marx makes the casual remark that in the Asiatic form of society "the individual never becomes an owner—only a possessor—he is therefore, *au fond,* the slave of him in whom the unity of the community exists."[6] It is the penalty of greatness that even the most casual rhetorical remarks of great men are likely to become foundations of whole new theories. This remark has been seized upon as proof that Marx regarded oriental society as simply an oriental sub-variant of slave society. It should therefore be pointed out that in spite of his rhetorical use of the word "slave" in this passage the whole chapter continues to speak of Asiatic and "antique" forms of society as two separate forms; that the distinction between an owner and a possessor, which Marx here applies to oriental society, is applied by him elsewhere in his discussion of European feudalism. Are we therefore to assume that he regarded European feudalism as a sub-variant of slave society? There is the added fact that Marx nowhere implies that "oriental" society is confined to the ancient period of Asian history. On the contrary, he implies in several places that in India oriental society persisted until the British conquest. He is particularly insistent on the enduring quality of this social form. Thus this a priori doctrinal support for the notion of slave society in China is quite as feeble as its empirical support.

When we turn from the notion of slave society to the notion of feudalism, we enter a truly dim and foggy realm. As applied to China within this scheme of periodization, the concept of feudalism is made to carry the burden of explaining the whole span of Chinese history from the Western Chou until just yesterday when it fades off in the unclear guise of semi-feudalism. There are differences of opinion concerning the time limits of the feudal stage but in all the available interpretations it is made to account for enormous stretches of Chinese history. It is therefore somewhat disconcerting to discover that the whole question of what feudalism is *in Marxist terms* still remains unresolved. In the former Soviet Union a discussion concerning the definition of the "basic economic law" of feudalism raged in the periodical *Problems of History* from 1953–1955. After a failure to reach any consensus, the discussion was brought to a close—at least temporarily—by an unsigned article in the issue of May 1955 entitled "Concerning the Basic Law of the Feudal Formation." After decades of textual exegesis we are amazed to find in this article the statement that the "classics of Marxism have not provided any generalized definition of this law."

However, most of those Soviet and Chinese scholars who have claimed that feudalism is a necessary stage of all human cultures have tended to seek their proof in *Das Kapital,* Volume III, Chapter 47. In this chapter which deals with the question of ground rent, there is one section which discusses forms of society in which "labor rent" has prevailed. In this passage Marx discusses certain salient characteristics shared by many economic forms. In his own language, these characteristics form the economic basis shared by these economic forms. This language is not very precise but, as I hope to demonstrate, there is no indication that what Marx here calls an "economic base" is to be identified with his more precise conception—"mode of production". On the contrary, if Marx's definition of the concept "mode of production" in his *Grundrisse der Kritik der politischen Oekonomie* is to be taken seriously, these characteristics are by no means sufficient to define a specific mode of production.

Marx speaks of forms of production in which "the direct producer is in possession of his own means of production and of the material labor conditions required for the realization of his labor and the production of his means of subsistence . . . He carries on his agriculture and rural household industry in connection with it as an independent producer." The "nominal owners" of the soil are thus unable to "filch their surplus product by any economic compulsion" and are forced to do so by extra-economic forms of constraint. Marx then adds significantly that the forms of property which accompany this "economic basis" may differ. The owner may be a private landlord who appropriates the surplus product in the form of rent (as in European feudalism) or a state which stands over the producer as his direct landlord and sovereign and extracts surplus in the form of taxes.

The whole procedure of the proponents of the universal necessity of feudalism is to assert that in enumerating these characteristics, Marx has provided us with his definition of feudalism. He has thus identified the medieval European social system and the social systems of Asia as variant forms of feudalism. Quite apart from the fact that Marx nowhere makes this claim, there is the hard fact that in his classical definition of the concept of mode of production Marx states that every mode of production is characterized by its own specific relations of property (which are merely a legal expression for the specific relations of production characterizing the mode of production in question). To assert that the individual property of European feudalism and the economic systems of Asia are the same, where, in Marx's view (based largely on his Indian studies), "no private ownership of property exists," is to deny that "relations of property" constitute an integral, organic part of any given mode of production.

It is true that in this passage Marx tends to underplay the importance of forms of property. The non-Marxist is free to speculate here
that while Marx began by placing the factor of "property relations"
at the heart of his system, his later investigations may have led him
to stress the greater importance of other factors. For the Marxist,
however, there is the irreducible fact that every mode of production
is characterized by its own specific relations of property.

Approaching the matter from a somewhat different angle, one
might, of course, contend that China's social development does not
correspond to Marx's concept of oriental society. China has certainly known the landlord-tenant nexus. Whatever the case in Peru
or India, China can therefore be classed as a feudal society. Here,
however, we confront other difficulties. Marx by no means identifies all forms of landlordism with feudalism where the mode of exploitation must be extra-economic. In his discussion of the emergence of the gentry in Tudor England he specifically states that this
new landlord class "abolished the feudal tenure of lands." The relations between landlord and tenant tend to become wholly economic. On the other hand, to the extent that the tenants possess
their own plots and work them themselves, we do not have the type
of landlord-tenant relationship which corresponds to capitalism.
We rather have what Marx calls (in *Das Kapital,* Volume III) an
"intermediate form" *(Zwischenform)* between money rent as the
last form of feudal rent and capitalist farming. As an intermediate
form it cannot be bracketed with either the feudal or capitalist
modes of production. Presumably as an evanescent, transitional
form it requires no categorization in terms of the Marxist inventory
of modes of production (although it has a long history in England).
It is interesting to note that this article, "Concerning the Basic Law
of the Feudal Formation," also underlines the distinction between
this type of land ownership and feudal land ownership. It speaks of
the "conversion of feudal land ownership into landlord-bourgeois
ownership, of the peasant possessor into a personally free leasing
tenant, of feudal rent into various transitional forms." In spite of
the use of the word "bourgeois" the article stresses that this type of
landlord-tenant relationship arose precisely in those areas where
feudalism was not transformed into capitalism. If the type of
landlord-tenant nexus which has characterized large periods of Chinese history resembles any form discussed in Marx, it certainly is

much closer to this "intermediate form" than to anything discussed under the heading of feudalism.

Furthermore, to the extent that China has known the small peasant proprietor we are again dealing with a phenomenon which Marx failed to bracket with any of his established categories of modes of production. Marx found "small peasant property," yeoman's property in the ancient world before slavery, in colonial America and in England during the period of transition between feudalism and capitalism.

How, then, are we to characterize China's "modes of production" during the immense period between the end of the Chou period and the recent past? To the extent that we have landlord-tenant relations, they tend to correspond to an unclassified "intermediate form." To the extent that we have the small peasant proprietor, we have a phenomenon which Marx himself failed to bracket with any specific mode of production. To the extent that we deal with the large *Chuangt'ien* (landed estates) of the T'ang and Sung dynasties, we are again dealing with a phenomenon which is not easily classified. Professor Niida Noboru attempts to demonstrate that the owners of these estates exercised extra-economic legal powers vis-à-vis the producers thus proving their feudal nature. On the other hand, it has been contended that the workers on these estates may have been agricultural laborers or even slaves or semi-slaves. It is thus uncertain whether we are dealing here with feudal estates, servile latifundia or something resembling the capitalist form. To the extent that the various attempts made to nationalize the soil and assign it to peasants on a temporary basis (as during the Northern Wei or early T'ang) had actually been realized, we have something which most closely resembles Marx's conception of oriental society.

In sum, then, it is doubtful whether there is to be found anywhere in the writings of Marx a name or rather names for the modes of production which have prevailed in China during the vast period from the Ch'in to the Ch'ing dynasties.

Why this tenacious insistence that China's development in terms of historic stages has been a duplicate of that of the West? It is always risky to speculate on motives, yet one reason for this insistence must certainly be the fact that within the Marxist framework "progress" takes place only within this scheme of periodization. Feudalism arises out of slave society and capitalism arises out of feudalism. To assert that China did not traverse this path is to assert that Chinese society did not bear within itself the immanent movement toward an industrial civilization. Since in terms of the values inherent in this Marxist view, the progressiveness of any society hinges precisely on its ultimate latent capacity to produce a modern industrial system—to deny this immanent capacity to China is to relegate China to an inferior historic position.

It is interesting to note in this connection that the Soviet article referred to earlier in this chapter, "Concerning the Basic Law of the Feudal Formation," while still asserting the universal necessity of a feudal stage, makes the striking assertion that feudalism does not everywhere automatically bring forth capitalism. "The classic path of the dissolution of feudalism actually consists of the approximation of the peasant to the position of the free commodity-producing owner. Such a path assures the best, the classical conditions for the genesis of capitalism. Only a few Western European countries took this path. Not only in Asia but in a whole series of areas in Europe (Italy, in part Spain, the countries of the 'second enserfment' after the abolition of serf law) the dissolution of feudalism took another path, a conservative path of the transformation of feudal property into landlord-bourgeois property, etc." The possibility is here envisioned that feudalism itself does not everywhere produce the same results.

Furthermore, if China's development is to be taken as a duplicate of Western development in Marxist terms, it must inevitably emerge as a defective duplicate. If, as is often stated, the emergence of a Chinese capitalism was inhibited by the aggressive intrusion of Western capitalist imperialism, the question remains—why did not Chinese capitalism emerge simultaneously with or even before Western capitalism? In most accounts, Chinese feudalism lasted much longer than Western feudalism. It had a much longer period for the contradictory forces within feudalism to grow and mature. If the maturation of the contradictory forces was inhibited by cultural or geographic factors, it must be admitted that factors outside of the mode of production played a dominant role in Chinese history. In any case, the duplicate remains defective.

One can, of course, never prove that Chinese society if left to its own devices might not, in the fullness of time, have produced an industrial system. All we would suggest here is that to hinge the whole study of China's history on the question of its presumed immanent tendency toward the creation of a modern industrial system is not a particularly fruitful approach to that history.

One should make oneself perfectly clear at this point. The question is not whether there existed in China the human capacity to produce a modern industrial system if the society's energies had been applied in this direction. Now that its energies are being so applied, there need be no doubt of its ability to do so. Nor does one mean that there has not been in China the type of normal long-range cumulative economic and technological development which we find in other pre-industrial civilizations. As of the time of Marco Polo or even later there is considerable evidence that in its development in this area China may have been ahead of other cultures. Over the centuries there was undoubtedly growth in commerce, money economy and urban development. None of this proves, however, that the peculiar type of exponential economic development which characterized the West in the late eighteenth and nineteenth century was just over the horizon or immanent in China's social system. Marx himself constantly maintained that such phenomena as growth in money economy, in the size of cities, in the merchant class have taken place again and again within the framework of many different societies, and were not sufficient in and of themselves to give rise to a modern industrial system.

It is possible to appreciate the dilemma of those who make an absolute value of modern industrialism and who nevertheless wish to find cause for pride in their national culture, which may have been oriented in other directions. It is doubtful, however, whether this state of mind is conducive to historic understanding.

In conclusion, we would suggest that the periodization of Chinese history—to the extent that periodization is a valuable undertaking—is a task which still lies ahead of us; that both the notion of a changeless China and of a China whose "logic of development" duplicates that of the West are obstacles in the path of fresh understanding. China's own path of development still demands much further investigation. It may well turn out that much of the evidence for change and the emergence of novelty in Chinese history—evidence which can provide the basis for a meaningful periodization—will have to be drawn from what the Marxists call the "superstructure" rather than from what they call the "substructure."

2

A Brief Defense of Political
and Intellectual History:
The Case of China

I shall begin with a confession. In my efforts to study the history of one non-Western civilization, China, I find that I have tended to focus on two areas of history—political and intellectual—which do not currently enjoy high esteem in many sectors of the historical profession. Owing to certain considerations which are not entirely methodological, my interest in political history has focused on contemporary China, while my concern with intellectual history has involved both traditional and modern China. There has, however, been a considerable interaction between both interests. In reflecting on the common denominators which may underlie these two areas, it occurs to me that both are involved with the realm of man's conscious life—with his conscious relationship to the situation in which he finds himself and to his conscious behavior within that situation. To the extent that politics involves ideology, policy, decision-making, and even power relations, it involves conscious intention and conscious activity. In this view, even power relations as they appear in political life are power relations as perceived by the actors.

In struggling to achieve a conception of political history, I find myself somewhat in sympathy with the current tendency to de-emphasize the history of political institutions and constitutional history. In the case of those structures known as political institutions, there has emerged a realization of how problematic and complex are the relations between formal structure and the human realities which they supposedly condition and constrain. Certainly, any effort to make sense of the political history of mainland China in the last twenty years could hardly depend entirely on the history of institutions, constitutions, and formal organizations, and yet we are dealing with a history in which there is considerable truth in the assertion that "politics are in command." If this phrase has any meaning within the context of contemporary China, it must refer not simply or even primarily to institutions but to categories such as policy, decision-making, power relations, and the interplay between ideas and political action.

At the same time the notion that political institutions are in some sense less real or fundamental than all those institutions and structures called social seems to me to be based on questionable assumptions. If it derives from the view that political institutions are often created and shaped by conscious intention and conscious activity while social and economic institutions are the products of deep, unconscious forces "independent of the wills of men," it seems to me that the contrast is overdrawn on both sides. Many American political scientists of the more scientific persuasion are as ardently bent on proving that the structures of political life and models of political development are as independent of the wills of men as any of the structures described by the economists, sociologists, and anthropologists. If one is prepared to believe Lévi-Strauss's assertion that "myths think themselves out in men,"[1] one can perhaps say that constitutions and political institutions think and act themselves out in men. On the other hand, the notion that deliberate purpose and conscious activity are absent in such preeminently "objective" areas as economics, the history of technology, or anthropology simply rests on unthinking dogma. A close look at the history of extended lineage structures in South China would indicate that the maintenance of lineages over time was by no means due simply to the preexistence of unconscious *gemeinschaftliche* kinship structures, but to the highly conscious organizational efforts of enterprising clan leaders.[2]

Nevertheless, one need not deny that in the case of political institutions, the role of conscious activity is often close to the surface. In China we are able to follow closely the collective deliberations which led to the formation of the Chinese Communist party and to the creation and destruction of various organizations which have emerged since 1949. This fact neither adds to nor subtracts from the reality of such institutions. Political institutions are neither less real nor less pervasive in their effects than other institutions, but they by no means provide the sole, or even the primary, substance of political history.

If political history involves conscious activity, it is, of course, by no means conscious activity in a vacuum, but conscious activity set within the framework of all the problems, pressures, and constraints imposed by the objective situation. In China one can hardly begin to discuss the programs, policies, decisions, and disputes of the political actors without constant reference to such factors as the overwhelmingly agrarian nature of China's economy, the crushing weight of its population, the persistence of cultural patterns inherited from the past, the contingencies of China's relations with the outside world, and so on. The political historian must welcome all the aid which economists, demographers, anthropologists, and others can provide to help him to understand the situation within which political action takes place. It is by no means demonstrated, however, that the responses of the political actors are the only obviously necessary effects of any or all these forces. It is thus quite clear that during the years 1960–1965 sharp differences of perspective developed within the Chinese Communist leadership concerning the policies to be pursued relative to the socioeconomic and cultural situation which had emerged after the Great Leap Forward. One might, of course, explain these divergent perspectives wholly in terms of power struggles within the leadership. Even if one were entirely prepared to settle for this account of the motivation of the various parties involved, the fact remains that power interests became indissolubly linked to different policy perspectives and that these perspectives in turn reflect divergent images, perceptions, and hopes on the part of the political actors involved. To assert that Mao Tse-tung's Cultural Revolution was the only obvious response to the imperatives of the objective situation of the early sixties is simply to indulge in spurious hindsight.

I am not here trying to prove the case for the freedom of political actors in the philosophic sense. If their actions are not clearly determined by the external objective processes, they may still be determined by internal structures and processes. The social backgrounds of the political actors, their personal biographies, their personality structures, and even the role of ideology as myth in Lévi-Strauss's sense may all be brought in to explain their conscious acts and decisions. One may psychoanalyze Mao Tse-tung. The point is that these forms of determinism are mediated through the conscious political acts of the political actors. This leaves open the relative autonomy of the political sphere. It also leaves open the possibility that political acts and decisions may substantially affect the course of history.

Here, however, we confront another ground for asserting the superficiality of political history—namely, that political history places undue stress on the acts of tiny groups of people or even on the acts of single individuals. It thus lends aid and comfort to the "great man theory of history" and is elitist in its very essence. It is an offense to both populist sentiment and to science—to populist sentiment in that it denies that the important movements of history are the cumulative efforts of vast masses of men[3] and to science because the general "laws of history" must manifest themselves through vast numbers of specific instances.

It is, of course, entirely true that the data on princes and prime ministers is infinitely more accessible than data on the political history of provinces and villages. This does not mean, however, that there is no political history of villages. Patrice Higonnet has written on the social and political history of the village of Pont de Montvert in southern France, indicating a complicated political life within the village as well as a complicated dialectic of relationships between the political and intellectual history of the village and of the nation as a whole. Frederick Wakeman has written a study of the political life of eastern Kwangtung province in the wake of the Opium War which lifts the veil on the complexity of the local political history of one small area of China.[4] Here we find an amazingly intricate web of political relations between local officialdom, clan politics, secret societies, local gentry, and interethnic rivalries. Other young scholars in the field of modern Chinese history have turned their attention to the political history of provinces and cities during the period before the 1911 Revolution and emerged with extraordinary accounts of local political history. All of these accounts combine political history with social history. The authors must make an effort to reconstruct local social life, but it is the dynamic and conscious life of local political history which reveals the concrete human reality of these social relations. There is no reason to think of political history as simply the history of the policies of kings or courts. It may just as well involve the frustration and deflection of leaders' policies in the capital by local power constellations and the local politics of villages. The policies associated with the Cultural Revolution in China were undoubtedly initiated by Mao Tse-tung and a small group of his supporters, but the turbulent evolution of China during the last three years has been influenced as much by the unanticipated deflection of these policies by various political forces as by the will of the leader.

To be sure, even though the web of political history is spread wide, it may be asserted that for the larger part of human history the masses of mankind have not participated in political life and that the political actors, whether they are monarchs or local clan leaders, are almost by definition part of the ruling class. Much, of course, depends on what one means by participation. If one concedes that political acts and political events may have profound and even devastating effects on the lives of men, then the masses certainly have participated in political history. The stereotype of the Chinese peasant village that lives a timeless life while the waves of political history flow over it may have a certain partial truth for certain times and certain remote places, but it is essentially not true. All of us know—at least in the abstract—about the vast peasant rebellions which periodically swept China affecting and involving vast populations. We also know about conscription of vast hordes of men for military activities and corvée labor far from home. We know of banditry and secret societies and of the voluntary and involuntary participation of peasants in the bitter feuds of local political life. We also know that peasants did not necessarily remain immured in their villages but were frequent visitors to market towns where they undoubtedly exchanged information concerning local political situations and perhaps even concerning the state of the empire. We know about many of these things in the abstract but, at least in the case of China, what we need if we are to clothe these abstractions with flesh is much more attention to the *histoire événementielle,* to the extent that the Chinese sources are able to supply us with materials. While it is true that all of these sources may be limited, we have hardly begun to exploit what they do contain.

The fact that political history tends to be closely associated with the history of events is, of course, another ground for asserting its superficiality. It is quite true that much political history has been concerned with the main events and the actions of the most visible actors, but presumably even a comprehensive political history which would provide an account of all political actions and events down through every province, city, and village would still be superficial because it would be a history of surface events rather than of the secular movement of underlying structures. I shall not dwell here at length on the procedures by which the variables which enter into these accounts of deep, impersonal forces are assigned an independent life of their own as the prime movers of history. It is thus possible to collect all the statistics available on a certain network of trade over a given period of time (no doubt this is a very valuable enterprise from many points of view), to suppress all considerations of political events, military events, shifts in mentalities, and other variables which may have profoundly affected this statistical series, and to emerge with the view that this pattern of trade is an absolutely independent "infrastructural" variable.

Similarly, one way of dealing with the history of mainland China in the last twenty years is to assert the ultimate importance of the "process of modernization," operating, as it were, behind the backs of all the participants, and to assert that all the shifts of political history are simply surface eruptions of this process or, if not, essentially insignificant. I shall not dwell here on the obscurities of the concept of modernization. It is based on the assumption that there exists an all-encompassing and apparently stable structure called "modern society," which provides the clear and unmoving target of all developing societies (since all development is development toward something). One need not deny that all societies now called modern share certain features, the most indisputable being a highly industrialized economy. Yet the notion that the differences between these societies are insignificant or the notion that these societies have achieved a kind of plateau of essential stability precluding sweeping future transformations is part of what might be called the ideology of modernization. The target itself is neither clear nor unchanging. Modern societies of the twenty-first century may exhibit features which run entirely counter to the dominant trends of the twentieth century. Without denying that the political leaders of China are interested in many of the elements which we tend to subsume under the category of modernization, the question of how China will modernize holds many obscurities and uncertainties for the leadership itself. The question of how to modernize becomes a political question and the political decisions of the leaders may have a profound effect on the nature and tempo of China's modernization. The Bolshevik seizure of power in October 1917 was a political act and part of the history of events. Can one contend that this event had no effect on the history of the Soviet Union during the last fifty years? One need not assume that the intentions of the original actors have been realized. Political intentions and political acts, like ideas, may have unintended consequences. Yet even the unintended consequences are inconceivable without the original action. It seems to me entirely reasonable to say that the political act of 1917 was one factor of enormous importance in shaping the history of the Soviet Union. Whether it will have any significance whatsoever a thousand years from now is a moot point. It is just as unclear, however, whether our present constellations of demographic, economic, and sociological trends will have any significance a thousand years from now. In the time scale of millennial history, single political acts and policies may shrink in significance, but this leads us to the question of whether the type of history which deals in millennia is necessarily more profound than the type of history which deals with the time scale of a generation or two. In the latter scale, political history retains its perennial significance. To those who happen to live in the time scale of one generation, politics are always with us.

There is in fact one way of regarding political history (and other forms of history as well) which runs quite counter to nineteenth- and twentieth-century historicism and reflects certain older ahistorical ways of looking at history. Political history is here regarded not as a single irreversible process but as a reservoir of instances of political experience. It provides the possibility for a kind of diachronic metahistorical and transcultural comparative politics in which it no longer is heretical to compare something in ancient Roman history to something in modern Chinese history provided that this is done with due deference to the insights which arise out of the "modern sense of history." Thus political actions and political events are significant not only for their place in some world-wide historic drama but also as comparative material for the study of man in politics in various times and places. This is not to deny the emergence of genuine novelty or the possibility of progress. It is simply to insist that together with novelty one also has the constant recurrence and recombination of political problems.

Linking political to intellectual history is the concern with the realm of conscious life. The English term "intellectual history" is most unfortunate since it seems to imply an exclusive concern with the intellect in the narrow sense of the term and hence also seems to imply an exclusive concern with the history of those called intellectuals. Intellectual history, as here conceived, involves the totality of conscious life—the life of the intellect, the emotions, the imagination, and every variety of sensibility—and not simply the realm of conceptualization. Furthermore, we are by no means exclusively concerned with the intellectual life as a self-subsistent realm—as the so-called "history of ideas"—but with human consciousness as related to the historic situations in which we find ourselves. To use Merleau-Ponty's trenchant phrase, "To be conscious is, among other things, to be elsewhere."[5] Ideas themselves may be concerned with matters which are entirely material. This view of intellectual history by no means precludes the history of ideas. It cannot be denied that the intellectually articulate in relating to their life situations tend to relate not only to life in its unreflective immediacy but also to the ideas of others about life. One must always understand their thought in relation to the thought of both their predecessors and contemporaries.

Like political history, intellectual history has been subject to the charge of elitism, although in my view with even less justification. While political action may be confined to small groups, even though the actions themselves affect the society as a whole, the conscious life of man is omnipresent wherever men are to be found. I am, of course, entirely aware of the academic conventions which assign the study of collective mentalities of the masses to sociology or cultural anthropology or social history. It is indeed possible to subsume even the intellectual history of intellectuals under these categories. Thus Lévi-Strauss is quite prepared to treat some of the ideas of his great contemporary Sartre under the category of anthropology.[6] Yet even those who concede a certain autonomy of intellectual history as the history of the ideas of reflective intellectuals insist on appropriating the mentalities of the masses for the social sciences. Presumably one basis for this assignation is that any phenomenon which is collective must seek its aetiology in sociology or some social science, although Norman Cohn and other psychohistorians have felt it quite possible to explain collective mentalities in Freudian psychological terms. More important, however, is the assumption that, whatever may be the case for intellectuals, the minds of the broad masses may be thought of as passive receptacles which are only able to reflect the mentalities produced in them by vast impersonal societal and cultural forces. Lévi-Strauss assigns a considerable causal weight to collective mental structures but the point is again that these structures, like language, are objective autonomous realities which manifest themselves through the essentially passive receptacle of the individual mind. To be sure, in the case of Lévi-Strauss, it is by no means easy to pigeonhole his thought. In his recoil from Sartre's contrast between the modern dialectical thinker (like Sartre) who is actually able to think and the primitive man whose conscious life is wholly controlled by preestablished structures, he tends to deny the distinction on both sides and points to the broad anthropological evidence concerning "primitive philosophers" who are quite capable of thinking through and justifying in their own terms the traditions of their tribe on a highly conscious level. If this is true of primitive men, it need not be less true of the mentalities of the masses in the so-called higher civilizations. The notion that the mentalities of the masses as opposed to the reflections of intellectuals are wholly passive and nonreflective and easily explained in terms of the social models which we impose upon them is not based on any genuine evidence. Whatever the claims of sociology, anthropology, or economic history, there is no reason whatever why the study of the conscious life of the masses should not also be subsumed under the category of intellectual history. Intellectual historians of China devote far too little attention to movements of popular religion, to the "ideologies of rebellion," to the interweavings of mythology and cosmological thinking on the popular level, and a host of other subjects.

Indeed, one of the barriers to a broadly conceived intellectual history of China has been the facile acceptance of the distinction between "folk culture" and "high culture." The distinction no doubt has validity as a heuristic device, but the notion that there has anywhere been an iron wall dividing the two has been most misleading, particularly in the case of China where, ever since the eighteenth century, there has been a tendency in the West to contrast the cool rationalistic Confucianism of the literati to the irrational superstitions and primitive folk religion of the masses. In fact, a closer look reveals that the literati most often shared in the "superstitions" and magical beliefs of the masses and were indeed able to provide a kind of rational basis for these beliefs in their highly developed cosmological theories (as in the case of geomancy). To a greater or lesser degree, they also shared in and were able to provide rationales for their participation in various aspects of popular religion. On the other hand, popular literature, proverbs, and other more immediate sources of evidence would indicate that the ideas of the so-called high culture circulated widely among the masses. The ideologies of rebellion are by no means simple products of the folk mind. They were most often fashioned by literati or semiliterati but were, of course, quite accessible to the masses. The rise of Christianity and the Reformation are two examples of vast movements of the spirit which have cut across the whole society. To be sure, the modalities of acceptance of these movements by various groups within the society could differ markedly. The same religious and ethical concepts could be part of Establishment culture and also figure in the ideology of rebellions. Buddhist scholasticism and Neo-Confucian scholasticism, like all scholastic refinements of doctrine, remained the preserve of the monk and literatus, but this does not imply that there was nothing in common among the religions of the monk, the literatus, and the peasant.

One reason for assigning the collective mentality of the peasant village wholly to the anthropologist is the assumption that peasant villages, like primitive tribes, have at some point in time reached a stasis of cultural forms which makes both political and intellectual history largely irrelevant. This, again, is an unproved assumption. There is thus considerable evidence that during the T'ang dynasty, when Buddhism was a vital encompassing force in Chinese life, a large part of village China was dominated by Buddhist beliefs, festivals, and the institutions of Monastic Buddhism. In later centuries, when Buddhism had retreated as a vital force, although one still finds definite Buddhist elements in the diversified popular culture of China, the spirit of that culture had changed.

While intellectual history as here conceived lays as much claim in principle to the mentalities of nonintellectuals as to the ideas of intellectuals, the ideas of the literate and the articulate are most accessible. Nor can we deny that for the greater part of human history (including the present) the literate and intellectually articulate have belonged to the more privileged sectors of society (particularly in the case of China's scholar-officials), or at least have been appended to it, as in the case of modern academic intellectuals. Hence, it can always be alleged in a quasi-Marxist spirit that their ideas either consciously or unconsciously reflect the interests of the ruling class. It is also frequently alleged that the intellectuals tend to concern themselves with matters which are their own exclusive concern and not those of the bulk of mankind. But intellectuals, unless they are blatant propagandists, have always regarded themselves as being engaged in a truth-seeking or truth-proclaiming enterprise designed to cope with the mysteries of the human and the cosmic universe. They have thus always implicitly assumed that their efforts transcended class interests and psychological motives. Indeed, most of them have tended to assume that their ideas could affect the world surrounding them.

This, of course, is no place to attempt to confront the enormous philosophic problems involved in giving an account of the human which tries to pay due deference to objective forces, to interest motives, and to psychological motives while taking seriously his claims as a truth-seeking animal. All I would suggest is that we ourselves are as deeply involved in these dilemmas as any of our predecessors; the devices used to separate our own intellectual enterprises from theirs will simply not bear scrutiny. One such device is to assume that at a given point in the historic process, it suddenly becomes possible for intellectuals to free themselves from the trammels of genetic conditioning and to confront the truth in all its fullness. To Hegel, the self-realization of the World Spirit coincides with his own lifetime. To Marx, the rise of the proletariat as a class which will finally overcome all the false consciousness of the past confirms the truth of his doctrine, while to Karl Mannheim his own life witnesses the final emergence of a free-floating intelligentsia whose views are no longer distorted by partial interests. Many American social scientists were convinced that they had achieved the happy state of scientific objectivity in the affluent fifties. The procedures here are almost too transparent to require comment.

Another way to achieve this appearance of transcendence is to lay claim to the precious mantle of science. Lévi-Strauss would have us believe that the purity and rigor of his science somehow lifts him above the cultural structure in which he is immersed. What is claimed now is that certain theories, ideas, and hypotheses have finally been, or are about to be, verified by the facts, thus placing these theories and hypotheses in an entirely different category from all the ideologies and theories of the past. A historian must, of course, be committed to the supreme value of empirical data. He must insist that all models and theories be constantly confronted with the richness of concrete experience. He must be committed to the view that facts may kill a generalization or challenge the universal claims of a model. He is convinced that only a confrontation with concrete experience can deepen and broaden our ideas. One might say that one of the main tasks of history is not so much to confirm given theories and models as to see whether they are falsifiable. It is, however, infinitely easier to falsify than to verify. The notion that certain sweeping hypotheses have been "scientifically" verified by certain types and quanta of facts will be infinitely more convincing to those who accept the models than to those who do not. The fact that one can find a high correlation between two series of statistics may represent a very local relationship and not a universal law of history. There still remains no royal road to verification in all the larger matters of human history and we have not lifted ourselves out of the dilemmas which confronted our intellectual ancestors. If their intellectual gropings and fumblings inevitably and exclusively reflected the interests of the ruling class, the structures of their culture, or their childhood traumas, then so do ours (as many of the young so vehemently insist).

The notion that the ideas and preoccupations of those who write and leave records are most often of concern only to priests, monks, religious visionaries, scholars, intellectuals, or effete ruling classes is based on what might be called a patronizing humanitarianism. In this view, masses who live in poverty should be properly concerned only with their poverty. Yet as Lévi-Strauss and others have pointed out, the Australian primitives who subsisted on berries and grubs developed vast mythologies, theologies, and cosmologies. There may be certain kinds of scholastic developments and certain kinds of learned jargon which are truly the preserve of the learned and inaccessible to the masses. This is by no means peculiar to traditional society. Many varieties of social science have developed precisely this type of scholasticism and learned jargon to an exaggerated degree, yet the practitioners of these scholasticisms remain firmly convinced that they are dealing with matters which are of universal concern. In short, the ideas of thinkers and intellectuals in the past must be taken seriously because they represent efforts quite as serious as our own to cope with the human condition in various times and places. Without assuming that these ideas are the embodiment of a *Welt-*

geist, they nevertheless represent preoccupations which may reflect matters of concern to all.

I have not, however, justified my particular concern with political and intellectual history in dealing with a non-Western culture in face of the present trend stressing "objective" "social scientific" history. In his *Pensée sauvage* Lévi-Strauss states that the ultimate goal of the human sciences is "not to constitute but to dissolve man;"[7] to dissolve him into the various impersonal structures—biological, societal, anthropological, and so forth—which make up his being. Within the French context this undoubtedly represents a reaction against certain forms of "existential humanism" with their emphasis on subjectivity and a reassertion of the pathos of objective scientism. In attempting this undertaking in the West, however, one faces a vast and profound literature concerned with "constituting man." Any effort to force Rousseau into someone's behavioral scheme must face a vast battery of Rousseau experts who know their Rousseau much better than the schematizer, while Jean Paul Sartre was quite capable of defending himself against efforts to fit him into someone's anthropological scheme.

In the case of China, however, the effort to establish the human reality of China across the centuries, of seeing Chinese responding consciously to the political and human situations which confront them, is a task which has still not advanced very far, at least in the West. This makes it far easier to impose our models and preestablished structures onto China. The Chinese will not contradict us because we know so little of what they have said. As John Habakkuk states in a paper submitted to the conference for which this essay was written, "Where the data are sparsest, one has to rely most heavily on reasoning based on a model." He might have added that where the data are sparsest, it becomes easiest to impose the model. China has already suffered far too much from premature structuralism. Lévi-Strauss refrained on the whole from attempting to impose totalizing structures on the so-called higher civilizations, perhaps because he suspected that cultures which occupy such vast areas of time and space do not in fact possess one all-embracing structure.

It may, of course, be urged that a good deal of Western sinology has concerned itself with Chinese thought, hence with the conscious life of the Chinese. In his *Pensée chinoise* Marcel Granet presents an image of the timeless essence of Chinese thought. Written under the influence of Emile Durkheim's conception of "collective representations," it attempts to provide us with the "deep structures" of Chinese thought in Lévi-Strauss's sense. The latter has, in fact, acknowledged his debt to Granet. If there have been synchronic and diachronic tensions and conflicts within Chinese thought, Granet dismisses these as "secondary manifestations."

Granet described a kind of Chinese cosmology which has indeed been a dominant and persistent strand of Chinese thought. It was, moreover, a brand of cosmology which was not displaced by any rival until modern times. Yet the fact remains that although this cosmology held center stage in the former Han dynasty, in the latter Han dynasty there was a distinct reaction against it. There is the fact that the Confucius of The Analects, while seemingly accepting elements of this cosmology,[8] refuses to place it at the center of his concerns. In the thought of many of the so-called Neo-Taoists of the Wei-chin period it was quite marginal, while there are many aspects of the history of popular religion which bear no particular relationship to the cosmological scheme (although efforts were made to fit them into the Procrustean bed). To Granet the range of possibilities covered by Chinese thought may seem to be "secondary manifestations." To the participants, the conflicts and issues may have been quite as fundamental as the issues dividing Lévi-Strauss from Sartre or French Marxists from American liberals even though it can be maintained that the latter both share important general notions. An intellectual history of China, as here conceived, would be concerned not simply with "Chinese thought" but with Chinese thinking and thinking within the framework of their historical situations. Similarly, a political history of China would involve not simply a reconstruction of the timeless institutional structures of the Chinese state (crucial as this undertaking may be) but a history of the living politics of those involved in these structures. Indeed, the evolution of the structure itself can hardly be understood apart from the context of concrete political situations.

It is, of course, not my intention to anathemize any method of historic investigation. Any kind of research procedure which provides us with new significant insights is relevant to any interpretation of history. It is rather my intention to defend against prevailing fashion an interpretation of history which is still concerned with constituting man rather than dissolving him.

To some this concern with man's conscious life may seem to be a manifestation of a peculiarly tender-minded view of the human situation. While not particularly concerned to establish credentials for tough-mindedness, it seems to me that a concern with conscious attitudes and activities has no necessary connection with any facilely optimistic view of human destiny. One may indeed contend that conscious attitudes, orientations, and visions of reality have more often than not played a devastatingly tragic role in human affairs.

3

❧

The Limits of "Tradition versus Modernity": The Case of the Chinese Intellectuals

The study of the role of intellectuals in developing society has been going on for some time now. To the extent that it has turned the attention of scholars to the concrete study of intellectuals in non-Western societies, it has been a spur to fruitful inquiry. To the extent that it has attempted to structure the whole experience of these intellectuals in terms of the conventional triad—tradition/development/modernity—without a deeper investigation of the range of meaning of these terms, to the extent that it has been unduly preoccupied with proclaiming universal laws or models of how intellectuals behave or ought to behave in developing societies,[1] it may have actually impeded deeper inquiry.

If the two terminal categories of this triad, tradition and modernity, do not refer to internally consistent and mutually exclusive entities, but only as a short-hand way of referring to vast inchoate areas of human experience, the unreflective use of these terms can only lead to what Alfred N. Whitehead called the fallacy of misplaced concreteness. One of the most dire results of misplaced concreteness is that it obstructs our contacts with true concreteness. To be sure, there are many who have in mind more specific polarities when they speak of tradition versus modernity. To some the crucial variable may be agrarian society versus industrial, to others authority versus freedom, to still others scientific outlook versus prescientific mentality, and so forth. However, all seem to share the assumption that every other aspect of the society or the culture—always conceived of as integrated wholes—is a function of whatever variable they happen to consider crucial.

What is proposed here is not the elimination of the use of the adjectives "traditional" and "modern." "Traditional" remains a shorthand way of dealing with the whole past experience of any society such as China before the impact of the modern West; furthermore, within this past one can indubitably find ongoing, recognizable, coherent traditions. The modern West has certainly witnessed the emergence of qualitatively new developments as well as the acceleration of other developments to a point where quantity almost seems to pass over into quality. There is, however, no reason to assume any preestablished harmony among elements called traditional, on the one hand, or modern, on the other—nor any necessary a priori incompatibility between modern elements and traditional elements.

It is worthy of note that in the triad the only truly dynamic term is the middle term, "development." Tradition is treated as a kind of static setting whose essential features can be described in terms of a few well-chosen propositions. It is not denied that diachronic change did take place within traditional societies. It is simply assumed that such changes are not important or relevant. Furthermore, while modernity is not contrasted to change—the acceptance of change as a value is one of the earmarks of modernity—the change always tends to be regarded as incremental change within the framework of an established modernity. Futurological speculations, for example, in spite of their stress on change, particularly in technology, are based for the most part on the extrapolation of certain variables which are regarded as established and irreversible. Indeed certain kinds of incremental change are themselves regarded as inexorably fixed.

In recent years,[2] however, there has emerged the notion that some traditions, far from impeding certain aspects of modernization, may have actually facilitated them in some societies. The variables which differentiate one traditional culture from another may be more important than the features they share. Yet in vast numbers of textbooks which still provide the intellectual food of innumerable schools of secondary and higher learning, the vulgar concept of traditional society has become almost a fixed dogma and has encouraged the philistine view that the total past experience of mankind is irrelevant and, on all important matters, homogeneous. Furthermore, while there has been some progress among those who deal in these matters toward a more complicated view of traditional society,[3] the notion that we all know precisely what we are talking about when we discuss the modernity pole of this triadic formula still remains, on the whole, unchallenged.

Tradition and Modernity—Some General Reflections

The difference between traditional and modern society is most often made to depend on some crucial variable. Among the most convincing and indisputable of these polarities is probably that of agrarian society versus industrial society. If one can assert that all peasant societies are alike in their *essential* features and that all change over time in such societies is inconsequential, one can of course go on to discount all the differences in the "high cultures" and in the historic development of these societies which in any event are assumed to affect only the ruling strata or intellectuals.

I shall not dwell here on the features which all peasant societies may share. While there are no doubt many, there is a tendency to accept them uncritically. I would question the assertion that even on the level of the rural village, differentiating cultural features are inconsequential. The difference between the caste structure of the Indian village and the various structures of Chinese peasant life are of crucial importance from any point of view. While it is often asserted that the political superstructures of these societies have little effect on the daily life of the villager, the differing political histories of China and India have in fact had a great deal to do with the endemic nature of widespread peasant rebellions in China and their relative lack in India. What is more, the iron wall which many erect between the "high cultures" and the "little cultures" is not easily maintained under close inspection. In fact, in all these societies Confucianism, Hinduism, Islam, and Buddhism cut across the folk culture/high culture barrier in both directions.

When we turn our attention to the so-called high cultures or Great Traditions themselves, the question of whether they concerned themselves with significant or real questions is ultimately a philosophic question, but it also bears most directly on whether traditional modalities of thought, attitudes, and sensibilities derived from the past continue to affect the outlooks of intellectuals in modernizing and modern societies. One of the most facile ways of dismissing the high cultures of the past is to assert that they encompassed a kind of closed symbolic world of concern only to limited strata and that they had little or no effect on or meaning for the lives of the masses. One might make precisely the same observation concerning the culture of academic and literary intellectuals in modern societies. The questions discussed and issues raised in our own intellectual media and the language in which they are discussed are more often than not quite inaccessible, even to the literate. In fact, quotations from the Confucian classics were probably more immediately available to the masses in China than passages from George Lukacs, Lévi-Strauss, or Herbert Marcuse are to the masses in the West. Yet this observation can hardly be used as a way of determining whether Western intellectuals deal with problems of the real world. Given our criteria of relevance, the issues which divided Ch'an Buddhists from Neo-Confucianists in Sung China, or Chu Hsi from Wang Yang-ming, may or may not appear significant. The fact that their discourses and debates may or may not have found an echo in every village, however, can by no means be used as a criterion for judging the general human significance and relevance of their preoccupations.

I have here spoken of issues, questions, and debates. These words tend to imply the existence of both synchronic and diachronic conflicts and tensions within the Great Traditions. This, of course, is quite contrary to the view of these Great Traditions as essentially static, integrated, unproblematic wholes which can be described in a few well-chosen propositions. It is by no means my intention to deny the presence of persistent and predominant tendencies within traditional cultures or to deny that there were in them limits to the range of alternative approaches to human experience. Yet the more closely we examine these Great Traditions, the more we are impressed with the broadness of the range and the variety of alternatives within them; also, the more we are conscious of the significance of change over time.

Even if we focus our attention on one coherent dominant tendency within the culture such as Confucianism in China, we soon find that Confucianism itself has had a complicated and turbulent history replete with unresolved problems. To be sure, it is possible to claim that the heart of Confucianism is the Confucian family ethic and that this has remained fundamentally unchanged over time. The Chinese social structure is marked by the centrality of the family; Confucian values provide the operative norms of this structure. Hence, whatever debates may have gone on among Confucian literati and Confucian philosophers can hardly have affected the central social function of Confucianism. They were probably concerned with matters of secondary importance.

One of the characteristic features of this particular sociological view of the role of norms within a social system is that it tends to ignore the gap between norms and the way things actually work. Yet many ethical philosophers have been concerned not only with the contents of given value systems but precisely with the question of how and to what extent any values are ever realized. Within the sociological perspective, the whole persistent tragic sense of tension between the ideal and the actual which has existed among sensitive spirits in every higher civilization simply disappears from view. In China, the lament that the ways of the world were far removed from the higher values of Confucianism was so persistent down through the ages that it became a cliché of Chinese literature, while those literati (probably the vast majority) who were complacently prepared to define the current state of affairs as Confucian were dismissed by the more creative intellectuals as *su ju* (vulgar or conventional Confucianists).

Even if one assumes that Confucian family morality was more or less successfully actualized over large areas of Chinese society and over long stretches of time, there is a serious question of whether Confucianism can be simply equated with the family ethic. The centrality of family values existed before Confucius and was rooted in pre-Confucian Chinese religion. Confucius may have already accepted filial piety as an ultimate value, but he placed it within a new context. His contribution lay in his attention to the problems of inner self-cultivation, what might be called the subjective springs of morality, and on the manner in which he related this problem to the whole sociopolitical realm. The family becomes simply one element within this larger frame.

If Confucianism is viewed in this light, one can immediately understand why the efforts to realize its higher values led to enormous and even tragic problems for serious thinkers. How is the Confucian ideal of individual self-realization ever to be attained? What is the relation of knowledge to ethics? What indeed is the relationship of personal ethics to action within the political realm? Is centralized bureaucratic organization compatible with Confucian values? What is the relationship of technical administrative capacity to morality? Was the bureaucratic state structure which had emerged after the Ch'in compatible with the Confucian stress on personal relations? Weber calls the Chinese system "patrimonial bureaucracy," but many Confucian idealists found it far too bureaucratic and far too little patrimonial. To what extent are Confucian ethical and sociopolitical values realizable in the world out there? What is the relationship of the aesthetic to the ethical realm? Some of the general problems which arise in the history of Confucianism when separated from the framework of specific Confucian assumptions within which they are constrained may be recognized as real issues even by those who live in modern Western society. As in all societies, of course, these issues became deeply enmeshed with conflicts of material and political interest, but in this respect traditional China was no different from any other society, traditional or modern.

I have dwelt here on the kinds of tension and conflict which can be found within the dominant strain of Confucianism. When one adds to this the counter-Confucian tendencies which have often been vaguely grouped under the headings of Taoism, Buddhism, and Legalism, and the complex relations of these tendencies to various aspects of Chinese folk culture, the picture of an immobile traditional setting fades. Incidentally, the notion that the countertendencies of Chinese culture simply faded away in the last few centuries of Confucian orthodoxy also becomes more doubtful the more we immerse ourselves in the concrete specificities of Ming and Ch'ing history.

Thus, a common conventional picture of the Chinese literati who first confronted the modern West in the early nineteenth century is that of somnabulant mandarins complacently embedded in the unchanging essence of Chinese tradition. Here again we must draw a sharp distinction between the unreflective mass of conventional literati and the serious thinkers. The latter were profoundly troubled by the situation in late eighteenth- and early nineteenth-century China and profoundly involved in the intellectual debates of their times. Thus at the end of the eighteenth century a strong reaction had set in against a kind of prevailing scholarly positivism which was found by some to be increasingly irrelevant to the problems of the time. There was also a revival of interest in statecraft and in philosophies of personal ethics. There was even some revival of interest in Buddhist philosophy. Within this context, the problems created by the western "sea-barbarians" were simply a novel problem in statecraft. Thus what we are dealing with is not so much paralytic immobility as a sense of assurance that somewhere within the rich and cumulative range of experience provided by the Chinese past could be found ways of coping with contemporary problems. The past provided not so much an integrated tradition as a reservoir of conflicting responses to human experience. There was in fact no Chinese word for tradition in this large and vague sense (the term *chüan-t'ung,* while Chinese in origin, came back to China from Japan as a neologism). It is only at the end of the century that we find a generation which finally began to question whether this range of experience was still adequate and which thus became open to new ideas from the West.

If tradition cannot be reduced to a simple integrated system, what can we say of modernity? Since our focus here is on intellectuals, we must be interested in modernity not merely as descriptive of certain processes of action but also as embodied in certain modes of thought and sensibility. For purposes of convenience, I shall here draw a distinction between modernization as referring to processes of development in economic, political, legal, military, and other realms of action and modernity as referring to certain modes of thought and sensibility. In dealing with modernization as a system of action I shall treat it in terms of Weber's conception of "rationalization," for it seems quite clear that the Weberian conception has been dominant in the American social scientific use of this term. Modernization refers to all those realms of life in which man can achieve the ends of world mastery by the individual and collective employment of rationally effective means. To the extent that modernization is linked to an idea, it is precisely this idea of the mastery of the world of nature as well as of the social world of man.[4] While many of Weber's conceptions of the prerequisites of *Zwecksrationalität* in various areas have been challenged, the validity of the general framework will be assumed for purposes of this essay.

What then has been the relationship of modernization in this sense to all those ideas, ideologies, attitudes, and orientations which have emerged in the modern world since the seventeenth and eighteenth centuries? One might presumably resolve this question by asserting that all ideas which facilitate the process of modernization should be labeled modern while all ideas which are contrary to the process of modernization might be considered nonmodern or antimodern. Leaving aside the controversial nature of this question, the overwhelming force of general usage has tended to label as modern all sorts of tendencies and ideas which may stand in a very questionable relationship to modernization (such as the modernist movement in literature). The force of ordinary usage seems sound and defensible, for in fact there is even less warrant for assuming that modernity is an integrated whole than that tradition is. The eighteenth-century Enlightenment itself contained many mutually contradictory tendencies. Yet all of these tendencies were new tendencies.[5] Some may insist on using the word "modern" as a eulogistic term descriptive only of the particular values cherished, but the term can never shed its primary sense of time reference. Rousseau was not less modern than Voltaire nor was Immanuel Kant a whit less modern than Jeremy Bentham. Many of the conflicts central to the French Revolution may have been quite tangential to the business of modernization as here defined. Saint-Simon, the creator of the term "industrialism," felt precisely that all the sound and fury of the revolution, all the frenzied moralism of the Jacobins, had been a diversion from serious technological business. Yet would anyone really deny that revolutions have continued to be an important part of the modern human experience or that Rousseau's pathos—which sees the whole question of society as a social ethical drama—has been as much a part of human experience as the pathos of those who have seen the problem wholly in terms of social technology?

What indeed is the relationship between modernization—the mastery of the world—and other values such as liberty, equality, democracy, and collectivity, which figure so prominently in the sociopolitical "isms" of the modern world? One cannot assume an a priori logical relationship because rational men have differed from each other profoundly concerning these matters. One can conceive of liberty, equality, and democracy without modernization as Weberian rationalization. Montesquieu, Jefferson, and Rousseau were convinced that obsessive concern with economic growth was detrimental to democracy, while Max Weber himself, who was a political liberal (and probably never thought of raising questions concerning the modernity of liberalism), was profoundly agonized by the implications of the bureaucratization of society incident to modernization for the survival of political liberty. He saw not a functional relation but a profound tension between these two elements of modernity.

The nineteenth and twentieth centuries have been rich in social philosophies which assert all sorts of necessary functional relationships between the process of modernization and particular political social values. One might say that an underlying shared assumption of these ideologies is that all the factors of progress must be harmonious with each other either immediately or ultimately. Such political and social values are often presented as either a necessary concomitant or function of the modernization process or a final outcome of this process. One way of viewing mature Marxism is to see in it the assertion that the process of modernization, here described as the capitalist mode of production,[6] must itself lead to the realization of socialism, while American social scientists have often seen in liberal values (as they understand them) the final culmination of the process of modernization. The doctrine of the "end of ideology" does not involve a rejection of given sociopolitical values. It rather involves the assumption that the modernization process, in its mature phase, will itself achieve these values without the intervention of moral and ideological passions. This is, of course, not the place to undertake a consideration of the modes of reasoning which enter into these various ways of linking modernization to sociopolitical philosophies. Suffice it to say that these controversies remain unresolved and that a non-Western intellectual looking in at the intellectual scene in Europe and America during the whole span of the twentieth century could not help but be aware of profound conflict and confusion on all these matters.

Beyond the unresolved controversies concerning sociopolitical ideals and modernization, what are we to say of such an important and recurrent movement of the modern spirit as Romanticism? Romanticism may share with modernization a certain Faustian striving for mastery, but in this case it is not so much mastering the machinery of material and social technology as conquering of the world of affective experience and sensibility. Of course, what it rejects most emphatically is what it regards as the desiccation of feeling in the cool and gray pathos of the machine-like world of modernization as a socioeconomic process.

What are we to say finally about the whole modernist movement in literature and art, which often reflects a range of attitudes toward modernization running the gamut from vehement negativity to indifference? C. P. Snow loudly lamented the lack of congeniality between one of his two cultures and the other, but it never occurred to him to impugn the modernity of the literary culture. One is reluctant to use the cliché "alienation," yet it does say something about the nature of much modern literature.

One could extend ad infinitum the discussion of the tensions, conflicts, and incommunicabilities within the world of modernity. One could point to such diverse phenomena as the lack of communication between the worlds of Anglo-American linguistic philosophers and French existentialists, or to the ambiguous relations to modernization of the various movements spawned by Freud, in spite of his own self-conception as a thoroughly modern engineer of the soul. Enough has been said, it seems to me, to make it quite clear that the word "modernity" refers to no simple entity.

It may, of course, be true that at a deeper level many of the disparate movements and clashing ideas of the modern West may rest on certain unexpressed common assumptions. Perhaps they all share a pervading anthropocentrism, a tendency to view the nonhuman universe as meaningless and irrelevant to human values. The various specific social and political ideologies may share with the more technocratic orientation a tendency to think in terms of the management and transformation of macroscopic social structures and of institutional frameworks or systems rather than in terms of personal self-transformation or personal ethics. Yet whatever may be the underlying common premises, the horizontal tensions and conflicts among the various currents and countercurrents of the modern world make it impossible to think of modernity as any kind of completed or synthetic whole.

Chinese Intellectuals, Tradition, and Modernity

If Chinese tradition refers to a vast and variegated experience which we have only begun to study in depth and if modernity refers to a complex and unresolved state of affairs, this does not suggest that we are likely to discover a simple development model which will adequately explain the behavior of the Chinese intelligentsia during the period of transition (a period which, it seems to me, has hardly ended) from one to the other.

What makes the construction of such a model even less likely is that in dealing with the concrete experience of intellectuals within any given society we must introduce between tradition and modernity another crucial variable, namely the concrete specificities of history. In China the end of the examination system in 1905, the Japanese incursion into China, Mao's all-out Cultural Revolutionary assault on the intelligentsia—to mention certain events at random—are specific historic movements which must figure in any effort to understand the experiences and the responses of Chinese intellectuals within the time period with which we are concerned. None of these specificities are reducible to the abstractions of tradition and modernity. One's interest in Chinese intellectuals cannot simply be in their role within some preestablished sociohistoric scheme. One must be intrinsically interested in the situations in which they find themselves and in how their ideas and passions relate to their situations. Out of this may emerge either an enrichment or stretching of the triadic scheme or perhaps even an abandonment of it in favor of more adequate conceptions. Whether we deal with large tendencies, groups, or single individuals, the tradition/modernity polarity will in itself seldom, if ever, be adequate to the subject of our investigation.

Thus, if we consider what might be called the transitional generation, which reached its creative peak in the last decade of the nineteenth century and the first two decades of the twentieth century, and which included among its leading figures such luminaries as K'ang Yu-wei, Yen Fu, Chang Ping-lin, Lin Shu, Liang Ch'i-ch'ao, Wang Kuo-wei, T'an Ssu-t'ung, and others, we find a group whose early life had been profoundly molded by traditional China. To a degree, this remains true of the younger generation of Ch'en Tu-hsiu, Hu Shih, Lu Hsün, and even of the student generation of May 4th. Depending upon a wide variety of social and geographic circumstances, many of the latter also spent their earliest childhood years in traditional China. Nevertheless, if one's conception of psychology allows one to concede that the second decade of the life cycle may be as crucial as the first, one must give enormous weight to the different life experiences of the two generations. The first decade of the twentieth century was to witness the demise of the imperial examination system and the scramble of the young to find new educational paths (often in westernized schools) into an unknown future. All of this took place largely within an urban environment which was itself undergoing unprecedented change at an ever-accelerating pace. In contrast, the older generation of intellectuals had still faced all the rigors and frustrations of the examination system and still had some expectation that the political system would continue to hold together.

The older generation of intellectuals was at home in the medium of classical Chinese,[7] with its rich burden of allusion, metaphors, and quotations derived from the culture of the past, and continued to be comfortable with traditional lifestyles. Some of its leading figures found the traditional family system quite tolerable on a personal level even when they were prepared to criticize it in the abstract. Few of them seemed to find traditional family practices as unendurable as they were to become for some young men and women of the next generation.

Above all, this generation lived sufficiently within the Chinese cultural stream to see it not as a harmonious integrated tradition but more as an arena of tensions, alternatives, and conflicts. They were thoroughly familiar with the intellectual tendencies of eighteenth- and nineteenth-century China, and the animosities aroused by the relations among the various schools of literati even continued to shape their relationships to each other. The youthful K'ang Yu-wei had turned against the narrow "irrelevance" of the still dominant scholastic philological school *(K'ao cheng-p'ai)* which, in his view, had little to say about the sufferings of men and the higher truths of Confucianism. He had for a time turned back to the thinkers of the Sung and Ming who had emphasized personal self-realization and had even been attracted by the radical transcendentalism of Buddhism. In the end, however, he believed that he found in a certain strain of early Han dynasty thought (the New Text School) the basis for a kind of redemptive philosophy of history which offered new hope for the collective future of mankind. He was probably already in contact with Western theories of progress which he must have read back into his New Text philosophy. Yet the point is that this new Western element was fed back into a mental world still formed by the *problematic* of nineteenth-century Chinese thought.

It was precisely this generation[8] which was to move well beyond the available range of Chinese thought and which was to prove eminently receptive to ideas from the West. Indeed, the more closely we examine their writings, the more impressed we are with the degree of openness and responsiveness to every variety of modern Western thought.

Their pervasive preoccupation[9] (particularly after the Sino-Japanese

War of 1894–95) was a concern for China's survival as a sociopolitical entity. As a group which still thought of itself in traditional terms as a state service class, one might say that its public concern with the nation's survival and its private status anxiety moved in the same direction. It was thus this generation that directly confronted the dread question: Were the resources of the culture of the past adequate to preserve China as an independent political entity? One of their number, Yen Fu puts the matter quite baldly: "We have no time to ask whether this knowledge is Chinese or Western, whether it is new or old. If one course leads to ignorance and thus to poverty and weakness ... we must cast it aside, if another course is effective in overcoming ignorance and thus leads to the cure of our poverty and weakness we must imitate it even if it proceeds from barbarians."[10] Having subordinated other values to the survival of the nation state, he has crossed the divide between what Western students of China call "culturalism" (what the Chinese call *pao-tao* or "preserving the Way") and modern nationalism. This is true even of those conservative nationalists such as Chang Ping-lin who continue to emphasize the importance of preserving the cultural tradition in the interests of identity. We are often struck by the degree to which Western ideas and "isms"—equality, liberty, socialism—came to be viewed in China in terms of their efficacy as a means to the achievement of national wealth and power as well as ends in themselves.

This concern with nationalist goals implies more than nationalism as such. It implies nothing less than a positive orientation to modernization and the Faustian-Promethean values underlying modernization. One is astonished by how Weberian are the prescriptions which one finds in the writings of K'ang Yu-wei, Yen Fu, and Liang Ch'i-ch'ao. Whatever their differences, they are all concerned with the rationalization of the economic, bureaucratic, military, and legal spheres of life.

Yet while Western ideas and ideologies are often viewed as instrumental to national goals, they are also viewed in terms of their own intrinsic meanings. One finds an influx of a wide variety of specific sociopolitical "isms" of eighteenth- and nineteenth-century Europe (albeit in a somewhat crude and simplified form) as well as all the puzzles involved in Western theories concerning the relationship of such ideologies to the process of modernization. Thus alongside of the scientific pathos of Yen Fu, who looks to nineteenth-century

England as the teacher of piecemeal social engineering, we find the passionate revolutionary pathos of those who steep themselves in their own versions of Rousseau, the epic of the French Revolution, and the activities of contemporary Russian revolutionaries.

This openness to the variety of Western thought when combined with the ongoing appreciation of the variety of Chinese thought leads this generation to perceive not only antitheses but also affinities, similarities, and compatibilities between specific elements of Chinese traditional thought and specific varieties of modern Western thought. Some of this is, to be sure, disingenuous and even puerile, explicable only in terms of the need to salvage national pride. Much of it is no doubt simply wrong and yet may reflect the brute fact that these people are inevitably forced to use the categories of thought and language available to them to assimilate the new ideas of the West.

I would submit at this point that there are no a priori grounds for assuming that all such attempts to find affinities and compatibilities are wrong in principle. There may indeed be elements of Chinese traditional thought which are similar to or compatible with elements of modern Western thought.[11] Only a careful study based on a thorough knowledge of the history of ideas and feel for language in both cultures can in the end determine whether any proposition of this type is valid or invalid. We find ourselves only at the very beginning of such transcultural investigations. When Yen Fu in his reading of T. H. Huxley[12] confronts the problem of whether human behavior can be wholly explained in terms of biological propensities or whether culture must be introduced as an independent variable, it occurs to him that *on the most general level* this debate had gone on in Chinese culture and that the Hsün-tzu had adopted a position strikingly similar to that of Huxley. He had also believed that the anarchic biological propensities which man derived from nature can be brought under the control of the countervailing force of human culture. At the same time, Yen Fu is also acutely and even insistently aware of what is radically new in the Darwinian interpretation of biological reality. When others see identities between Rousseau and the book of Mencius, we cannot dismiss their claims out of hand but must examine the extent to which they may or may not be founded. We should not be deterred by culturalistic-historistic dogmas that there cannot possibly be any comparison between the thoughts of a

Chinese literatus living several centuries before Christ and those of a neurotic social philosopher in eighteenth-century France.

Again, when T'an Ssu-t'ung finds in Buddhist philosophy as well as in Taoism and even some strands of Confucianism a kind of transcendental ground from which he can carry out an all-out attack on the ontological foundations of many of the forms and structures of contemporary Chinese society, he can find such grounds because they did indeed exist and had even been used in the past for similar purpose. When he uses this antiformalistic mysticism as a kind of bridge to a cult of energy and dynamism of the Western type he has obviously added something new. Finally, while China may have never known revolution in the modern Western sense, there were available utopian motifs and apocalyptic themes which could be fused in a potent blend with certain revolutionary tendencies out of the West as in the writings of some anarchists and revolutionaries before 1911.

The complex dialectic of conscious and unconscious relations between the culture of the past and modernity is not confined to the pre–1911 generation, although it was most clearly illustrated in the life experiences of that generation. It continues on into the present in complex and unresolved forms.

To be sure, in the generation which reached intellectual maturity after the 1911 revolution,[13] the concept of Chinese tradition or culture as an integrated whole to be rejected as a whole, does indeed emerge. Here we have a generation obviously less inside the Chinese past than the older generation. It was also a generation which keenly experienced the failures of the 1911 revolution and the political disintegration which followed that revolution. The experience of the years 1911–1919 certainly lent plausibility to a totalistic view of the traditional culture as a vast, inert, and uniform incubus strangling the vital spirits of the nation. One Chinese scholar, Lin Yu-sheng, has suggested that this totalistic rejection of Chinese culture in the May 4th period (which was, of course, not universal at this time or later) may itself be an unconscious reflection of a predominant traditional tendency to regard the cultural and political order as one and indivisible. (This had not led even in the past to any necessary consensus on the true nature of this cultural-political order.) With the collapse of the political order all aspects of the culture of the past lost their credibility. A totalistic view of culture led dialectically to a

totalistic rejection of culture and beyond that to the yearning for a
new totalistic cultural-political order of the future. Even in this generation, as Mr. Lin would gladly concede, when one focuses one's attention on its more creative individual representatives such as the
writer Lu Hsün, one finds that the totalistic rejection of the past is
often complicated by countermotifs. One thus finds in Lu Hsün both
a vehement fury against the "man-eating" Confucian society of the
past combined with a sensibility which is still under the spell of
many aspects of Chinese folk culture and even of certain strains of
the high culture of the past. Alongside of the rejection of the past we
find a profound suspicion of many aspects of modern European
urban culture and particularly of the contemporary Chinese "all-out
Westerners" who represent this culture in China.

Nevertheless, the rejection of the Chinese past did lead to a general search for answers in the modern West. So powerful had the
categories of Western thought become that even those who now
chose to defend tradition sought their arguments not in Chinese literature but in the writings of Bergson and Babbitt, Eucken and Rus-
sell. The modern West, however, yielded no unitary answers. One
could find totalistic formulas which would sum up the Chinese past
but one could not find unitary formulas which would sum up all the
conflicting ideas and "isms" of modernity. Chinese intellectuals
were confronted with all the conflicts and unresolved tensions of
modernity as well as with the difficulty of applying any variety of
modernity to Chinese conditions. Ch'en Tu-hsiu, one of the great
spokesmen of totalistic antitraditionalism, drifted from a kind of
French liberalism to Marxism-Leninism to a quasi-Trotskyite version of Marxism-Leninism to social democracy, while Hu Shih
came to regard himself as a spokesman of John Dewey's variety of
liberalism. Accidents of individual fate often partially conditioned
such philosophic decisions. The fact that Hu Shih was a student at
Columbia University under John Dewey led him to a quite different
version of modernity from that of many of his peers who studied in
Tokyo. This reminds us once more of the degree to which the varieties of modernity in the West itself have been defined by the confin-
ing boundaries of disparate national cultures. Again, others of a
more literary-poetic bent such as Hsü Chih-mo, Yü Ta-fu, and Kuo
Mo-jo fell under the spell of Western Romanticism. They saw
China's cultural crisis much more in terms of the mystery of their

individual existence than in terms of national destiny or the tasks of modernization.

We shall not attempt to recount the troubled intellectual history of China (that is, the intellectual history of the small but crucial intelligentsia) between 1920 and the rise of the People's Republic. The intellectuals who rejected the past did not arrive at common conclusions concerning the essence of modernity nor did the totalistic rejection of the past abolish the continuing influence of that past, for good or ill, on the shaping of the present. For one thing, the vast majority of the Chinese rural population still continued to live habitually within the framework of a popular culture inherited from the past and continued to look to types of local intellectuals such as secret society leaders, Buddhist monks, Taoist priests, leaders of Confucian uplift societies, and popular sects. The latter did not look to Bergson or Babbitt for justification although some Western notions did creep into their fund of ideas. Not only were the intellectuals forced to confront this fact but their own relationship to the past continued to be complex on many conscious and unconscious levels. Nor can one dismiss the ideas of such neo-traditionalists as Feng Yu-lan, Liang Sou-ming, or Hsiung Shih-li merely on the ground that they defended Chinese traditions—to some degree—in terms of Western categories.

One can perhaps make a certain case for the assertion that the intellectual history of China after 1920 conformed to a certain pattern common to all developing countries. Certain types of political and economic liberalism were not to flourish among the Chinese intelligentsia although they continued to be represented. All the objective factors which have proved inimical to Western liberalism elsewhere could certainly be found in China. One might add that however much the "higher civilizations" of the past may have differed from each other in terms of their ethical orientations, they have, on the whole, shared a negative attitude toward the pursuit of individual material self-interest as a value and striven for consensus rather than for pluralism and dissent. From this point of view, to the extent that Western liberalism is identified with a capitalist ethic and pluralism as an ideal it is probably the most exotic and subversive product of modern Western thought. The resistance to these aspects of liberalism has gone on in the heart of the modern West, and antiliberal tendencies in China, whether of right or left, have from the outset been able to draw much of their doctrinal sustenance from the West. In this sense, antiliberal intellectuals in China and the developing world in general have been thoroughly contemporary with powerful ongoing tendencies in the Western world.

One must add that the word "liberalism" is a semantic monster burdened with an enormous accumulation of meanings. Looking at the fate of Chinese intellectuals on both the mainland and Taiwan from the perspective of 1971, one becomes aware of the fact that they had not remained untouched by all strands of liberalism and that Mao Tse-tung is not entirely wrong when he accuses them of a kind of ineradicable liberalism. It would appear that even intellectuals who had long since committed themselves to the Chinese Communist movement had to a greater or lesser degree continued to believe in intellectual autonomy and in the much abhorred doctrine that "all men are equal before the truth." In any event neither liberalism and antiliberalism nor tradition and modernity are dichotomies that adequately explain the specificities of Chinese developments since 1949, particularly as they affect the intellectuals.

This is, of course, not the place to consider the intellectual biography of Mao Tse-tung. Yet if we are to say anything about the fate of the intellectuals in the People's Republic we must say something about their main antagonist. Mao's mistrust of the intellectuals[14] has early roots and was highly developed by 1949. In his view, the urban intellectuals were isolated from the realities with which he had been contending since the early Hunan-Kiangsi days. Their individualistic vanity led them to insist stubbornly on the validity of their own mistaken ideas. They had a built-in tendency to complicate simple truths and to seek ironies and ambiguities. They could not give themselves unreservedly to the battle and submit to the general will of the masses as Mao understood that will.

Nevertheless, it never seemed to occur to Mao before 1949 that the intellectuals were dispensable. Their thoughts would have to be transformed but they were necessary to the tasks which lay ahead. If the tasks of revolution in China had been reducible to simple maxims, the tasks of building socialism would probably be difficult and complex (as Soviet experience had demonstrated). During the Hundred Flowers experiment of 1956–57, he even offered more freedom for intellectuals on the assumption that they had been "basically transformed." The results of that experience were, of course, to reconfirm his worst suspicions of them and to lead to the grander visions of both the Great Leap Forward and the Cultural Revolution— visions which projected the truly radical possibility of a Chinese road to modernization without intellectuals. The older intellectuals continued to embody all the corruptions, ambiguities, and cultural superfluities of both traditional China and the modern West. They were the inveterate enemies of that new morality which would show the world that modernization and national power were not incompatible with a life of collective simplicity.

When one asks whether this vision is traditional or modern, one emerges with no clear answer. To the extent that it involves commitment to further modernization, it is, of course, modern. To the extent that it embodies primitivist yearnings, it may draw on Mao's early and ardent admiration for that type of Chinese literature which depicts the untutored yet purehearted tough guys *(yu-hsia)* of Chinese history as contrasted with the corrupt mandarins. It may owe something to the primitivist critique of the overcomplexity and corruption of "higher civilization" which finds expression as early as the Book of Lao-tzu and which remains a persistent motif of Chinese culture. It may even draw on the facile moralism of certain varieties of Confucianism. One can look here to the Sage-Kings of hoary antiquity who transformed the hearts of men through their mana-like virtue.

Through Marxism-Leninism and other Western influences, one can also point to Western sources, to the kind of deep resentment of the vanity, insincerity, and selfishness of fellow intellectuals which one finds in Rousseau. One can point to many highly relevant attacks of Robespierre on the treachery of *les esprits* and their exasperating inability to align themselves with the general good. One can even point to *The Greening of America.*

If one asks oneself how it is conceivable that the primitivist critique of high civilization can be found in both "undeveloped" traditional societies and in the modern West, it must be pointed out that development may be very much a matter of perspective. To the author of the Lao-tzu, Chinese society of his time was already overcomplicated, full of needless artificialities, and therefore corrupt. In all of this we may be dealing with an orientation which transcends the dichotomy of both East and West, of both tradition and modernity.

But what of the intellectuals themselves? Their experience since 1949 has indeed demonstrated that the Chinese intelligentsia, like intellectuals everywhere, do dwell on complexities, are attuned to ambiguities and ironies, and do indeed tend to develop a strong stake in their own ideas. In this sense they are the enemies of simplicity although in other contexts they may also be the great yearners for simplicity. When the opportunity arises, they continue to find meaning in the culture of the past, they continue to be attracted by various tendencies in the West, and they continue to stress theoretical complexities.

What then of the future? If Mao's experiment does not succeed and a new generation of intellectuals does emerge (the Maoists have practically succeeded in stilling the voice of the older generation), where will it go? If it reacts against the Cultural Revolution will it finally achieve modernity? The entire drift of what has been said above would suggest that the only proper approach to these questions is one of Socratic ignorance—an openness to unforeseen possibilities. Since Mao has carried out an across-the-board attack against the Chinese cultural past, the whole gamut of modern Western culture, and the pretensions of technological expertise, one might, in China, expect, at least for a time, a common front among the representatives of all these tendencies. What they share in common, after all, is a defense of cultural complexity and the values of high culture. Under conditions of relaxation one would expect to see Chinese intellectuals renew their interest in the West, but the modern West of 1972 is not the West of 1919. It is more deeply involved than ever in its own unresolved intellectual and moral crises. One would thus expect a new Chinese intellectual generation to be far less passive and far more critical in its relations to various tendencies in the West. (This is already visible in some of our Chinese students.) Some tendencies out of the past might witness a strong revival, and the dialectic of relationship of traditional and modern factors would continue to produce novel combinations. Since China's objective situation remains vastly different from that of the West (for example, in the overwhelming weight of its agrarian population), China may indeed have to develop its own patterns of modernization. Thus neither tradition nor modernity provide the image of China's future in a world where the future of modernity itself remains unclear.

4

The Age of Transcendence

*I*t has frequently been observed by Jaspers and others that the first millennium B.C. (or perhaps more accurately the first seven or eight hundred years B.C.) witness the roughly simultaneous occurrence of such developments as the rise of classical Judaism through the prophets and the beginning of rabbinic Judaism, Zoroastrianism in Persia, the Upanishads and Buddhism in India, Confucianism, Taoism, and the "hundred schools" in China, and Homer, Hesiod, the Pre-Socratics and classical philosophy in Greece.

What is the significance of this observation? Does the significance lie in the fact of simultaneity itself? Is the simultaneity significant because it suggests the possibility of cross-cultural influences or because it suggests that all the "higher civilizations" of the ancient world had reached a roughly similar point in a kind of unilinear evolution? If the latter is true, to what extent is it true? In what sense can one speak of common lines of development and in what sense are the qualitative differences among these cultures and among the various spiritual and intellectual developments mentioned above more significant than the shared features?

For purposes of argument I shall here postulate that the question of "influence" or of "diffusion from a center" versus "independent origin" is not a particularly interesting or significant question from the point of view of the issues here considered. Undoubtedly, the entire evolution of man, both pre-historic and after the rise of the higher civilizations, has been marked by the diffusion of separate material and social technologies and perhaps even of religious and scientific ideas over vast areas. Yet in dealing with the developments of what is here tentatively called the age of transcendence, the question of how ideas are used in given contexts seems to me much more significant than the supposed paternity of such ideas.

Nevertheless, the fact of simultaneity may have a profound significance if one is prepared to recognize the existence of common features in the evolution of all the higher civilizations. If such common features exist, one may postulate that all of these civilizations had reached a period of crisis which called forth new spiritual, intellectual, and moral visions among certain groups and individuals.

The definition of higher civilizations is by no means easy. Jaspers feels quite self-assured in drawing a sharp line between the higher civilizations and the "Naturvölker" (primitive peoples). Yet, as Lévi-Strauss insists, the so-called primitive peoples have structures of language, religion, and mythology which are neither more "natürlich" nor necessarily less complex than those of the higher civilizations. What strikes one first of all in the higher civilizations is the imposition of common cultural patterns and often political authority over extensive areas and vast masses of people. One of the implications of this difference of scale is the division and specialization of labor over a vast society rather than within the tribal unit. Writing, spectacular advances in material technology, "universal kingship" and bureaucracy, large-scale military organization, law codes, the rise of cities, and large-scale religious organizations all argue for a kind of broad frontal advance (over centuries) of material and social technology—a kind of first "rationalization" of society in the Weberian sense.

To be sure, the Weberian coupling of "rationalization" with "disenchantment of the world" hardly applies. In all of these civilizations we find a world permeated throughout with the divine, the sacred, and the mythic. The divine forces support—are indeed consubstantial with—the powers and manifestations of both the world of nature and the world of human civilization. Even the demonic is in some sense affirmed. There is as yet no clear association between religion and other-worldliness or world denial.

None of this implies that the higher civilizations of Egypt, Mesopotamia, or China were essentially alike. There were enormous differences in the rate of development in various sectors of material and social technology, and as Henri Frankfort vehemently insisted, the religious developments of ancient Egypt and Mesopotamia were profoundly different. The orientation to "ancestor worship" in ancient China had specific implications for the subsequent development of Chinese culture. The cultural differences which existed before the age of transcendence unquestionably conditioned the direction assumed by the transcendental "breakthroughs" within these various cultures.

Again, the schematic distinction drawn here between the age of transcendence and the previous period is heuristic as are all periodization schemes. Jacobsen has stressed the strain toward transcendence which can be found in ancient Mesopotamian religion and even in the Gilgamesh epic. In Egypt, one need hardly dwell on Ichnaton and other elements in Egyptian literature. In India, the transition from the religion of the Vedas to the religion of the Upanishads is long and involved. Confucius and the Lao-tzu book were preceded by centuries of moral and spiritual development which are reflected in the authenticated portions of the *Book of Songs* and *Book of Documents*.

By transcendence I refer here to what seem to be common features—the standing back, the looking beyond, the negation of the actual which is a kind of common strain symbolized by Abraham's departure from Ur, the much more radical negations of Gautama, Confucius turning inward to the source of *jen*, the Lao-tzu book's yearning for the reality which is nameless, and the Pre-Socratics' search for ultimate principles lying behind the messy multiplicity of the world. Judaism negates the immanence of the divine in either nature or civilization, but does not devalue the world of the finite, the individuated and the multiple, while early Buddhism tends to find in individuated existence itself the source of ultimate evil.

In the Middle East, as Jaspers points out, the most radical bearers of transcendence are to be found within two fringe outsider groups—the Greeks and the Jews—while the Mesopotamian, Egyptian, and Canaanite cultural spheres do not experience a fundamental "breakthrough." In "Aryan" India and China the strain toward transcendence takes place within the framework of a more or less established culture.

These strains toward transcendence effect only small groups of people and do not immediately effect the progress of the higher civilizations in the sphere of material and social technology. The shift from the bronze age to the iron age is largely culminated within this millennium while the achievement of a centralized universal state follows rather than precedes the age of transcendence in India and to a degree in China. Some "materialist" and cultural-holistic historians have indeed seen in the rise of the higher religions and transcendental tendencies an organic concomitant of the accelerated "progress" of this period. It might actually be more fruitful, however, to see a profound tension between material and social technological development and these transcendental movements. The spectacular developments of civilizations in China during the Chou do not dissuade Confucius or Mencius from the view that they live in an age of profound spiritual and moral decay and, if it is possible to speak of the Hebrew prophets as fathers of the idea of progress, this progress has absolutely nothing to do with advances in material and socio-political technology. These profound tensions were in fact, in convoluted and complex ways to shape the whole subsequent development of all the higher civilizations.

5

Review of *Law in Imperial China*

As a layman in the law and a student of things Chinese, I must confess that my major source of fascination with the 190 legal cases which Professors Bodde and Morris have culled from a Chinese casebook compilation containing well over 7,600 legal cases has been with the enormous variety of social and cultural data which they contain. Here we have a collection of *tranches de vie* based on undeniable actualities which shed new light on every aspect of Chinese culture. Bodde and Morris have made a highly representative selection of cases, and it is to their credit that what they provide simply whets our appetite for more of the enormous material available. Like all forms of documentation this may have its own problems and inherent limitations, but henceforth it will no longer be possible to ignore this source of evidence when making large generalizations about traditional Chinese society.

If the book has a much broader reference than the study of law as a separate discipline, it is certainly a major landmark in the Western literature on Chinese law. To appreciate its value and scope, a brief description of its contents is in order. The core of the book (Part 2) is the collection of 190 cases translated from the *Conspectus of Penal Cases (Hsing-an Hui-lan)*. The *Conspectus* is a private compilation of cases drawn from the archives of the Board of Punishments by Chinese legal scholars of the nineteenth century. The *Conspectus* proper was compiled by Chu Ch'ing-ch'i and Pao Shu-yün in 1834, and the work was later augmented by two supplements, the last of which is dated 1886. Drawn from the archives of China's highest court of appeal, these cases all found their way to the state's highest tribunal. They are thus cases which are problematic and contradictory, and the motive for their compilation, stated by Professor Bodde, is "to supply jurists with a body of precedents in readily accessible form."[1] The translation of these cases was hardly a routine undertaking given the enormous difficulties of the technical language employed. Furthermore, Professor Bodde has copiously interlarded his translations with illuminating annotations rendering comprehensible circumstances which would appear entirely baffling to the Western reader.

The text itself is preceded by a lengthy and extraordinarily valuable introduction (Part 1) on the whole subject of Chinese law. The section on basic concepts summarizes some of the generally accepted views on the nature and role of law in Chinese culture. I would like to record at this point a slight dissent from Professor Bodde's assertion that the "continuing penal emphasis" in the imperial codes is due to "Legalist" influence.[2] While Legalism as an outlook has undoubtedly profoundly influenced the whole course of China's political development, and while the idea that every crime has its exactly fitting punishment may owe something to Legalist "objectivism," the notion that the legal sphere (the sphere of *fa*) is the realm in which the state maintains social order by the application of physical force is quite as Confucian as it is Legalist. The most utopian variant of Confucianism may dream of a society in which harmonious relations among humans are maintained wholly by the uncoerced obedience of the customary rules of morality *(li)*, but other variants of Confucianism seem to accept the existence of the principle of evil in human society which makes it regrettably necessary to control certain elements of society and certain modes of behavior through the use of physical force. To Confucius no less than to the Legalist, the realm of litigation is the realm of brute force.

Other sections of the introduction, however, represent new contributions to the Western literature on Chinese law. The section on the organization and functioning of the Board of Punishments is most illuminating, and the description of the Ch'ing legal code and of the Chinese penal system provides the student with the most vivid and succinct account of these matters which I have seen anywhere. Section VI on the social and political implications of those cases touches, it seems to me, on most of the important themes. It does, however, lead to further questions which I would like to explore briefly below.

Professor Morris's juridical commentary in Part 3 is an excellent and original discussion by an American legal scholar who, like Professor Jerome Cohen at the Harvard Law School, is able to bring to bear his vast knowledge of the theory and practice of law in the United States. His ability to compare the cases from the *Conspectus* with *Lanzetta v. New Jersey*[3] and *State v. Provenzano*[4] introduces an entirely new dimension into our discussion of these matters.

Finally, the painstaking care which Professor Bodde has lavished on the compilation of appendices, glossary, and bibliography make this work as a whole an entirely exceptional contribution to Western scholarship. It is designed to be of equal value to the Chinese specialist and to the student of comparative law.

Turning for a moment to the realm of law itself, one finds that Professor Morris provides us with valuable correctives to some of our accepted conventional wisdom. There is a widespread impression that traditional Chinese law was judge's law, that the local magistrate was often able to decide cases on the basis of his own judgment and sense of equity (or lack thereof) with infrequent references to the codes. This judicial discretion was presumably based on the Confucian view that one must rely ultimately on the judgment of good men in dealing with the infinitely varied circumstances of life. Professor Morris has convincingly demonstrated that at least on the level of judicial review represented by the Board of Punishments every effort was made to create a systematic, reasoned, and consistent structure of law and legal procedure. The feeling for the infinite variety of circumstance and the aversion to generalized formulas is, to be sure, present. From the Western point of view, many of the statutes are almost ridiculously specific in reference. Yet every effort is made to subsume new cases under existing statutes either directly or by "analogical" reasoning. When one realizes that an enormous proportion of legal cases (e.g., all cases involving homicide) did come under review in Peking, one feels obliged to modify some of our notions concerning the legal powers of local judicial authorities.

On further reflection, this tendency toward consistency and system was probably inherent in the whole centralized bureaucratic system of legal institutions, and here, as elsewhere in the Chinese state, one finds a constant tension between the Confucian emphasis on personality and the systematizing and impersonalizing tendencies of centralized bureaucracy. To be sure, many of the decisions made in Peking also seem to be based more on socio-ethical considerations than on rigorously systematic legal reasoning (although legal grounds are always found), but it is quite clear that the local magistrate and even the provincial legal authorities operated (at least during periods of stability) within a system whose severe constraints they could not ignore.

If the book modifies some of our notions about how the law itself worked, it confirms our views about the place of law in the society as a whole. The magistrate's yamen is concerned above all with the punishment of crimes, and the state itself is consciously bent on making the realm of litigation a realm of dread and fear. "Litigation tricksters" who use their literacy to act as informal lawyers are punished with amazing severity, and we have several incidents of the suicide of persons who are driven to this recourse by the prospect of involvement in a legal case. Neither the good nor the circumspect would betake themselves to the magistrate's yamen if they could possibly avoid it.

While the law was thus less arbitrary than we had supposed, while every effort was made to have the punishment fit the crime, the aggregate picture which emerges both of the law and of the society which became entangled with it is somber and unflattering, at least to the western eye. The idealized China of peace and social harmony is not very much present in these pages. Everywhere we find the prevalence of violence, suicide, and the cruel abuse of the privileges provided by the law to those in authority, particularly parents and senior relatives. The draconic nature of the punishments, as has often been pointed out, is of course not so different from what prevailed elsewhere before the rise of nineteenth-century humanitarianism.

In all of this we are dealing not only with the usual discrepancy between ideals and actualities. On the contrary, these cases confirm the enormous impact of Confucian ideas and ideals on the fabric of Chinese life. Everywhere we find evidence of the "Confucianization of the law." Precisely because the family relationship is the *sacrum tremendum* of Confucianism we find hierarchic family authority protected in law with a zeal which seems almost grotesque. From the Confucian belief that family relations can easily be rendered benign and harmonious, we arrive at a situation in which an adulterous father who kills his protesting son escapes with an extraordinarily light punishment. Images of reality and ideals do affect life, but this is not always a heartening fact. The fact that their effect is often quite far from the intentions of the founding fathers is not due simply to the unregenerate Adam but also to the blind spots and one-sided nature of the ideals and images themselves.

The crucial question remains. If the 190 cases present a generally sordid and dark picture (at least from our point of view), to what extent do they provide us with a picture of Chinese society "as it really was?" Was traditional China a violent society (in comparison to others)? Was the abuse of privileged family authority (as well as status positions of all types) universally prevalent? Here we must take into account some of the inherent limitations of our data. Professor Bodde notes that most of these cases belong to the early decades of the nineteenth century which he describes as a period of "relative cultural and political stability."[5] Others would stress that this was a period of growing demoralization and depression. Are we therefore dealing with perennial China or with a particular historic moment? There is the further fact that the 7,600 cases of the *Conspectus* are difficult and interesting cases and that one would expect a relatively high proportion of sensational cases in such a collection. There is, above all, the fact already stressed that by the very nature of the role of law courts in Chinese life, the most sensationally seamy side of Chinese life was bound to occupy a central place within the legal sphere.

We can thus not derive any statistical conclusions about the typicality of the varieties of experience found in these cases. They certainly cancel out some sinophilic idealizations of Chinese society, but one suspects that life in the average was no more like this than it was like Voltaire's image of China. The "truth" about China is probably as complex and paradoxical as the truth everywhere.

6

Social Role and Sociologism in China, with Particular Reference to Confucianism

In approaching the subject of individualism and social role in China, I shall begin by focusing on the latter. The term "social role" is a modern Western term based on a theatrical metaphor. It immediately calls to mind Shakespeare's "all the world's a stage" with its underlying implication of the illusory quality of the whole social game. Given the enormous ontic weight ascribed to "social role" in much modern Western thought, it seems somewhat paradoxical that in its origins the term referred to a category which suggested unreality. Even now in ordinary discourse we often say of someone that he is "merely playing a role." How one moved from this concept of social role to the concept which one finds in much modern sociological literature is a puzzle one would like to see unraveled. I shall dwell on the Western sociological conception in order to focus our attention at the outset on how complicated (and unresolved) the whole problem of individualism and social role is in the modern West. Turning at random to a textbook written in 1953 by Gerth and Mills—*Character and Social Structure*—we find it asserted that "man as a person is composed of the specific roles which he enacts and of the effects of enacting these roles upon himself." Social roles are, in turn, embedded in and determined by the total social structure and "changes of the social structure make up the main course of human history." In this absolutist version of sociologism the social system "internalizes" its pattern of roles in the individual. Since every social role comes equipped with its own behavioral norms, the ethical norms which inhere in a given social structure are instilled in the individual through

the medium of the various roles which the individual necessarily enacts. The Actor here is the social structure acting through its various
orders, spheres, institutions, and roles while the existent individuals
are the passive receptacles through which it acts. In this view we
find a total rejection of Steven Lukes' "methodological individualism."[1]

The same attitude can be found in a myriad of sociology textbooks
whose authors are all sincerely committed to individualistic goals.
One need, by no means, doubt the sincerity of their commitment to
"autonomy, respect for human dignity, privacy and self-development."
How is this possible? It becomes possible if we regard all these goods
as goods internalized in the essentially passive individual by changes in
the social structure. It is difficult to believe that the sociologistic absolutist when he speaks of autonomy can mean anything like the "self-
determined deciding and choosing" mentioned by Lukes.[2] To the
extent that Lukes himself falls into the language of absolutist sociologism (as he frequently does) it is difficult to see how he can believe in
this image of autonomy.[3] If a person is nothing but a congery of determinative social roles, all his choices will be determined by the role he is
playing. Hence autonomy in this view refers not to a dynamic capacity
of the individual but to a socio-political condition. The crucial question is how does one bring into being a social structure which confers
these goods on the essentially inert and passive entity which is the individual? One answer is that one simply has faith that the history of
society is inexorably moving in a direction favorable to individualism.
Another possible answer is that those who have the knowledge and
power to shape the social structure shape it in a way to favor individualism. This latter assumption, however, inevitably involves the reintroduction of a certain form of "methodological individualism."
There is the tacit assumption that *certain exceptional individuals* have
the inherent capacity to stand beyond the social structure and even to
change it. Thus Steven Lukes first rejects "methodological individualism" and then goes on to assert that "one will need to look very closely
at the structural determinants of status ranking . . . if one is concerned
to maximize autonomy and self-development throughout all sections
of society."[4] The puzzling question here: Who is the "one" referred to
in this sentence? One must assume that it refers to those individuals—
whether intellectuals or politicians—who have the capacity to do
something about changing social realities. These individuals—*as*

individuals—possess transcendent dynamic capacities. They can shape social realities.

When we turn our attention to China, most of us are immediately struck by the primacy—the ontic weight—of what we call social role within Chinese culture in general and in Confucianism in particular. Indeed one even tends to see this primacy prefigured in the Shang oracle bone inscriptions. The rituals and ceremonies of ancestral worship are indissolubly linked to a network of familial role relationships which even cross the divide between life and death. Certainly by the time of Confucius one already has the concept of an all-encompassing cultural-social-political order made up of networks of interrelated social roles. The ceremonial prescriptions of *li* do not concern themselves with categories of human behavior abstracted from role-activities such as stealing or killing (as in the Ten Commandments) but with role-related behavior. The rules relate primarily to norms of behavior within and between given social roles. Thus ancient Chinese social thought in general and Confucianism in particular seem overwhelmingly "sociologistic."

I would nevertheless argue that the Confucianism of the Analects actually provides more space for one form of individualism than do Gerth and Mills or perhaps even Steven Lukes. In saying this, however, I do not mean to imply that Confucius is more of a "modern liberal" than they. In Gerth and Mills, "social role" is not only a self-subsistent reality, it is a self-subsistent dynamic force; or rather, it may be more accurate to say that it is one of the mediating forces through which the entire social structure acts as a dynamic organism. Not only is the social role internalized in the individual, its governing norms are also internalized. Society internalizes its values in the individual. In Confucius, a given social role ought to be linked to certain governing norms. The actual father or actual ruler ought to embody the norms of fatherhood and rulership. In fact, they may not. The brute facticity of an ascriptive social role by no means assures the actualization of the norms associated with it. The same role may be enacted well or badly and the question of how it is enacted is wholly dependent on the moral quality of the person who enacts the role. The crucial question is—*how* are the roles enacted? Many individuals possess the extraordinary power of moral self-direction and self-improvement. All good behavior, to be sure, expresses itself through the articulations of a preestablished social order and a system of preestablished prescriptions of proper role behavior, but the dynamic principle which leads to the actualization of these norms lies within individuals. All human beings may potentially possess this power of moral self-determination and some may actually initiate self-improvement.

Yet we should not overstate our case. Does everyone possess the power to initiate self-improvement? One has the impression in the Analects and in Mencius that in most it remains only a potential. The mass of mankind is heavily conditioned by its social environment. The Confucius of the Analects would probably have emphasized the limits of their capacity and opportunity to acquire the kind of learning required for the achievement of true self-perfection. Mencius emphasizes the evil environment brought about by those within the political order who have the power for moral self-determination but who do not exercise it. Occupying roles within society which confer power, they do not have the will to actualize the norms inherent in their roles. Thus within the Confucian-Mencian framework there is no yes-or-no answer to the modern Western conundrum: Does one improve society by perfecting individuals or does one improve individuals by perfecting society? *Most* individuals can be improved only by improving society. The improvement of society is, however, wholly dependent on the moral self-determination or intellectual initiative (Hsün-tzu) of certain individuals who constitute the ethico-political vanguard of society. Here "methodological individualism" is quite ingeniously combined with social determination.

There is a curious affinity between certain modes of Chinese thought and certain strands of eighteenth-century Western Enlightenment thought (which does not, of course, preclude profound differences). The Sinophile *philosophes* of France were not wholly wrong in seeing such a resemblance. Within this strand of Enlightenment thought, most men are determined by their social environment and this environment is decisively shaped by the whole sociopolitical order. We have here what might be called a limited sociologism. There are, however, individuals within the social order who have the intellectual capacity to transcend and transform this order and who ought to have the political power to do so. Those who act within the political order have the power as legislators to transform the society. The point of view is closer to Hsün-tzu than to Mencius. It is not the legislator's virtue but his transcendent intellectual insight. In either case, the initiative lies with transcendent individuals.

The kind of all-embracing sociologism which emerged in nineteenth-century Europe was a critical reaction against the inconsistency and naiveté of this partial sociologism. If some are socially determined, then all are. Who are these educators and legislators who stand outside of and above the whole social process? In Marx's words, in the "Theses on Feuerbach," "who educates the educators?" The political order is as much determined by the whole social structure as any other sphere of the social order.[5] Furthermore, while this strain of eighteenth-century thought posits the power of the social structure to determine the lives of most, it does not seem to ascribe to social process as such any immanent dynamic historic principle of self-transformation. The social structure must be changed "from without" by enlightened legislators. Here also one can compare the eighteenth-century view to the Confucian view. The normative social structure can be actualized only through the efforts of creative individuals. In both Confucianism and in this strand of Enlightenment thought—*ceteris paribus*—we thus have the attribution of extraordinary transcendent powers to *some* individuals.

The modern West has been enormously concerned with the creation of social and political conditions for the realization of the "liberty and equality" of individuals.[6] Yet this concern has gone hand in hand with an enormous diminution of belief in the powers of individuals to shape their own lives, to influence the lives of others in interpersonal relations, or to shape the socio-political order as a whole.

The theory of political democracy as expounded by John Dewey, which struggles with these issues, really presupposes a large measure of some aspects of "methodological individualism." It presupposes that *all* human beings as individuals have the capacity to participate in shaping the socio-political structures in which they are involved. Yet if all men are essentially determined in their behavior by their social roles, statuses, and social interest constellations, how can they shape that by which they are determined? John Dewey wrote many turgid pages on the problem but never solved it. Steven Lukes's book seems to vacillate between any number of positions. At times he writes in terms of a totalistic sociologism. "His (the individual's) distinctively human qualities, even his very capacity (and of course, opportunities) to achieve autonomy and self-development are in large measure socially determined."[7] Quoting George Mead, he states that "the individual self is not merely essentially asocial in its formation and nature; its very individuality is to be seen as formed of social elements."[8] At other points he seems to be highly critical of absolute sociologism as in his assertion that we must see persons "not merely as the bearers of certain titles, the players of certain roles or the occupiers of certain social positions, or as the means to given ends but as the concrete persons who—for one reason or another—bear these titles, play these roles or serve those ends."[9] At times he seems to revert to the Enlightenment model outlined above.

The mainstream Confucian view, on the other hand, attributes at least to some individuals enormous powers of moral self-determination (some might say extravagant powers)—an ability to shape themselves and others as well. The moral autonomy of the *chün-tzu* is not socially determined. Some may occupy socio-political niches which should provide the opportunity to realize these powers and yet fall short. Others (*chün-tzu* out of office) are able to realize their moral potentialities within the limits of their own personal and familial lives even though they are not provided with the opportunity to bring their moral or intellectual influence to bear on the society as a whole. This moral autonomy has nothing to do with Lukes's version of "ethical individualism." It does not by any means signify that every individual creates his own system of values. On the contrary, there is an assumption that there is a given system of normative ethical values which finds its expression both in certain determinate inner virtues and certain determinate outer prescriptions of "role behavior." The values are realized within the framework of a given normative social structure. As in many other systems of ethics—Judeo-Christian as well as Confucian[10]—the ethical freedom of the individual does not reside in his power to create his own private system of ethics but in his power to actualize and realize an already existing ethical system. The whole fallacy of Fingarette[11] resides in his highly Western assumption that ethical inwardness and inner moral autonomy presuppose the power of each individual to create his own ethical values rather than the power to *realize* values which are accepted as given. There are modern Confucian thinkers who contend that the "subjective" Confucian values can be separated from their historic connection with a particular conception of normative socio-political structure. Whether or not this is true, I shall not presume to judge in this paper. I do think, however, that these thinkers are not wrong in their claim that Confucianism has within limits preserved a certain conception of individual autonomy that is now singularly weak in the modern West.

7

On the Absence of Reductionism in Chinese Thought

We are already well supplied with a surfeit of books and treatises which purport to provide us with the timeless essence of Chinese thought. General characteristics of Chinese thought no doubt exist. One can certainly find common notions and themes which are shared by many diverse strands of thought both synchronically and diachronically and there surely are dominant currents within Chinese thought. There are also modes of thought which can be found in other cultures which may not be found or found only minimally within the Chinese cultural stream. Yet it is my own personal conviction that the major task which now confronts the Western student of Chinese thought is not so much to dwell on timeless essences but rather to explore the range, variety and problematics of Chinese thought. In large part our tendency to see only the monochrome forest is a function of cultural distance, while in dealing with Western thought we closely scrutinize the nuances of shading of every leaf. The concrete and highly significant diversities and tensions within Chinese thought will reveal themselves clearly only when we study ideas and thinkers within the context of living historic situations. When one focuses one's attention on this level, one is often more impressed by the degree to which Chinese ideas and orientations are involved with trans-cultural, universal human problems rather than by the degree to which they are frozen within the matrix of a changeless "Chinese mind."

Yet in what follows I shall proceed to violate my own injunction and discuss what seems to me a general characteristic of Chinese

thought. In self-defense, I would simply urge that the concern will
here be with the implications of the absence (which may not be total)
of a definite mode of thought rather than with the definition of some
unchanging positive essence of Chinese thought.[1] To some it may appear that what is here called reductionism is simply the obverse side
of what Professor Joseph Needham calls China's "philosophy of organism." Quite apart from the obscurities of the term organism as
used by Needham, reductionism and organismic philosophy are not
two poles of an exhaustive dichotomy. The world—including the
Western world—is rich in varieties of non-reductionist philosophies.
In Chinese thought figures as diverse as Chuang-tzu, Mo-tzu, Tung
Chung-shu, Chu Hsi and Wang Yang-ming may all be called non-
reductionist thinkers even though the term organismic philosophy
may by no means furnish the best way of describing what they have
in common. What is more, their differences may be no less significant
than the features which they share. The absence of reductionism may
tell us something about the limits of the spectrum of Chinese thought.
It tells us little about the chromatic variety within the spectrum.

The word "reductionism" has, of course, been used in many ways
and in many contexts. What we refer to here is that view of reality
which regards the cosmic manifold in all its variety as reducible to a
kind of "stuff" (or even a kind of energy) with minimal physical
properties of extension, of mass, and of a capacity for mathematical
arrangement in space (the so-called primary qualities of the Newtonian universe). Such stuff may be conceived of as a continuous substance, as a primitive particle or even as "energy."[2] The atomic (or
in our terms sub-atomic) particles may actually possess unimagined
properties, but from the point of view of a reductionist naturalism,
one need concern oneself with nothing but their strictly physical and
mathematical properties. Thus the variety and manifold qualities of
reality are explained as appearances resulting from the structures
built up out of the primary stuff. The metaphor most closely associated with reductionism is that of building or structure (e.g. "the
structure of the universe"). One speaks of the world being constructed either out of building blocks or of some primitive clay-like
stuff. Another form which reductionism may assume in a more epistemological view of reality is the reduction of the world of experience to nothing but sense data.

It has often been pointed out that the ultimate source of reductionist thought in the West is to be sought among the Pre-Socratic thinkers. There has, however, been no agreement on details. When Aristotle suggests that the Ionian thinkers such as Thales, Anaximander, and Anaximenes were mainly interested in the question "What are things made of?" he seems to attribute to them a "scientific" motivation (whether the motive was practical-technical or one of disinterested curiosity or both). Thus the search of Thales and Anaximander for some simple homogeneous stuff out of which the world might be made, would be the clear origin of a "scientific" reductionism. On the other hand, scholars such as W. W. Jaeger[3] and F. M. Cornford[4] have suggested the presence of other concerns in these early thinkers. They point out that neither the water of Thales nor the "boundless" *(apeiron)* of Anaximander are elementary stuff with universal purely physical properties. Water, to be sure, is a known physical element with observable properties, yet Thales still speaks of it as being "full of gods," while Anaximander's "boundless" is not an empirically observed element at all. It is an indeterminate stuff "from which arise all the heavens and worlds within them." It is pregnant with all the possibilities of being and hence probably much more like the Chinese conceptions of *ch'i* (vital force) than the matter of any reductionist materialism. Anaximenes, whose primary stuff was air, developed further than his predecessors the notion of condensation and rarefaction as an explanatory device[5] and thus seems to approach more closely a full-scale reductionism. Again, Pythagoreanism with its implication that "differences in nature were based on differences in geometric structure"[6] seems to point to the kind of mathematically based reductionism which was to play such a dominant role in the scientific revolution of the sixteenth and seventeenth centuries. Yet Pythagoreanism was a kind of religious sect dominated by all sorts of religious and ethical concerns.

The clearest realization of reductionism in ancient thought can be found in the atomism of Leucippus and Democritus. Here the effort to reduce reality to particles endowed solely with the properties of solidity or impenetrability and differences of shape is clearly visible. Yet it is again not entirely clear whether the basic preoccupations were strictly "scientific." Democritus is supposed to have written some fifty-two works ranging from technical subjects to ethics.[7] If we regard Epicurus as Democritus's main disciple, we would be obliged to conclude that the concerns of this follower was existential and ethical rather than strictly scientific. Epicurus and Lucretius seem to have regarded a universe divested of religious and cultural meanings (meanings which were in their view mainly anxiety-producing) conducive to the absence of fear and anxiety, the promotion of individual serenity, and a kind of comfortable ataraxy.

In sum, then, while the reductionist impulse did indeed arise in ancient Greece, the concerns behind it may have been only partially scientific. It was, however, to survive as a predisposition which would not realize its full scientific implications until the sixteenth and seventeenth centuries. Within ancient thought it was only one strain among many and was indeed rejected by Socrates, Plato, Aristotle, the Stoics and a host of other philosophers. Needham's statement that "Europeans could only think in terms either of Democritean mechanical materialism or of Platonic theological spiritualism"[8] is a gross simplification not only as applied to European thought in general but even as applied to Greek thought in particular.

Another possible source of the reductionist impulse in the West which has often been cited is the Hebrew heritage. In the cosmogony of Genesis, the gods and spirits are banished from nature and the manifestations of nature are reduced to the status of creations of God. The relation of God to his world is one of creating—or making or fashioning, and the idea of making seems to suggest some simple and primary raw material or materials out of which things are made. In the account of man's creation we read that Adam is formed from the dust of the earth. The relationship of the reductionist view to the notion of God as creator is of particular interest to us here because the notion of a creator or a creative or fashioning dynamic principle is, we shall find, by no means entirely absent from Chinese thought.

It is probably true that the Hebrew conception of the world as created or made could be easily combined with Greek reductionism in the stream of modern Western thought to produce the watchmaking god of eighteenth-century Deism. It is by no means clear, however, that the Biblical view of reality is itself reductionist. The concerns behind the cosmogony of Genesis are clearly religious and ethical rather than scientific. Divinity and the sacred are banished from nature but there is little evidence in Biblical descriptions of nature that its manifold variety and qualities are not accepted in the spirit of a naive realism. The revelation is that creation is made by one God rather than any notion that we can know what it is made of. To the extent that the account in Genesis is explained in terms of *creatio ex nihilo,* we are confronted with a mystery rather than with reductionism. Man is formed of the dust of the earth but God breathed life into his nostrils.[9] The concern here seems to be with the mystery of a creature who is both made and ensouled with the divine breath. Otherwise, the Hebrews of the Bible seem to be as little inclined to probe the ways of heaven as is the Confucius of the Analects. Yet it may be true that the Judeo-Christian heritage probably provided a more favorable environment for a mathematized reductionism than might have been the case with the dominant religio-philosophic tendencies of Chinese thought.

Finally, it should be pointed out that the radical nature of reductionist naturalism in the modern West can only be understood when seen in conjunction with an anthropocentric subjectivism. The qualities, values and meanings (and with Kant even the mathematical structure of reality) which are banished from the world "out there" are all introjected into the human subject, which becomes the only available receptacle for these phenomena. Much of modern Western philosophy revolves about the insoluble problems of the relationships of a reductionist materialism or positivism to a completely subjectivized symbolic world. There are to be sure quasi-Platonic philosophers of science (such as Einstein) who continue to regard the mathematical structure of the world as objective and as full of an almost religious significance even when they are prepared to subjectivize everything else. Perhaps those very special spirits who respond most vibrantly to the divine beauty of mathematics detached from human subjectivity ought not to be classed as reductionists. For the majority, however, a universe constructed of bare matter or simply energy which behaves in the most beautifully mathematical fashion remains a reduced world stripped of most of the qualities and values which they cherish.

Professor Needham in his work on science in China has, of course, paid due attention to the role which reductionism has played as a method of inquiry in the scientific revolution of the seventeenth century. He has, however, insisted that while the method has been fruitful in the past, the world picture which has emerged from science has been more favorable to what he calls the Chinese "philosophy of organism" rather than to a reductionist naturalism. Many might be inclined to agree that the image of the world which emerges from modern physics and biology does not inexorably support a reductionist view of the universe.[10] Yet the fact remains that so long as the natural sciences continue to concern themselves with the same type of questions which inspired the fathers of the scientific revolution, they will probably continue to employ a reductionist method of inquiry and some will continue to draw reductionist philosophic conclusions from their reductionist methodology.

In dealing with Chinese thought, our concern will not be so much with the polemics surrounding the word science as with its relevance to such spheres as religion, ethics, and aesthetics. In the latter realm, a reductionist view of the objective world combined with a radical subjectivization of all religious phenomena has provided us with the clearest definition we have of irreligion or what might be called a radical humanistic (in the philosophic sense) view of the world. This does not mean, of course, that we can issue semantic decrees on how words such as religion or humanism should be used but it does alert us to the need for an extraordinary degree of semantic awareness when we apply these Western categories (even in their conventional Chinese translations) to the Chinese cultural sphere.

When we turn to the first evidences of thought in ancient China in the oracle bones, the *Book of Poetry (Shih Ching)*, and the *Book of Documents (Shu Ching)*, we find the same sort of religious pluralism and naive realism which we find in other cultures. On both the level of sacred and ordinary life, the world of the manifold is accepted in all its plurality. Ancient Chinese religion may already have its own characteristic features such as the striking prominence of the orientation to ancestor worship (an orientation which may have had many implications for the entire development of the culture). There may already be signs of a movement toward something like an immanent cosmic order. From the very outset, however, this order tends to embrace rather than to reduce the manifold variety of the natural and cultural world.

I would submit that even the more reflective thought of the age of the "Hundred Schools" offers little or no evidence of any reductionist impulse although one must immediately add that only a tiny fraction of the written record has been preserved.

As has often been pointed out, the Confucius of the Analects, like Socrates, is basically concerned with the realm of man. In the case of Socrates we have a very deliberate turn away from centuries of speculation about the ways of nature; but in the case of Confucius we are simply informed that he seldom discussed the "Way of Heaven" *(t'ien tao)*. Since much of what we have about cosmology in China dates from post-Confucian sources, we cannot have any definite knowledge of the contents of this phrase. Heaven appears in the Analects as both a conscious power ("Only heaven knows me") and as the principle of order in nature ("Heaven does not speak and the four seasons run their course") and, while Confucius uses the word *Tao* mainly in reference to the normative order of society ("When the Way prevails in the World"), there is a strong presumption that the normative human order is part of a normative cosmic order. Whether heaven is a conscious power or the principle of an impersonal order,[11] it is quite clear that the Confucian cosmos is not reductionist and that Confucian humanism has no relationship to any humanism predicated on the notion of man against the meaningless universe.

In Confucius's famous opponent Mo-tzu, however, we find a deep resistance to the growing Confucian tendency to explain the world in terms of an immanent all-embracing order and a highly conscious effort to revive the religious pluralism of the past. The good ethical order is not an immanent order. It is an order achieved by the arduous efforts of gods and dedicated men. Mo-tzu represents the assertion of a pluralist universe against what Needham calls the "organismic" main current of Chinese thought. A pluralist universe is, however, as uncongenial to a reductionist monism as is any philosophy of organism or mysticism.

When we turn to the cosmological thought which emerges in the period spanning the Warring States and early Han dynasty we again find a kind of thinking which begins by accepting the world in all its irreducible variety and plenitude. The four seasons, the five cardinal directions, the patterns of the heavenly bodies, the social and political structures of human society and in the "Hung Fan" cosmology of the *Book of Documents,* even details of human psychology are accepted as primary data. These phenomena are not reduced but correlated to each other in the type of "resonantial" association so well described by Needham and others. It is already clear in the fragments of Tsou Yen who is the first identified thinker within this line, that the underlying preoccupation of this mode of thinking is neither simply scientific curiosity nor a search for philosophic serenity but the proper ordering of human affairs—the proper alignment of the human world with the ordered patterns of the universe whether by ritual, magic, or proper ethical behavior.

This does not mean that there was no interest in ancient China in the disinterested and accurate observation of nature. Indeed, many of the separate components of this correlative cosmology (which are probably much older than the cosmology itself) are obviously based on the close observation of nature, but close observation of nature does not in itself necessarily lead to reductionist explanations. Yet even the presence of reductionist speculations cannot be ruled out, particularly in the case of the so-called theory of "five elements." Does this not represent a primitive effort to explain the entire cosmos as being composed of water, fire, earth, metal, and wood (or vegetation)? Even if it does, the reductionist impulse seems to have been feeble. The five elements in their plurality are already associated with a vast a variety of properties and we find no inclination to reduce them further. Indeed, the very fact that they appear in a group of five and that this numerical group tends to be linked in the earliest evidence with other numerical groupings would suggest a numerological concern from the very outset. In the posthumous collected essays of the historian of philosophy Tu Kuo-hsiang,[12] we find an essay on the Liang dynasty thinker Yang Ch'uan, "Yang Ch'uan ti shui i yuan-lun" (Yang Ch'uan's theory of water as the ultimate substance) which quotes Yang to the effect "that by which heaven and earth were established was water. That which brought them to completion was *ch'i* . . . The stars and planets arise out of water." This may suggest reductionism but again there is no evidence of any effort to give a clear and simple account of the properties of water. Since all things arise out of water, water seems to be the pregnant mother of all possibilities. The same is true of chapter 30 of the Kuan-tzu book, where again water is posed as the ultimate substance of all things. Here it is quite clear that water contains within itself all the possibilities of reality including monsters, prodigies, and the highest ethical qualities. Thus the Chinese term *wu hsing*, which we translate as five elements, means something like five doings or phases. Ch'en Meng-chia has speculated on the basis of an ancient bronze inscription that a ritual activity involving the use of fire may have suggested the association of fire with a certain proper ritual activity.[13] At any rate, the early association of these natural elements with certain kinds of movement or process suggests that they were associated at a very early point with the kind of correlative thinking which is a dominant feature of Chinese cosmology. There is in fact no particular reason to think that they were put forth even at the outset in answer to the question: "What is the world made of?" Ch'en Mengchia explicitly denies that they are the Chinese equivalent of the Greek four elements on the ground that the "five elements *(wu hsing)* are the interacting flow of five forces and not five passive elements *(yüan su)*."[14] The durability of the five elements idea down through the ages as a fixture of Chinese cosmology makes it quite clear that the concerns with which it was associated had little to do with the disinterested search for scientific hypotheses about the structure of the natural universe.

Lying beyond the all-embracing machinery of Chinese correlative cosmology we also find in Chinese thought words which refer to a transcendental reality both enveloping and transcending the world of the ten thousand things with all its realms and categories. Tung Chung-shu, who provides us with the most architectonic and elaborate account of Han cosmology, sees it all as an emanation of the "heart of heaven." There is, of course, also the *Tao* of the Taoists and the concept of *ch'i,* which when it emerges as the "primordial stuff" of a monistic philosophy (as in Chang Tsai and Wang Fuchih), is most often treated as the true Chinese equivalent of western "matter."

I shall not linger on the *Tao* of Lao-tzu and Chuang-tzu. Even those who attempt to play down the mystical core of philosophic Taoism can hardly make a case for reductionism in these early Taoist classics. By invariably translating *Tao* as the "order of nature" one may, of course, avoid the ultimately ineffable and unnameable nature of the *Tao.* Yet an order of nature which spans and embraces the entire manifold of the world is clearly a "more than" rather than a "nothing but."

In 1959 an interesting debate was conducted among the historians of philosophy in the People's Republic on the question of whether Lao-tzu was a materialist or idealist.[15] Apart from certain fanciful efforts to find atomism in the Lao-tzu book, the most plausible arguments on the materialist side emphasized the absence of a providential theistic form of religious orientation and the presence of an "impersonal order of nature" in Lao-tzu's conception of the *Tao.*

The protagonists of the idealistic interpretation were quite effective in demonstrating the inadequacies of the materialist view. In any event, these particular Marxist-Leninist notions of materialism in China are quite devoid of reductionist implications.

The concept of *ch'i* has often been made the focus of discussions of materialism in China. Its origins, like so many of the key notions of cultures of the ancient world, tend to reflect a state of mind which draws no sharp distinction between physical and spiritual realities. The underlying image seems to be one of vapor or breath. In the earliest texts, it seems to refer to a kind of energy emanating from all sorts of phenomena of nature as well as to a kind of psychological "soul" energy and moral energy in human individuals.[16] Whether used pluralistically as a kind of energy associated with all sorts of entities and activities (e.g. the *yang ch'i* and the *yin ch'i*) or monistically as in the philosophy of Chang Tsai, it never becomes anything like the matter of Newton. In the philosophy of Chang Tsai of the Sung dynasty it encompasses properties we would describe as physical as well as properties we would describe as spiritual or mental. It is pregnant with all the possibilities of reality including the gods and spirits, the rules governing the harmonious relations of human society, and the individual's capacity for moral self-realization. To be sure, Chang Tsai uses the physicalist image of condensation and rarefaction to explain the emergence of individual entities, but that which is being condensed and dispersed is by no means the matter of Newtonian physics. In its dispersed form it is called "emptiness" *(hsü)*. It is made quite clear, however, that this emptiness has many of the connotations of the Taoist *wu* (non-being); that is, emptiness of all determinations, yet full of the capacity to produce all determinations. In fact *ch'i* in itself is discussed in the rapturous language of the mystic.

It may, of course, be argued that thinkers such as Wang Fu-chih and Tai Chen use the word *ch'i* in a truly materialist sense. What characterizes them is a vehement emphasis on the reality of the manifold variety of reality. To Wang Fu-chih, while *ch'i* may ultimately be an underlying principle, it must always be thought of as immanent within the variety of the differentiated world. It should not be thought of as a transcendent something apart from the world of the manifold, for to think of the world in this way is to encourage mystical quietism or a morality of pure inwardness. To the extent that the world of the manifold is taken as real in itself, however, there is no impulse toward reductionism. The world of the senses is real. The world of the hexagrams of the *Book of Changes* is also real. For Tai Chen, in fact, it makes great sense to attribute the value of goodness to the universe as a whole. He insists on the immanence of the Mencian moral qualities in the *ch'i* but the ethical categories themselves remain an integral part of the furniture of the universe. Neither in the case of Wang Fu-chih nor of Tai Chen can one say that they are unconditional pluralists. The *Tao* and the *ch'i* are often described as all-encompassing and unifying principles. There is simply the constant insistence that these principles can only be discerned only as immanent within the manifold.

If these central terms of Chinese thought *(Tao, t'ien, ch'i)* can almost never be interpreted in a reductionist sense, this does not mean that all of Chinese thought is "religious" if the term religion implies a providential God or gods or a providential cosmic order—that is a god or an order concerned with or involved with either the weal or woe of human individuals or even human collectivities. In both Chinese high culture and folk culture one can in fact find much evidence of providentialism, but there are powerful beliefs and modes of thought which run against it. The kind of "correlative" cosmology which we associate with Tsou Yen and Tung Chung-shu and which remains a powerful current until the twentieth century may well be described as a providential view of the cosmos although it is not clear whether we should here speak of theodicy or cosmodicy. The cosmos is intimately involved with the fortune and misfortune of both human individuals and collectives and reveals its concern through an elaborate mechanism of omens, auspicious signs, and natural disasters.

As we know, however, this type of providential cosmology had its vehement opponents. The "philosophic" Taoists as well as Hsün-tzu and Wang Ch'ung come immediately to mind. It may seem odd to place in the same category mystics and men who have often been cited as the very epitome of "irreligion" within the Chinese cultural sphere. Yet one of the characteristics of certain forms of mystical religion everywhere has been the indifference to providentialism. The good tidings of this type of religion are not to be found in the faith that God is concerned with the human enterprise but in the realization that mystic, ineffable reality renders the human earthly enterprise unimportant. Thus, Lao-tzu's statement that "heaven is not benevolent, it treats the ten thousand things as straw dogs," when taken in context, does not reflect the dour pathos of modern Western naturalism but rather the kind of mystical exultation which permeates the whole book. The meaningfulness of the universe does not depend on the fate of its individuated manifestations.

What we find in the Hsün-tzu book is a very explicit and emphatic denial of any concern of heaven—any theological involvement with either man's happiness or his virtue whether individual or collective. "The processes of heaven are constant. They are not present for Yao and are not destroyed for Chieh."[17] The human nature which man receives from heaven in his genetic endowment actually runs counter to the higher ends of human culture. Thus here we find a theme which seems to resemble most closely the modern Western view that man must create his moral and cultural values in the very teeth of a universe intractable to human purposes. In the end, however, the pathos underlying the whole book is quite different. The kind of resonance between man and the universe found in the correlative cosmogony is rejected, but the dissonance between man and heaven is only provisional. The universe is neither reduced nor devalued. In addition to the disordered human nature which most men receive at birth, the sages—the lofty fashioners of human culture—are able to employ their heavenly intellects to bring into being the patterns of normative behavior which must govern human culture.[18] Thus the human intellect which brings order into the chaos of human affairs is itself an incarnation of the powers of heaven. Heaven's workings in the non-human sphere are described in a language which is almost mystical. Once the normative human culture is realized, man is aligned with the harmonies of the universe.

The most relentless and thorough enemy of a cosmological providentialism is, the late Han thinker Wang Ch'ung. Indeed, while Hsün-tzu provides for a realm of autonomy in the human sphere which allows sages and kings to shape recalcitrant human nature into the ordered universe of human culture, Wang Ch'ung denies autonomy to the sages themselves. The same *Tao* which spontaneously engenders and determines the phenomena of nature determines the moral and intellectual capacities of men and also determines the cyclical patterns of human history. Men of sagely endowment may appear in history but whether they can bring their wisdom to bear on society is wholly dependent on the conjuncture of the times. Not only is the non-human cosmos indifferent to the fate of men, but the same cosmic forces hold sway within the human realm itself so that man is held in bondage by a plethora of determinisms. Again, however, there is little evidence of reductionist thinking. The *ch'i* of heaven[19] and earth commingle and spontaneously *(wu wei)* engender out of their limitless potentiality all the manifold categories of reality including the ethical capacities of humans.

> The man of supreme virtue and of profound purity is richly endowed with the *ch'i* of heaven and is thus able to model himself on heaven. He acts spontaneously, effortlessly, without set purpose. He who is poorly endowed with (heavenly) *ch'i* does not comply with the Way and its virtue and does not resemble heaven and earth.[20]

The qualities are haphazardly endowed in a sort of genetic determinism but they are irreducible qualities grounded in the nature of the universe itself. One senses that the pathos which accompanies his statement that men are like lice on the garments of the universe is by no means incompatible with a certain natural piety toward that universe even though one can hardly speak of mystic ecstasy.

Mou Tsung-san[21] is thus probably quite right when he sees in Wang Ch'ung the beginning of the movement which was to culminate in the "Neo-Taoism" of the post-Han period. Here we find an orientation which was no longer deeply hopeful or committed to the success of the moral cultural enterprise on either the individual or collective plane. While Wang Ch'ung does not share the aestheticism or the deep mysticism of the later generations, his view of man's place in the universe does not seem to differ markedly from theirs. The *Tao's* indifference to the fate of its individual creatures does not reduce the majestic plenitude of the universe. If we are to call Hsün-tzu and Wang Ch'ung materialists we must detach that word materialism from all reductionist implications.

There is one more motif in the history of Chinese thought, which may provide at least indirect evidence of the presence of reductionism—what might be called the minor creationist strain. While the dominant strain in most Chinese accounts of cosmogony leans heavily on the image of procreation, of heaven and earth (or in Lao-tzu the *Tao*) engendering *(sheng)* the ten thousand things, one can find in Chinese philosophic literature from Chuang-tzu and Lieh-tzu down

through Neo-Confucian philosophy, constant reference to the workings of a "creative (or fashioning) process" *(tsao-hua)* or even of a creator or fashioner *(tsao-wu-che)*. The image of procreation may have
seemed inadequate to account for the enormous variety and intricacies
of natural phenomena. The fact that objects of nature seemed to have
structures which were contrived like the artifacts of human artisans
hardly escaped the attention of the Chinese. As A. C. Graham states
with reference to the famous story of the mechanical robot in the Lieh-
tzu book, "It is interesting to see how easily Chinese writers fall into
this kind of language[22] when admiring constructed models of nature
such as automatic toys and armillary spheres."[23] Yet if the image of
the creation of the universe in the book of Genesis had no necessary
reductionist implications the same is true a fortiori of the Chinese concept of the creator or of a creative principle. The principle of *tsao-hua*
first appears as a kind of subordinate principle in the literature of
philosophic Taoism. It is clearly subordinate to such principles as *Tao*,
non-being *(wu)*, being *(yu)*, *yin*, and *yang*, and seems to intervene precisely at the point where these higher principles give rise to all the particularities of the "ten thousand things." In Chia I's poetic image
"heaven and earth are like the smelting furnace, the creative process
(tsao-hua) is the workman, *yin* and *yang* are the fuel, and the ten thousand things are the metal." In some sense it is more like Plato's Demi-
urge than a transcendent creator. In fact, in most of Taoist and
Confucian high philosophy there is a general tendency to assign a subordinate position to the creative or fashioning principle or creator. In
much of Chinese philosophy there is a distinctly pejorative connota-
tion surrounding words which mean making, fashioning, or contriving
(tsao, tso, ku-tso, etc.). If there is a fashioning principle or god operating within the ultimate order of things, neither the Taoist sage nor the
Confucian gentleman will emulate this model. A little noted fact of
Chinese thought is that often the Taoist or Confucian sage is modelled
on the *Tao* itself in all its spontaneity *(wu wei)*, lack of set purpose,
and impersonality. Lao-tzu's famous observation concerning the non-
benevolence of heaven is, after all, designed to furnish a model for the
Taoist sage. If one wishes to define the main thrust of Chinese philosophy as non-theistic in this sense, we must posit the possibility of something like a non-theistic view of the ideal human being. In any event,
the creationist strain in Chinese thought remains subordinate and
seems to bear with it no reductionist implications.

If reductionism seems to be largely absent from the available record of Chinese thought, what implications may this have for subjectivist tendencies within Chinese thought? As observed, the radical nature of reductionism in modern Western thought has been intricately tied in many problematic ways to an anthropocentric epistemological subjectivism. The human subject has become the source and receptacle for all sorts of contents banished from the "world out there." Now there certainly are Chinese modes of thought and belief which seem to stress what we call the subjective side. One finds this in certain varieties of Mahayana Buddhist philosophy as well as in that whole strain of Sung and Ming thought running from Lu Hsiang-shan through Wang Yang-ming and the various schools which derive from him. It has often been pointed out that for both Kant and Wang Yang-ming, the moral law arises from within, and in the writings of Lu Hsiang-shan we find a passage which suggests that the categories of both time and space are projections of the "mind" *(hsin)*. I would, however, suggest that in China, the emphasis on mind or consciousness never implies the kind of anthropocentric subjectivism which has emerged from the Cartesian revolution. For Descartes himself, to be sure, behind nature there still existed a God who was soon to become the watchmaker God of the Deists. There is a powerful stream of Western thought running from Leibniz and Spinoza through Goethe and German objective idealism rejecting both reductionism and a purely "humanistic" subjectivism. Yet what might be called the ordinary Kantian, positivistic and even naturalistic outlook of the modern West has insisted on lodging the entire "symbolic world" and "world of values" within the realm of a human subjectivity or in the collective mind of human culture, which is treated either as an "epiphenomenon" or some other kind of inexplicable intrusion into a reduced natural world.

In Chinese "subjectivity" the human mind or the essence of the human mind is almost invariably treated as merely a manifestation or projection of a cosmic mind. This is true of that form of Mahayana Buddhist philosophy which is prepared to speak of the absolute in terms of "mind-only" or "store-consciousness" (as opposed to types of Buddhist philosophy such as Madhyamika which are not prepared to use any known category to describe the absolute). It is also true of that brand of Neo-Confucianism which speaks in terms of the ultimacy of mind *(hsin)*. Whether one refers to the ultimate reality—the Ultimate One—as indescribable or as mind or conscious-ness, the universe constitutes a plenum which is the source of all value and the human remains indissolubly bound up with that plenum. It is in this sense that most forms of Chinese thought must be called world-affirming. Wang Yang-ming's thought may represent a kind of ethical individualism, as Professor DeBary insists,[24] when it is viewed within a socio-political context, but Wang is by no means asserting his individual autonomy vis-à-vis an indifferent or blind universe. On the contrary, he ardently stresses the human identity with the transcendental mind. The cosmos, however construed, remains the source of value and meaning.

Finally, it need hardly be pointed out that the world of Chinese folk culture[25] is not a reductionist world. The natural world of Chinese folk culture is neither disenchanted nor de-demonized. It is full of gods, spirits, and magical phenomena most often associated with the kind of correlative cosmological thinking which was a common possession of both high culture and folk culture. Nor were there any overwhelming impulses on the part of the high culture to reject in toto the "polytheism" and magical dimensions of folk culture.

For the most part, the higher philosophies of China—whether Buddhist, Taoist, or Confucian, were not impelled by either monotheistic or reductionist motives to banish the gods and spirits from nature. The spirits and gods simply came to be explained as manifestations of the *Tao* or *ch'i*, or of the Buddhist world of *sam-sara*. The views of Hsün-tzu and Wang Ch'ung which assaulted providential correlative cosmology did indeed involve an attack on many "superstitions," but these philosophies were not to become the dominant ones of Chinese high culture. Indeed, even Chu Hsi's variety of rationalism was able to provide a detailed philosophic account of the ontological status of the ancestral spirits and spirits of nature. They are all manifestations of *ch'i* and they all have their own princi-ples of being *(li)*. The cosmos can accommodate them.

If this thesis is valid, one is tempted to speculate on why it may be so. Such speculations would carry us far afield and all I would sug-gest at this point is one of two highly tentative notions. It has already been noted that ancient Chinese thought about the world was domi-nated by the metaphor of procreation. The dominant image in Chi-nese cosmogony is the image of engendering. The image of procre-ation turns one's attention to the thought of a pre-existent fullness of being, of a kind of emanation rather than of making or creating. May the dominance of this image have something to do with ancestor worship as a dominant form of religious orientation in early China? The notion of heaven and earth engendering the ten thousand things as well as the world of man does, of course, provide an ideal coalescence between the realm of the ancestors and the realm of the divine forces of the natural world. It suggests that these forces are pregnant with all the manifold variety of the world.

Another line of speculation points to the early emergence within Chinese culture of an all-embracing socio-political order organized on a bureaucratic principle. The bureaucratic view of reality does not attempt to reduce the manifold realities of human society and culture. It rather attempts to classify them and establish routines for governing them from a center—a center which in Confucianism is the fountainhead of a kind of spiritual power. While the normative role of society which Confucius refers to in the Analects as the *Tao* is not, strictly speaking, a purely centralized bureaucracy, it is nevertheless conceived of as a total system in which everything moves along its proper grooves and is thus bureaucratic in some broader sense. It is the projection of such a view onto the cosmos which may produce the 'organismic' view so favored in Professor Needham's writings, and which may militate against the kind of preoccupation lying behind the emergence of reductionist thought in ancient Greece.

Such notions of the projection of the image of the social order onto the cosmos generally gain ready acceptance in a sociologistic age. They are particularly satisfying to those who regard images of society (presumably based on the cultural structures of society) as ultimate facts which require no further elucidation. While I find this notion suggestive, it still leaves open the question of why such an image of society won an early ascendancy in the Chinese cultural sphere. Professor Wittfogel, in his *Oriental Despotism*, has provided us with one answer. For myself the question remains open. At least for the present, it may be as important for us to examine what lies within the range of and outside of the range of Chinese thought as to determine why it may be so.

8

Area Studies as a Critical Discipline

*T*he modest, colorless, and ambiguous term "area studies" emerged during the course of World War II as a way of describing one minor enterprise in the war effort. It was an enterprise designed to achieve an encapsulated understanding of the unknown areas of the world with which we suddenly found ourselves engaged. During and after the war, most area studies were contemporary in orientation and, given the circumstances of their origin, extremely vulnerable to the charge of serving "nonscholarly" political or military interests.

Now the question of the relationship of area studies to political, economic, and other interests—and of their use for utilitarian purposes good or bad—remains a topical one. Yet they have for some time been disengaged from the circumstances of their origin. They are no longer exclusively modern in orientation. They involve a wide array of disciplines and theoretical approaches, and many are concerned with matters that certainly do not have any obvious relationship to immediate pragmatic goals.

I confess that I remain somewhat attached to the term "area studies" precisely because of its modesty and even because of its ambiguity. One might use such terms as the study of non-Western "cultures" or "societies" to describe our field of inquiry, but both the terms "culture" and "society" have been claimed by the disciplines of anthropology and sociology, respectively, and come to us laden with connotations and assumptions derived from those disciplines. The term "area studies" asserts no particular theory of society or theory of culture and no particular views of the relations of society and culture to history or other areas of human experience. The word "area" refers quite literally to some portion of the earth's surface inhabited by human collectivities, more or less marked off from other collectivities by virtue of the fact that they constitute relatively autonomous fields of human interaction among various life-realms. An area is, so to speak, a cross-disciplinary field of collective experience within which one can discern complex interactions among economic, social, political, religious, and other spheres of life.

The people who are attracted to an area approach are people who, despite their specific disciplinary commitments, share such an overriding, even burning interest in areas such as India, China, and Japan that it leads them to communicate with each other across the formidable barriers and jargons set up by their disciplines. The communication may occasionally be acrimonious, but the desire to communicate exists. Occasionally, they may even raise skeptical questions about the shibboleths of their disciplines on the basis of experience derived from their area studies. This, of course, may be an ideal. I am not aware of the extent to which those who attend panels on modern Indian economics are also impelled to attend panels on medieval Indian poetry.

I have spoken above of the ambiguity of the term "area studies." At times, when we speak of an area, we speak of a separate collectivity constituting a field of intensive cross-disciplinary interaction. At other times, we seem to refer to common cultural features shared by several societies. Specialists in East Asian studies often use the word "area" to refer to the East Asian cultural area as a whole. It is also used to refer to China, Japan, Korea, and Vietnam considered separately. If this is ambiguity, I suggest that is a fruitful ambiguity. The extent to which Chinese culture has or has not shaped the cultures and histories of Korea, Japan, and Vietnam remains a matter of lively dispute and discussion. If I may be allowed to apply the term "area studies" to Western civilization, equally fruitful questions are raised when we consider the relationships of various Western national cultures to Western civilization as a whole. The kind of questions raised are by no means exclusively factual—they are pregnant with theoretical implications.

While the term "area studies" may be ambiguous in reference, it successfully avoids the pitfalls of the shapeless term "Orient," against which Professor Edward Said fulminates in his book *Orientalism.* However much the focus of the word "area" may change, it is always based on some concrete principles of coherence, which give due weight to the specificities of local conditions. The area specialist can sympathize with Said's rage against those for whom everything from Iran to Morocco, and from the Abbasids to Khomeini, is simply part of one homogeneous, unchanging Islam, which in turn fades into a blur called the "Orient." Said is quite right, it seems to me, when he contends that the concept "Orient" is often used simply to provide a counter-image to the "Occident." While "Orientalism" has made enormous contributions to positive knowledge, it remains true that the Orient becomes in the minds of many not so much a place as a kind of receptacle for dreams, frustrations, facile polarities, and vapid generalizations about the oriental and occidental minds. To the extent that the area approach has been quite unwilling to treat "everything east of Suez" in this fashion; to the extent that area specialists emphasize the vast differences between Burma and Malaysia, between the T'ang dynasty and the Sung dynasty, and between the thought of Confucius and Mo-tzu, one would think that area studies would be relatively immune to the kind of accusations that Said hurls at Orientalism. Yet he insists on regarding area studies as the linear descendant of Orientalism and subject to all its vices.

What I shall consider here are some of the attacks on the enterprise of "area studies" that have emerged in various quarters. I will consider in particular the hostile views that have emerged in various social science disciplines as well as Said's attack on area studies as a mode of intellectual imperialism. I will also refer briefly to the "globalists" and the followers of Immanuel Wallerstein who would have us believe that area studies represent an escapist diversion from the study of "global models" and "world systems."

While many of you may agree with my defense of area studies as one approach to human experience, you may still question my use of the august and portentous word "discipline" to describe our approach. I will confess that my use of this word is meant not so much to inflate the status of area studies as to deflate the overblown and oversold status of the established disciplines in the field of human and social studies. It is not particularly my intent to challenge the present method of cutting up the cake of human knowledge in the American academic world. For the time being, we can live with it. We would nevertheless do well to remind ourselves that this division of labor grows out of quite recent trends in Western intellectual history. We would also do well to remind ourselves that many of the general notions that pervade many of these disciplines, such as the idea of "modernization" and the idea of a "behavioral science," are ideas that have shaped these disciplines, rather than ideas that have emerged from them. The disciplinary ideas of human knowledge arise out of the general intellectual discourse of the times. Yet let me stress that I am neither proposing a revolution in the present departmental structure of the university, nor am I even suggesting that area specialists not have bases in the various disciplines, whatever doubts they may have about absolute disciplinary claims. However much one may wish to stress that area studies are inherently cross-disciplinary, it is impossible for the individual specialist to encompass the whole, and such specialists naturally tend to approach their fields from a variety of vantage points and perspectives. Nevertheless, I would urge that, to the extent that area studies *have* established institutional niches within the academy such as area centers and area programs, these niches should be tenaciously defended.

The problem is not whether the area specialist can adapt to other disciplines, but whether the disciplines are prepared to accommodate the needs of the area specialist. The systematic tendency to downgrade the area approach within the human disciplines is not so much a function of the present division of labor among the disciplines, as it is a function of the scientistic pretensions within these disciplines. The craving to achieve the supposedly apodictic certainty and high status of the natural sciences has, of course, been a feature of the human sciences ever since the Enlightenment. It has, however, become particularly virulent in the American academy during the past few decades. Among the characteristics of this scientistic self-conception is the tendency to treat the disciplines not as roughly demarcated areas of human experience, but as sharply discrete, self-contained domains, each characterized by its own pure theories, models, hermetic vocabularies, and research methodologies. It is, as always, economics which here provides the supreme paradigm. Since political science, to take one instance, has its own pure theory, when the theorist of comparative politics seeks out political data from various areas of the world, he presumably has no need to trouble himself with the question of whether these strictly political data can be treated in isolation from the cultural and historical context from which they are extracted.

The only discipline within the area of human studies that occupies a somewhat anomalous position within this entire development is, of course, that of general history, which, as a kind of "area studies" in a time dimension, raises questions of a cross-disciplinary nature. Many efforts have been made by historians to "come in from the outside" by appropriating the theoretical frameworks of other disciplines. Yet to many practitioners of the other disciplines, historians fundamentally occupy the same status as area specialists—humble gatherers of facts. Nevertheless, for many historic reasons, history continues to enjoy the status of an established separate departmental discipline.

I might note in passing that this clear scientific demarcation of the disciplinary territories has by no means put an end to fierce conflicts about the scope of the explanatory claims put forth by the various disciplines. Imperial expansion is a constant reality. The ideological struggles concerning the relative causal roles of psychology, sociology, and anthropology continue unabated. Theoretical conflict also continues within the boundaries of the various disciplines. The scientific claims of the disciplines have not made it possible for them to wall themselves off from the general intellectual conflicts of the age.

Nevertheless, a major consequence of these scientistic claims has been the tendency of the disciplines to inflate the theoretical and methodological requirements imposed on students. Ostensibly, one of the great drawbacks for area students is that their fields of study have their own formidable research requirements, such as the need for in-depth study of language, and the time devoted to these requirements supposedly detracts from the time available for the use of the infinitely more important research tools of the discipline. The inflation of the discipline's requirements goes hand in hand with a tendency to provide less and less space for the requirements of the area specialist. To the extent that his presence is tolerated at all within the discipline, he is often regarded simply as a furnisher of empirical data. I am, of course, drawing this picture in somewhat bold strokes which may exaggerate the current state of affairs, but my effort here is to highlight a general situation.

The questions that confront us at this point are: What is a theoretician, and what is a gatherer of facts? What is a theory, and what is a fact? Anyone familiar with current literature in the philosophy of science will be aware that these are not simple questions. At one ex-

treme one can find the view that there are no such things as bare
statements of fact. In the words of Karl Popper, "all observations are
theory-impregnated." Said, who is not a philosopher of science,
states in his book that the vast edifice of positive scholarship erected
by nineteenth- and twentieth-century orientalists is in some sense un-
true because of the underlying assumptions of the orientalists who
produced this scholarship. Personally, I remain convinced that there
are such things as relatively pure statements of fact. In our ordinary
public discourse, we often make reference to simple spatiotemporal
events, such as the assertion that "it rained yesterday" or "the chair
is in the room," which I think will serve as statements of fact (even
though the question, "what is a chair?" raises profound philosophic
problems). I would even venture to suggest that on rare occasions a
fact may kill a theory. Yet, in our observation of the world, we seldom remain for long in the realm of what can unambiguously be
called the domain of bare fact. Words such as "fact," "event," and
"observation" have been used to refer quite promiscuously to vast
segments of human experience. The French Revolution has been
called an event, and entities such as the "Chinese examination system" and the "Indian caste system" have been referred to as facts.
Here we are indeed dealing with facts that are thoroughly impregnated with theory and high-order generalization.

Area specialists who proudly accept the description of themselves
as people who deal strictly in facts are as deluded as those who describe them in these terms. It may be simply the case that, in dealing
with large segments of experience within their area of study, they
rely on certain *idées reçues* deriving either from the culture itself or
from elsewhere. Yet, if they are of a theoretical bent, the theory-
impregnated facts with which they deal provide them with ample occasion for theoretical reflection. The books that they write (including
dictionaries) either reflect the theories of others or their own theoretical cogitations. Thus, when comparative theorists from the established disciplines read their book in search of "facts" to fit into their
models, what they will find is not bare fact but an inextricable mix-
ture of fact and theory. The theory will often reflect one point of
view within the theoretical debates that rage within the field itself.
Comparative theorists may even find that the books they read have
already taken into account ideas derived from the disciplinary theoreticians themselves. Certainly, area specialists should be open to any

insight that the theoreticians within the other disciplines may have to offer, but they need not treat these theories as sacred doctrines in terms of which they passively categorize the "facts" derived from their field. On the contrary, they have an admirable vantage point from which to test the logical rigor and universal claims of the models they are being asked to validate. Area specialists may, indeed, find that many of the theoretical problems suggested by their own experience cut across the boundaries so sharply drawn by the disciplinary theoreticians. They certainly have every reason to be a critical participant in their own right in the debates surrounding the conflicting causal claims of the various disciplines.

If the area specialist is inevitably a theoretician, what are we to say of the claims of those in other disciplines to be the guardians of pure theory? The term "pure theory" suggests something like the Kantian deduction of the categories—a process of pure reason based strictly on logical or mathematical implication. In fact most of the theories in the disciplines are based on empirical generalization. If fact is "theory-impregnated" as Popper asserts, then these theories are impregnated with reference to particular segments of observed experience. Some of them are even heavily based on the experience of given localities. It would be interesting to know how much of American academic economic theory is based on the study of the American economy. It may, of course, be claimed that the mature industrial economy of the United States represents a certain universal stage in a generalized theory of economic development and that the laws of this economy (which can often be stated in mathematical terms) have universal scientific validity. I am in no position to challenge this claim. Yet we are reminded that within the area of development theory, theory is often directly based on the observation of particular areas. For example, in the 1950s many Western development theorists assumed that, because the Soviet Union represented a certain universal stage of economic development, certain basic features of the Soviet model were applicable to all economies assumed to be at that stage. The arguments were, of course, logical as well as empirical, yet the reliance on a given historical experience is unmistakable. Not only are we here dealing with empirical generalization but with generalization in trouble because of its tendency to universalize a particular experience that may have been heavily influenced by noneconomic factors. We are hardly dealing with theory uncontaminated by reference to particular experience.

Another notion prevalent in the other disciplines is that the area specialist as such is incapable of engaging in comparative analysis. He is so transfixed by the unique and idiosyncratic nature of his field of study that he is resistant to the notion that any aspect of the society which he studies is comparable to anything else. Comparison, as we know, can only take place within a framework of general and universalizable categories. Hence, comparative theory is the proper preserve of the theoretician within the several disciplines. What has happened is that area studies have been identified with certain extreme forms of cultural anthropological theory or certain extreme forms of linguistic determinism in the manner of Benjamin Whorf. Such points of view are, to be sure, represented within area studies, and their advocates have made their own creative, albeit controversial, contributions to the field. Ironically, these points of view derive from certain general theories present within the discipline of anthropology and linguistics. I would nevertheless venture to say that most area specialists are firmly convinced that the phenomena which they study are eminently comparable to similar categories of phenomena elsewhere. Thus, the Chinese political experience both in its synchronic and diachronic aspects is certainly different from any other political experience, but it is nevertheless eminently comparable in all its aspects to the political experience of other systems.

Offhand, I would think that Western area specialists trying to understand a society other than their own would be comparative-minded by the very nature of their situation, although one would expect them to be somewhat more conscious of the profound difficulties involved in the comparative enterprise than the comparativist in other disciplines. If asked to compare "kingship" in their area to "kingship" elsewhere, they must be conscious of the relationship of kingship in their area to other aspects of the society they are studying, and, above all, they must be aware of change over time. They must be fully aware of the various theoretical interpretations of this matter that are to be found within the field itself. They must be acutely conscious of the fact that they are not dealing with bare facts, and of the demanding preconditions of any honest comparative effort.

It has always seemed to me highly regrettable that more comparative communication does not take place among area specialists themselves. Comparative theorists from other disciplines should be

welcome participants in such communication and should be invited
to put forth their theories and models (but not to deliver ex cathedra
pronouncements from on high). Their theories should be as subject
to critical scrutiny as the theories engendered by the area specialists
themselves. May it not be a fact that some of the most interesting
problems cut squarely across the boundaries of the disciplines? Some
of the most fruitful comparative ideas of Max Weber—who has been
conventionally identified as a sociologist, but who was in fact a
cross-disciplinary thinker—are cross-disciplinary in nature. It is no
accident that Weber was also deeply aware that honest comparative
work required an immersion in what we now call area studies. His
several volumes on the sociology of religion, whatever their limitations and defects, are based on what I would call a profound respect
for area study.

There is finally one other aspect of the relationship of the human
disciplines as now constituted in the United States to area studies that
I would like to consider—namely, the heavily behavioral bias that
dominates so many of these disciplines. In discussing this aspect, I
suspect that I am expressing my own particular point of view rather
than representing the point of view of the area approach in general.
Certainly, the behavioral approach is amply and even heavily represented among area specialists. It is, nevertheless, my contention that
when a purely behavioral point of view is applied to the study of non-
Western society, its capacity to obstruct balanced understanding and
its culture-boundedness become particularly apparent.

The issues involved are profound and complex and can hardly be
resolved here. What I call the behavioral approach is, of course, also
based on the craving for the apodictic certainty of the natural sciences mentioned above. The physicist can treat his particles as simple
instantiations of the general laws he is interested in. He need not
trouble himself with the conscious dispositions and subjective intentions of his quarks and protons. He is, thus, the undisputed master
of all he surveys. The behavioral social scientist also aspires to eliminate the queer and bothersome factor of subjective intentions and
the conscious truth-claims of the human particles he examines. In the
fashion of the true Cartesian ego, he asserts his own conscious truth-
claims by excluding the conscious truth-claims of others. He is, of
course, just as interested in explaining his own social environment
"behaviorally" as he is in explaining the behavior of far-off societies.

Yet, within his immediate environment, he is constantly exposed to the counterclaims of rival "scientists": The Freudian can explain the behavior of the Skinnerian in terms of his infantile traumas; the Skinnerian can explain the behavior of the Freudian in terms of his negative conditioning; and the sociologist can explain the behavior of both in terms of their social strata. In the face of all these claims and counterclaims, it becomes impossible to escape genuine intellectual debate or to dismiss completely the ideas in the heads of others. However, in dealing with far-off societies, one can presumably impose one's behavioral models and conceptual schemes in complete oblivion of the conscious, intentional life of the inhabitants of those societies. So dominant and intimidating has the dogmatic sway of the behavioral approach become that, even in history departments, those who are concerned with intellectual history and human conscious life in general must often struggle to survive.

While the behavioral approach is represented and ought to be represented in area studies, there is still a substantial body of area specialists who remain firmly committed to the investigation of the conscious life of the societies they study. They are firmly convinced that the only honest way of studying far-off societies is to give as much weight to the subjective life of those they study as they give to their own. The question of how the world of conscious intentionality relates to the world of social behavior remains in the West one of the unresolved problems of post-Cartesian thought, and I do not propose to resolve it here. Nevertheless, I suspect that it can be pursued with greater philosophic freedom in the field of area studies than it can in the closed world of those disciplines dominated or intimidated by behavioral dogma.

The attack on area studies as a legitimate approach to human experience has come not only from the overweening scientific pretensions of the established disciplines but from other quarters as well. Edward Said, in his book *Orientalism,* attacks the legitimacy of area studies from another point of the compass. As already stated, he insists that area studies are simply the latest variant of the orientalism that he attacks with such unrelieved vehemence. Indeed, so deep is his animus against area studies that at times he seems to align himself with the kind of disciplinary attack we have just discussed. In an uncharacteristic mood of piety toward the end of his book, he contrasts "disciplines defined intellectually" with fields like orientalism

"defined canonically, imperially and geographically." Actually, it is
quite clear from Said's exposition that he by no means approves of
everything to be found in the "disciplines defined intellectually." But
this remark forcibly calls to our attention the degree to which his
ideas are solidly rooted in modern Western thought.

What are the features that orientalism and area studies share in
Said's view? First of all, he points to the undeniable fact that the rise
of orientalism and of area studies coincided at least for a certain
epoch with the expansion of Western dominion throughout the
world. These two facts are obviously related in many complex ways.
There is no doubt that a confident sense of superiority permeated
both the imperial expansion and the attitudes of many orientalists.
Nor can one deny that it is also to be found among area specialists.
(Said does concede at one point that attitudes of cultural superiority
have by no means been unique to the modern West.)

Said maintains that orientalism and area studies have been designed to serve political purposes or have at least been used to serve
political and other interests. The latter statement is indeed true but
probably not a whit more true of orientalism and area studies than
of the human sciences in general and even of the natural sciences.
The sense of superiority that he finds embedded in orientalism, after
all, found its spiritual source in such disciplines as philology, ethnol-
ogy, and Darwinian biology interpreted in racial terms. Ernest
Renan, who is Said's particular *bête noire*, drew most of his sustenance from these sources.

At one level of Said's discourse, he does not seem to deny that orientalism and area studies, in spite of their enmeshment with economic and political interests and deplorable attitudes, have in fact
produced positive knowledge which has its own validity as knowledge. At this level, he is even willing to acknowledge that certain orientalists, such as Louis Massignon and Maxime Rodinson, have
been able to rise above their historic conditioning to achieve genuine
understanding.

At another level, however, Said implies that orientalism and hence
area studies taken as a whole are a dominating total discourse in the
sense of Michel Foucault or a kind of ideology in the sense of a vulgar Marxism or sociology of knowledge operating behind the backs
of all the individual orientalists and area specialists. No matter what
their intentions, however much they may strive to achieve some gen-

uine understanding, "objectively" everything they do reflects political and societal power interests. On this level, one cannot even speak of contributions to positive knowledge as having any objective validity. All knowledge is a mode of domination. Even the possibility of using knowledge as a vehicle for achieving understanding *(Verstehen)* in the Weberian sense is ruled out a priori.

We cannot solve these larger cosmic questions here. I would simply point out that, if we apply Foucault's concept of discourse as a world of language which controls everything within its orbit or, if we accept a completely deterministic sociology of knowledge, these notions must be applied across the board. If all ideas and all discourse simply reflect historic and social interests, there seems to be little reason to single out orientalism or area studies for special treatment. Foucault himself would certainly not differentiate between these pursuits and what Said calls "disciplines defined intellectually." They are all equally part of a dominating discourse. Foucault's own theory of discourse when applied to the Orient would be fully implicated with this posture of domination.

What is it, however, that leads Said to believe that orientalism and area studies are particular embodiments of ideological bad faith? It seems to me that it stems from his identification of orientalism (and hence of area studies) with an extreme form of culturalism, of the cultural anthropological type discussed above. The orientalist treats the Orient as an exotic, totally integrated cultural system, one radically different from the culture of the West. This stress on essential difference is further compounded in the writings of many by recourse to a kind of philological theory of the absolute differences of language systems, as in the case of Renan who posited a qualitative difference between the Indo-European and Semitic languages. In the nineteenth century this stress on a changeless, essential difference was even further exacerbated by a racialist version of Darwinism. To the degree that Renan and others tacitly assumed that man's true humanity had been realized in the modern West, I think that Said is quite right when he asserts that this variety of orientalism involved the dehumanization of the entire non-Western world.

To what extent are such notions of the absolute, changeless, and irreducible differences of other cultures still present in contemporary area studies? No doubt representatives of an anthropologically based cultural relativism are still with us. Many of our cultural and linguistic relativists are no longer convinced of Western superiority, however. Their relativism has now become quite genuine. Such ideas do not necessarily constitute the mainstream of contemporary area studies. Yet the fact remains that, if area specialists do not on the whole think of their subject in terms of the absolute "Other," they are still committed to the idea of significant difference—Japan, India, China, and Bali *are* significantly different from each other. The relationship of the political order to the religious *is* different in India than it is in China. Apparently, it is in this ongoing stress on significant difference that Said finds the continuity between orientalism and area studies. It is also apparently here that he finds the superiority of "disciplines defined intellectually," since these disciplines presumably deal in universal ideas and the universal seems to imply sameness rather than difference.

The recognition of significant difference, however, does not necessarily involve the denial of a common humanity. On the level of individual life, it would not occur to any of us to assert that our common humanity is incompatible with the existence of significant differences in temperament, personality, life history, and outlook. All of these differences are universally human, because they represent varied human responses to common human concerns. If this is so on the individual level, how much more must it be so when vast segments of collective experience, such as politics, religion, and social life, are in question. Such differences belong to the universally human because they are eminently comparable and, one hopes, ultimately penetrable and comprehensible. The Latin epigram *nihil me alienum puto* ("I consider nothing human alien") was not meant to assert that all other humans are exactly like myself, but rather that, through empathetic imagination, I can hope to comprehend highly different human experiences.

Indeed, at times the assertion of universal sameness may itself involve the denial of a common humanity because of the tendency to identify the universally human with what may actually be a very particular historical and cultural configuration. It is interesting to note that one of the few orientalists whom Said regards with favor is Rodinson, who has written a book entitled *Islam and Capitalism*. According to Said, it refutes Max Weber's denial of a capitalist system to the Islamic world. Rodinson attributes to Weber the notion of the "Oriental's incapacity for trade, commerce and economic rationality." I must say that this is a grotesque distortion of Weber's conception of capitalism as an organized system. The main question here, however, is the following: Does the absence or presence of the particular configuration that we call the capitalist system have anything to do with the humanity of the Islamic world? Does Weber's denial of capitalism (he certainly did not deny trade, commerce, and economic rationality) in the Islamic world mean that he has denied the humanity of that world? Does Rodinson's assertion of its existence confirm the humanity of that world?

One mode of thought which dominated the nineteenth- and twentieth-century West is neglected in Said's book, although it has profoundly affected both Orientalism and area studies. (I suspect that one reason why he has not discussed it is because he may himself share its premises.) It is a mode of thought that posits a conception of a universal normal path of societal growth, evolution, development, or history for the entire human race. The underlying metaphor is that of the growth of a biological organism applied to total societies. Its enthusiastic acceptance in the nineteenth-century West was based on the belief that Western humanity had finally made the breakthrough to the maturity of the human race. Much of the hubris and sense of superiority of the modern West derived not so much from the kind of biological and cultural absolutism so much stressed by Said as from the confidence so clearly expressed in the writings of Hegel, Spencer, Comte, Buckle, Marx, Maine, and others that the West had clearly forged ahead of the non-Western world and its own past. It was as much a temporal as a spatial hubris.

One might argue that such a mode of thought is at least potentially more universal than a cultural, linguistic, or biological essentialism. It does, after all, assign the non-Western world to the same categories of "feudalism," "backward society" or "traditional society" to which it assigns the West's own past. Since the non-Western world is, however, contemporary with us, one must inevitably use such images as "retarded growth" or "arrested growth" to account for its failure to achieve immanent growth in terms of the general accepted criteria. In accounting for such failures, some are indeed tempted to have recourse to the same unchanging cultural or geographic factors so deplored by Said—as in the case of Marx's conception of the Asian mode of production. One wonders in the end whether the image of arrested growth is less dehumanizing than the image of eternal and irreducible cultural difference. One wonders whether the notion that one particular configuration of evolution or historic development derived from the West as the only model of "normal" societal growth either confirms the human dignity of other peoples or makes it possible to write a true history of their societies.

It is precisely the area-oriented historian who should be capable of liberating himself from the frozen alternative of either an ahistorical culturalism or the notion of a path of history that must seek its paradigm of normalcy in the spurious universality of holistic configurations derived from the West. In writing the histories of other areas, it may in the end be necessary to rid ourselves of the stale categories, which now dominate our discourse, and to seek new nomenclatures, some of them perhaps even derived from the cultures we are studying. This does not preclude the use of the metaphor of growth as applied to concrete areas of human experience where its use is appropriate. Technologies, economies, and systems of military and political organization have developed at different rates in all cultures at all times. It is when the concept is applied as a totalistic biological metaphor that it inevitably leads to distortion. To assert that the larger configurations of the histories of different areas may be different from each other in all kinds of significant ways is no more dehumanizing than to point out that different individuals have quite different biographies.

I have discussed certain attacks on the validity of area studies as a mode of inquiry. There are attacks from other quarters—both left and right—which deserve an essay of their own. I will simply refer to the "globalist" thinkers—disciplinary and cross-disciplinary—and the adherents of Professor Wallerstein's "world system analysis." However much they may differ in political orientation, all insist that the study of the contemporary world should be left to them. Since the world has already become one interdependent system in terms of the criteria that they deem to be important, it no longer makes sense to ascribe causal weight to factors operative within separate societies. Here, too, there is much to discuss.

In summation, I suggest that there is little room at present for complacency or self-congratulation in the area of human and social studies in general and in the established disciplines in particular. At such a time, the academy can ill afford to ignore any perspective. I do not mean to suggest that area studies provide the sovereign cure for all our ailments, and I would certainly concede that area studies are as enmeshed with human passions, interests, presuppositions, and utilitarian goals as any truth-seeking endeavor. Yet they do represent the aspiration to bring the experience of the entire human race to bear on our common concerns. They do aspire to achieve a complex and deep understanding of other societies, cultures, and historic experiences. Area specialists should henceforth be vigorous participants in all comparative enterprises and vigorous critics of the restrictive and culture-bound comparative theories put forth elsewhere. As area specialists, we are engaged in an enterprise that deserves our whole-hearted defense.

9

The Primacy of the Political Order in East Asian Societies

One of the most striking characteristics of Chinese civilization is what might be called the centrality and weight of the political order[1] within that civilization. As a historian strongly biased toward an insistence on the reality of historic change and the emergence of novelty within Chinese culture, it is with some hesitation that I here focus attention on what seems to be a more or less enduring dominant cultural orientation. We may not be dealing with a dichotomy between mutually exclusive terms, however. The dominant cultural orientation operates on a high level of generality and it is most easily discerned when we contemplate the whole sweep of Chinese history. It is a general orientation which remains quite compatible with vast and significant changes operative within its wide boundaries.

Since this chapter will deal with large but tentative generalizations, I shall allow myself to extend these generalizations to other areas of the East Asian culture sphere and to ask in particular whether the Chinese orientation did significantly affect the evolution of those societies in East Asia such as Japan, Korea, and Vietnam which were influenced by Chinese civilization.

The idea of an all-embracing socio-political order centering on a particularly powerful conception of universal kingship seems to have emerged very early within the Chinese cultural world. One can indeed discern its beginnings even in the Shang oracle bone inscriptions. The universal king (universal in that he presides over the universal human civilization) surrounded by his ministering elite soon comes to embody within his person both the supreme political[2] au-

thority and the spiritual-ethical authority of the entire society
(zhengjiao heyi). The kingship or locus of the authority which he occupies *(wei)* is an institution which comes to constitute the major
link between human society and the ruling forces of the cosmos. It is
itself a cosmic institution. Certainly as early as the *Book of Poetry*
and the genuinely pre-Confucian texts of the *Book of Documents,*
the king and the ruling stratum under him were responsible both for
what we would call political administration and the ethico-ritual
order of society.

This conception of political order, whatever the actuality to which
it related, thus seems to have emerged well before the rise of the centralized bureaucratic state which emerges out of the developments of
the Warring States period and finds its universalization in the Qin
revolution.

In speaking here of a conception of all-encompassing authority,
one is not necessarily speaking of the concentration of power and
authority at the territorial center, but rather of the conception of the
supreme jurisdiction of the political order in all domains of social
and cultural life. When in the so-called feudal period of the Zhou,
local power-holders shared a portion of the king's politico-religious
authority within their own domains, they also shared the king's jurisdiction over the "spirits of mountains and streams" within their
domains. The centrality and weight of the political order was as
much present in their exercise of power as in that of the king himself.
In speaking of the "weight" of the political order we refer to its ultimate authority in every domain of social-cultural experience as we in
the West would tend to define these domains. This highly general
shared orientation by no means precluded the emergence of highly
diverse and even conflicting modes of thought concerning the interpretation of the orientation itself. The conflicts among the Mohists
and Legalists were not necessarily less significant than conflicts
among modern Western ideologies which often share the same implicit assumptions. Indeed this dominant orientation did not even
preclude the emergence of tendencies of thought which minimized or
even negated the role ascribed to the political order (e.g. the Yang
Zhu strain and the genuine Zhuangzi strain in the book of
Zhuangzi).

What do we mean by words such as "centrality" and "weight"?
The implied contrast is to other high civilizations and cultures in

which the political order did not in general come to occupy this degree of centrality. A general glance at the history of India—with all
due reservations—suggests that in India the religious order is quite
independent of and pre-eminent in relation to the political order and
one may indeed say that the Hindu social order is itself, to a degree,
independent of the political order. The Indian concept of the role of
the political order as the policing agent of society seems much more
modest in its scope of application. In quite a different way we have
the model of ancient Biblical Judaism in which the priesthood is depicted as emerging before the kingship and in which bearers of spiritual authority such as prophets and later rabbis remain essentially
separate from the political order. In medieval Europe we have, of
course, the authority and power of the Catholic church in the spiritual sphere, leading to sharply demarcated conceptions of sacred and
secular power and to bitter conflicts concerning the boundaries between the two. Out of this emerges a sharply defined concept of the
"secular" state. I would even suggest that the role of Catholic Christianity in medieval Western feudalism sharply differentiates that feudalism from the feudalism of medieval Japan (despite the actual
politico-military powers of certain Buddhist monastic establish-
ments). In the West, the prominence of the legal order will greatly facilitate the establishment of the separate "rights" of estates, institutions, and various domains of social experience sharply defined in
legal terms.

The fact that in China the political order presides in principle over
every area of socio-political life seems at least on the surface to lend
strong support to the notion of "Oriental despotism" and to further
suggest that the more "totalitarian" aspects of Chinese Communism
represent a natural continuity with the "Oriental despotism" and the
"totalism" of the traditional order. I would, however, contend that
the all-encompassing jurisdictional claims of the traditional political
order did not necessarily—or even ordinarily—imply an aggressive,
positive interventionism in every area of life. The modern word "totalitarianism" refers to an eminently modern phenomenon. It implies
not only the state's claim to ultimate authority in every domain of
experience, but to an aggressive intervention in every domain of life
in order to control and shape the lives of groups and individuals in
the service of collective future goals. The totalitarian polity is goal-
oriented rather than maintenance-oriented. Even its vehement attack

on the autonomy of various spheres of social and cultural life represents a kind of highly conscious dialectic antithesis to a fully articulated liberalism.

Something like a "totalitarian aspiration" can at times be discerned in Chinese history, as in the case of Qin Shi Huangdi. Yet I would argue that if we consider the entire sweep of Chinese history, one can say that the basic impulse of Chinese political order did not move in this direction. Some would argue that it did not move in this direction simply because of the lack of opportunity provided by the modern instruments of material and social technology. Others might argue that on the whole the aspiration to totalitarian power did not become a dominant aspiration. To the extent that Confucianism was a factor, one can argue that the main line of Confucianism ran counter to the notion of aggressive state intervention in every domain of society, and that on the contrary, it favored light government. On its most idealistic level it envisions the entire society permeated by the radiation of the spiritual-educational influence of an exemplary Confucian ruling class. On a more mundane level, it can be asserted that this non-interventionist philosophy often coincided with the elite's perception of its own interests. None of this implied any inclination to conception of freedom of thought or pluralism. On the contrary, the ideal continued to be that of total consensus. The fact remains that the orthodoxy was loosely defined. It did not, in the centuries from the Song through the Qing dynasties, preclude the emergence of highly diverse schools of Confucian thought and did not on its outer boundaries preclude the accommodation of Buddhism or "Religious Taoism." It did not preclude the notion that the normative *Tao* of Confucianism was transcendent vis-à-vis the current status quo of the political order, nor that the emperor and the bureaucracy could be judged and found wanting in terms of the *Tao* (even though it provided no legal protection for those who appealed in a prophetic spirit to the higher norms). The truly great Confucian thinkers felt no obligation to regard the current holders of power as the embodiers of the *Tao* and hence the sense of a gap between the normative ideals and the prevailing status quo could be maintained.

The political culture was indeed unambiguously authoritarian and based on a positive evaluation of hierarchy and status. There was nothing which precluded the ad hoc, arbitrary, and often brutal in-

tervention of state power in the lives of groups or individuals. Yet
the dominant orientation did not ordinarily lead to systematic intervention by organizational means for either good or evil goals.

In the religious spiritual sphere, the political order was regarded as
an integral part of the cosmic order. Rather than speaking of the
state religion, it might be more accurate to speak of the religious status of the political order. It remained a crucial link, in its own self-
conception, between human society and Heaven as well as with the
numinous world in general, and hence claimed jurisdiction over all
social organizations including those which concerned themselves
with the religious sphere. Below Heaven, all the "legitimate" manifestations of numinous powers in the world should themselves be
subordinate to and "canonized" by the political order. Yet the fact
remains that in the long history of the exuberant popular religion of
China there was much that remained beyond the control of the political order. In later centuries spontaneous cults and sects remained in
constant tension with the claims of the political order to preside over
all organized manifestations of religious life. Religious sects were always suspect, yet in their non-apocalyptic phases were often reluc-
tantly tolerated. In the end, the strikingly foreign institution of
Buddhist monasticism was "brought into" the boundaries of the
socio-political order, as were the institutions of the "Taoist church."

All of this would seem to argue for a fairly heavy control of the religious domain by the political order. Yet the fact remains that on
the level of "high cultural" religious life, it does not appear that the
political order ever claimed a monopoly of access to the world of the
transcendent, and the ineffable-mystic Chan (Zen) masters, "Taoist"
adepts, and hermits could pursue their particular forms of gnosis,
bypassing the religious claims of the state. On the level of popular
religion there was often a swifter reaction to the potentially dangerous claims of direct access to the numinous sphere by shamans and
sorcerers. But even here the state could not control the vast, protean
world of popular religion with all its regional variations. Indeed the
term "popular" may be a misnomer to the extent that a considerable
part of the ruling elite itself participated in popular religion. Brutal
persecution of the ill-defined realm of the heterodox was an ever-
present possibility. Yet the aggressive and insistent efforts of the
modern totalitarian state to internalize in the popular mind its own
spiritual intellectual claims and exclude others was not to be found.

Whether this was wholly a matter of incapacity or whether it had something to do with the inherent nature of the traditional orthodoxy itself, is a question I shall not attempt to resolve.

In the sphere of general intellectual life, the orthodoxy/heterodoxy dichotomy was always present, yet the line between the two was by no means clearly defined, even though individual literati and officials often had very definite views on this matter. The range of outlooks within Confucianism remained broad and the lines between Confucianism, Buddhism, and all the modes of thought which have been grouped under the category of Taoism were often crossed without leading to state repression. While literati were forced to be enormously circumspect in their language about the present holders of power, there was no assumption that the current occupants of the throne necessarily embodied the Confucian *Tao*.

In the realm of economic life, there did not develop in China (nor in the West before the eighteenth century) the notion of the absolute discreteness of the economic as an entirely separate discipline nor any notion of the economic realm as lying outside the jurisdiction of the state's authority. While no strong orientation to economic development seems to have arisen (as opposed to continuing concern with economic subsistence) and while the usual generalization about the inferior status of merchants may be generally true for broad sweeps of Chinese history, the operation of the free market was generally accepted within the commercial economy, and in later ages, commercial economy, commodity production and the buying and selling of land were certainly present. Hence the application of the dichotomy "command economy" versus "market economy" is highly misleading for large parts of Chinese history. While Confucianism as a doctrine may not have been favourable to commercial growth and development, it also did not favour heavy intervention into what was regarded as the proper domain of merchant activity. None of this, however, was at all incompatible with intervention by the political order in the economy at any point or with state monopolies based on collaboration of "government merchants" and the state. Land in later dynasties could be bought and sold although the full Lockean legal definition of private property or property rights was never established, and property was certainly subject to confiscation. Professor Wittfogel has argued that private property was weak in China. Yet this statement itself indicates that in some sense it existed. Many modern historians argue that in the Ming and Qing, with the growth of commodity production, empire-wide commerce, and the growth of manufacture, the command role of the state vis-à-vis the economy actually declined. Yet others have shown that the state initiatives continued to play a considerable role in regulating empire-wide trade, flood control, and famine and in policies governing the internal migrations of population.

The same combination of the notion of the ultimate authority of the political order with the absence of any active unremitting interventionism can be found in other spheres of social and cultural life. Beyond all this, we find that the question of centralization versus decentralization of power within the political order was to remain a constant issue in Chinese political thought. Different views of the distribution of power and authority were entirely compatible with the general maxim of *zhengjiao heyi*.

In light of the above, it becomes exceedingly difficult to provide neat affirmative or negative answers to many categorical questions which we tend to direct to Chinese traditional culture. Not only were there shifts and changes over historic time, but the culture will not yield clear responses to the antitheses which we impose. Was there or was there not freedom of religion in China and East Asia? Was there or was there not intellectual freedom? Was a critical stance toward the government possible? Was the economy a "command economy" or a "market economy"? Did organizations such as guilds and religious organizations enjoy any autonomy or were they completely controlled by the political order? Much of Chinese history occupies the borderlands between those stark alternatives.

In the light of these uncertainties it seems highly doubtful—despite the all-encompassing jurisdictional claims of the traditional political order—whether the victory of Chinese Communism and the more totalitarian propensities of the People's Republic of China before Mao's death can simply be explained in terms of cultural continuities. In accounting for the victory of the Communists due weight must in the end be given to the contingencies and conjunctures of twentieth-century Chinese history as well as to the specific historic circumstances which made the ideas of Marxism-Leninism particularly appealing to those who formed the nucleus of the Communist movement. The ideas themselves—whatever their affinities and resonances with traditional ideas—were of foreign origin. I do not myself subscribe to the dogma that the inhabitants of one culture cannot be deeply affected by ideas which come from outside the cultural orbit. It is always possible in retrospect to single out those features of a complex cultural heritage which seem to favor current developments. Such features undoubtedly exist but they exist as aspects of a larger complex within which opposing tendencies can also be found.

A strong case can be made that the world of present-day Taiwan— where de facto autonomy in social and cultural life is combined with the presumption of the ultimate authority of the political order— may resonate more directly with traditional practice than the aggressive totalitarian dynamism of the first thirty years of the People's Republic. Indeed, in other modernizing or modernized societies of East Asia such as Japan, South Korea, and Singapore certain traditional East Asian attitudes toward the centrality of the political order continue to affect the evolution of these societies.

To be sure, each of these societies must be treated separately and the question of the weight of the Chinese influence in each of them remains a matter of much dispute. This is particularly true in the case of Japan where many scholars are inclined to stress the specificities of Japanese culture and history rather than general "East Asian" propensities. Japan is very much a case in itself. Not only is it fully modernized in every tangible meaning of that word, it is also a functioning constitutional democracy, however Japanese the style of its constitutionalism. Japanese history has also run a unique course. The long history of the decentralized feudal order has led many to discern a presumed parallel role to the organic development of modernity out of a feudal past in the West. For purposes of argument I would raise some doubts about the importance of the latter consideration. An argument can be made that the East Asian matrix of Japanese feudalism made it radically different from the feudalism of the West with its conflict between church and state as well as its legalistic Roman law background. Some of the characteristics of what has been called the East Asian concept of political order can be found within Japanese feudalism itself. However fragmented the territorial distribution of power and authority may have been, the Japanese feudal lord often claimed the same jurisdiction over every sector of social and cultural experience within his domain as the Confucian bureaucracy. The same was certainly true of the Tokugawa Bakufu.

While constitutionalism in Japan has indeed established tangible and definable legal constraints on the authority of the political order in Japan, in many areas of social and cultural life, for better or worse, there nevertheless remains a resistance to sharp and dogmatic demarcations among the political order represented by the administrative bureaucracy and other sectors of social life. Western dogmas concerning pure centralized planning or pure free market have not sunk deep roots despite the fact the Japanese economy is essentially a market economy. The merchant-capitalist manager is no longer despised, but the official continues to enjoy high prestige and the cooperation between officialdom and the economic elite takes place on every level of the economy. It is widely accepted that state bureaus may play a guiding role in economic life. The dichotomy of the public and private is blurred by the enormous emphasis on cooperation and the achievement of consensus where possible.

In Japan and other East Asian cultures which are familiar with the Chinese terms often translated as private and public *(si/gong)*, these terms often referred not to the notion of two separate domains of the social order, but to attitudes of individuals or groups toward their roles in society. There were those who were public-minded *(gong)* in their ethical attitudes and those who were selfish or ego-oriented *(si)* without regard to the social field in which they were operating. Whatever the actual motives of industrialists and businessmen, it was the firm conviction of personalities such as Shibusawa Eiichi in Japan and Zhang Jian in China that in their role as leaders in the private sector they were also answering the public and national interest. They did so not simply in the terms of Adam Smith's notion that the pursuit of enlightened self-interest—through the operations of the "unseen hand"—in the end serves the best interests of society as a whole, but in the sense that they were really public persons even in the private sector. To the extent that such self-perceptions continue to exist, they greatly diminish the abyss between officials, entrepreneurs and managers.

The entire Anglo-American tendency to see individualism and modern industrial society as two sides of the same coin is certainly not as dominant in most of these East Asian societies (even in Japan with its constitutional democracy) as it is in America or Western Europe. The word "individualism" is, of course, a many-layered word, and it is not my intention to deny that certain definitions of individualism may apply to certain aspects of East Asian culture. Yet what is probably least marked is that mode of aggressive libertarian individualism— particularly economic individualism—which posits an inevitable conflict between the aggressive individual and the group. Indeed, do theories which insist that individualism is at the heart of industrial progress do justice to that vast complex of phenomena which we subsume under the word "industrialism"? The very Max Weber who played a large role in developing the theory of the individual entrepreneur, in his image of a developed industrialism, was above all impressed by the dominant role of bureaucratic rationalization in corporate industry, and by the need for iron discipline and subordination of individuals on all levels to the requirements of organization. Whether advanced industrialism as such is inherently more favorable to "rugged individualism" than to hierarchy, status, and emphasis on group cooperation and group morale remains an unresolved question. The experience of Taiwan, South Korea, Japan and even Singapore would indicate that even a "capitalist" economy in an East Asian setting may favor the latter values as much as the former.

Again it must be pointed out that modernity in East Asia has thus far, for better or worse, not led to the degree of prominence of the legal order that it has in certain Western societies, despite Max Weber's insistence that a fully developed legal system of the modern Western type is an absolutely essential ingredient of rationalization. In Japan, the establishment of constitutional democracy has led to an impressive development of constitutional law and civil rights laws, yet the legal profession continues to be far less important than in the West and law has not penetrated every nook and cranny of other spheres of life including the economic.

In the spheres of intellectual and cultural freedom (again with the notable exceptions of Japan and Hong Kong) we continue to perceive a kind of resonance with the lack of clear boundaries which we find in the tradition. In the late 1980s in South Korea, Taiwan, and Singapore, there are considerable, though varying, degrees of de facto intellectual autonomy in academic life, although much less in the media. There is also considerable freedom in the arts and literature. Yet the ultimate authority of the political order in these spheres has not been relinquished, and arbitrary interventions are a constant possibility. They can still be justified in terms of the larger social good as determined by the state.

Finally, in speaking of possible future developments of the People's Republic of China in the post-Mao period of ferment and change, one of the possible scenarios suggested by the experience of the past might be a movement away from a full totalitarian control of society, not only in the economic sector but in other domains as well, to situations in which the political order will provide spaces of autonomy without renouncing its ultimate authority. If such a posture of retreat from actual control endures for an appreciable length of time, it may become customary practice. One need not necessarily expect that the policies will remain the same in all arenas. The experiment in a mixed economy might continue even while spiritual control is reasserted. Such de facto autonomy would not remain immune to intervention and to shifting boundaries of the permissible from area to area. Without in any way predicting this outcome I would simply urge that it would not be out of line with the cultural orientation discussed in these pages.

10

Hierarchy, Status, and Authority in Chinese Culture

*H*aving spent over forty years in the society of China scholars it has long been my feeling that one of the most intractably problematic aspects of Chinese culture for most contemporary Western scholars has been the perceived role of hierarchy, status, and authority—or to use a harsher "unmasking" vocabulary, domination, subjugation, and repression—not only in the actual history of Chinese society but even in its shared cultural norms. Most Westerners are to a greater or lesser degree children of the Enlightenment or at least of that strain of the Enlightenment which negates and repudiates hierarchy, status, and authority and looks forward to the elimination or drastic reduction of these aspects of "traditional societies." This strain of the Enlightenment is shared in disparate ways by a host of modern Western socio-political ideologies such as liberalism, Marxism, and anarchism. The theoretical dilemmas concerning the relations of liberty, equality, and democracy have by no means been resolved. Whether one attacks the concept of authority from the vantage point of individual liberty or of equality, the shared Enlightenment orientations remain. I must confess that to the extent that I accept the generalization that human beings have, on average, handled hierarchy, status, and authority poorly, I probably also share the Enlightenment bias.

Some might be inclined to say that these biases need not affect our work as "objective" scholars of Chinese culture. Yet the perennial question of the nature of objectivity and of the relation of fact to value has most recently been called to my attention by a review by

Thomas Metzger of my book *The World of Thought in Ancient China*.[1] In his review Professor Metzger takes issue with my treatment of the roles of hierarchy, status, and authority in the texts of early Confucianism. He also raises the larger question of whether these views may not reflect some of the presuppositions of a Western liberal and whether I still cherish the illusion that I can interpret an ancient Chinese text "objectively" while suppressing my own "value attitudes."

Like Professor Metzger, I am strongly skeptical of notions of objectivity which imply a presuppositionless tabula rasa on the part of the scholar. We all bring to our study of China an accumulation of intellectual assumptions which may be ultimately related to value attitudes. Such assumptions decisively influence our view of what constitutes an important problem. While Matteo Ricci was certainly interested in the structure of Chinese society and of the Chinese polity, he did not bring to his study of these matters some of the concerns which post-Enlightenment scholars bring to the study of hierarchy, status, and authority. Metzger like myself, also shares the faith (perhaps irrational) that these intellectual assumptions do not preclude the possibility of reaching out to an understanding or *Verstehen* in Max Weber's sense of other cultures and societies.

Metzger does acknowledge that in my interpretation of early Confucian texts like Professor de Bary and himself, I emphasize the notion of individual moral autonomy within Confucianism. I do stress the role of individual moral agents who are able to transcend the limits of the actual social environment in which they live. His critical stance toward my interpretation is, however, based on statements in the book such as the following:

> This [the normative social order] may be a "sacred community" in Fingarette's sense but it is a sacred community that accepts unblinkingly what it regards as the need for hierarchy, status, and authority within a universal world order. While the ultimate end of *li* may be to humanize hierarchy and authority, it certainly is also meant to maintain and clarify their foundations ... To many modern sensibilities this frank acceptance of hierarchy and authority as a necessary and even good aspect of a civilized and harmonious society creates an enormous barrier to *Verstehen* ... The fact that the extended traditional state of

ancient civilizations necessarily involved an unequal division of power, hierarchy, and authority was, of course, taken for granted not only in China but in all ancient civilization which came under the control of large territorial states.

While Metzger by no means totally denies the role of hierarchy, status, and authority in Chinese culture in general and in Confucianism in particular,[2] he believes that statements like these grossly overemphasize this moment in Confucianism and grossly underestimate the considerations which run in an opposite, mitigating direction.

Before considering these countervailing factors, I should like to comment on the assertion that the Confucian texts regarded hierarchy, status, and authority not only as a necessary but even as a good aspect of a harmonious society (and a harmonious family). Here I am reminded of the depiction of the ancestral ceremonies of aristocratic families in *The Book of Odes* where everyone from the main familial participants to the humblest ceremonial functionaries play their duly assigned roles with the utmost dignity and decorum. The important thing is not whether the role played is august or humble but that one plays one's part in the beatitude of the entire ceremonial pageant. Such an attitude can be found illustrated as recently as in the roles of the butler and cook in the British television series "Upstairs, Downstairs." However alien such views may be to many and however prone some may be to explain them in terms of "false consciousness," such attitudes have existed in all human cultures.

Can such attitudes be at all reconciled with the notion of the latent or actual spiritual and moral autonomy of individual human beings? Here, of course, one deals with the problem of potentiality and actuality. Donald Munro in *The Concept of Man in Early China* stresses the innate equality of all human beings which can be found in the dominant Confucian conceptions of human nature. In Mencius, the entire human species is equal in its possession of a uniquely innate moral capacity. Yet even in Mencius, the capacity is by no means equally active in all men. It is only a creative minority of truly noble men who are capable both of realizing their own moral potentialities and of creating a socio-political environment which will make it possible for others to realize theirs. When we read Mencius's account of the origins of civilization, we are equally struck by the passive latency of the goodness of the mass of mankind and the extraordinary initiative of those called "the sages" who alone seem to possess the spiritual power to transcend the constraints of an adverse environment. The notion that at a certain deep level of being all humans are equal can also be found in different forms in other ancient civilizations and seems compatible there as well with the notion of unequal moral and intellectual powers and even with the idea that hierarchy, status, and authority are necessary aspects of any highly organized society.

Professor Metzger seems to accept the notion of these natural inequalities when he speaks of the "Confucian respect for moral authority figures" who enjoy their authority because of their recognized moral and intellectual power, even when they are outside of the centers of established authority. I would agree with him that probably one of the main contributions of early Confucianism is this notion of the role of the *chün-tzu* who operates outside of the political center and yet presumes to stand in judgment on the actual holders of political authority. Metzger also acknowledges that while their authority is essentially moral, they nevertheless aspire to fulfill their moral vocation in government since it is the objective structures of political authority which provide the only truly effective lever for enforcing their moral authority. Yet at other times he comes perilously close to saying that Confucianism respects the objective authority embedded in institutions and loci of power only when such structures are in the hands of "sages" and "noble men."

The facts seem to be more complicated. If the objective structures of the political order are to serve as a lever through which sages and noble men can exercise their transformative influence in society, these structures must themselves embody an inbuilt sacred aura of objective authority. The universal kingship which is at the pinnacle of the order is not a person, it is a sacred locus of authority *(wei)* which enjoys its own cosmic grounding. This sacred space may be occupied by the entirely unworthy and the sacredness of the institution by no means has the power to turn foolish kings into sages. Yet even a sage king must draw on the sacred aura of his position of authority in order to affect the society. Thus the Confucius of the Analects by no means asserts that the symbols of political authority can be easily undermined even when the authority is in the hands of the unworthy. The Zhou dynasty during Confucius's lifetime found itself in a state of profound debility. Yet he remains loyal to this corrupt and wraithlike remnant of legitimate authority. When a dynasty declines radically and irremediably, a change of mandate is possible, but even then the sacred aura of universal kingship as a locus of socio-cosmic authority remains.

In Book 10 of the Analects—a section which many modern Western and Chinese interpreters of Confucianism find disturbing, we find a description of Confucius engaged in scrupulous and meticulous ceremonial practices. There has been much dispute over whether this section of the Analects is authentic. The painful question which emerges is the following: Can the same Confucius who fiercely maintains his moral autonomy and integrity and who seems to believe that Heaven has endowed him with a mission to reform society be the Confucius who "when he entered the palace gate seemed to bend his body" . . . and who "when he carried the ceremonial scepter of (his ruler) seemed to bend his body as if he were not able to bear its weight"? I would suggest that this may indeed be the same Confucius. It is entirely possible that the same Confucius who deliberately employs what we might view as a self-demeaning body language may actually despise the present occupant of the princely throne. He may still fervently believe that the sacred symbols of long-established legitimate authority must be treated with reverence and awe. If the objective structures of authority which have their own cosmic basis are to serve as levers for sages and noble men, they must be revered even when they are controlled by the unworthy. The same consideration may hold for the Confucian moral heroes of later ages who never hesitated as officials to perform the *ketou*.

I would suggest that what we have here is a radically different approach to the relationship between individual moral autonomy and social role than that which we find in much modern Western sociological theory. In much of this sociology "being an autonomous individual" and "playing a social role" are almost mutually exclusive categories. When one enters into the field of a social role, the role determines one's behavior. The autonomous individual is the residue which is left when the individual is not playing a role and a truly free individual is one who frees himself to the greatest extent possible from the subjugating power of all social roles. In Confucianism, social role is a dominant category and there are very definite moral and ceremonial prescriptions for proper behavior in given roles. Yet the role does not automatically enforce its own norms. Whether the role of a father is played well or badly is determined by the moral quality of the individual who plays the role. Thus the individual autonomy of the noble man largely manifests itself in the way in which he plays the multitude of roles with which he is confronted although there may also be circumstances in which he feels entirely constrained from playing certain roles. Since the human reality is inevitably hierarchically articulated on the familial, social, and political levels, the man of *jen* will play his role well whether he finds himself in a subordinate or superordinate position.

From this point of view the family itself is ideally a school not only for the socialization of the individual but also for individual self-development. While the patriarchal family is a naturally hierarchical social unit it is also a unit in which some role relationships are naturally mutable. Sons become fathers and daughters become mothers and mothers-in-law. The contingency of death may even shift the order status of brothers and sisters. Thus in the bosom of the family, the individual learns how to manifest his individual moral qualities both in the posture of subordination as well as in the posture of superordination. If his heart is governed by *jen* and *li,* his moral superiority will pervade his role behavior. If not, he will prove that he is a mean man *(hsiao-jen).* What we find here is a normative conception of individual autonomy and social role which sees the two as inseparable polarities, rather than as mutually exclusive antitheses. This does not mean that there are no problems concerning the relations between the two poles. Over the centuries, a vast ongoing discussion concerning the causal relations between the two has taken place. Yet even a Mencius who finds the only source of the moralization of society in the heart of those human beings who are able to actualize their moral capacities—sages and noble men—still accepts the premise that such capacities can transform society only within the framework of a socio-political order which rests on hierarchy, status, and authority.

Professor Metzger is disturbed by what he regards as my tendency to exaggerate the moment of hierarchy both within the family and in what he calls the "moral community." One must first of all mention the esteemed value of friendship where the role of hierarchy, status, and authority is reduced to a minimum. Metzger points out that in the Confucian ideal all of these relationships have a strong element of "reciprocity" strongly diffused with sentiments of respect *(jing)*, love *(ai)* and empathy which he calls "egalitarian" sentiments. I would agree that in an ideal Confucian society, all relations are indeed "reciprocal" and diffused with and maintained by such moral sentiments. The fact remains that reciprocity does not imply equality. While the moral sentiments such as love and respect which ideally infuse these role relationships bring a kind of transcendental dimension to bear on them, the structures of hierarchy, status, and authority remain intact.

I thus remain unconvinced that the above considerations undermine in any serious way the assertion that Confucianism (at least pre–twentieth century Confucianism) unblinkingly accepted hierarchy, status, and authority as essential—and even potentially positive—aspects of a civilized human order.

There are, however, other mitigating (from the point of view of our Enlightenment biases) factors which merit serious consideration, particularly from the point of view of the current discussions among Westerners and dissident mainland Chinese about the degree to which the People's Republic has been largely shaped by the authoritarianism of the "feudal past."

Normative Confucianism down through the ages drew a sharp distinction between authority vested in the objective structures of the state—however sacred and cosmic—and the moral quality of those who occupied the positions of authority. The famous dictum that "governing and teaching [true doctrine] proceed from the same source" *(zhengjiao heyi)* was in Confucianism treated as a prescriptive rather than as a descriptive maxim. This described the way things ought to be. "When the *Tao* prevails," states the Confucius of the Analects, "ceremonies, music, and punitive military expeditions proceed from the Son of Heaven." In a Confucian paradise sages would always occupy the throne and families would always be governed by ideal patriarchs. Yet no one is more aware than Confucius that the world of his time is "without the *Tao*." It is an awareness which is shared by eminent Confucianists down through the ages long after the Chinese state had in some sense become a "Confucian state." The sense of an abyss between the ideal state of affairs and the fallibility and even the corruption of the current political establishment appears throughout the vast body of Confucian literature. It is adumbrated in the idea of the "Heavenly Mandate" and becomes almost a cliché in the widely shared idea of late Confucianism that ever since the ancient Three Dynasties, the *Tao* had not prevailed or had only been very partially realized in the flux of human history. Within the constraints imposed by the rituals of authority, we find a vast debate about the wisdom of prevailing government policies. It was rarely assumed by either the "moral community" of the literati or even the masses as a whole, despite the ceremonial fictions of state documents, that the present holders of power at all levels actually "incarnated" the wisdom and virtues of the ancient sages.

If a distinction between the cosmic authority of the political order and the all-too-human fallibility of the occupants of the *loci* of authority was, in the main, generally accepted by the society over the centuries, it stands in sharp contrast to the Leninist conception of the party which, at least until recently, assumed that the present holders of authority "immanently" and virtually embodied both the infallible claims of Marxism as a science as well as the general will of the masses. The prevailing party line is thus in concept beyond all external criticism.

Similarly, it seems to me that it would be incorrect to call the traditional political order totalitarian in the sense in which that term has been applied to the modern Marxist-Leninist-Maoist regime. One can speak of a kind of all-encompassing claim of jurisdiction by the traditional political order (here, again, I overlook all significant changes over historic time) over all sectors of human experience which involve a social dimension—over religion, economy, family, and law. If by totalitarianism, however, we refer to an aspiration to achieve total control of every aspect of human culture and society down to the grass-roots level in the interest of future-oriented societal goals, then it must be stressed that "jurisdiction" is by no means the same as "total control." As a cosmic structure, the state, while accepting the overlordship of "Heaven," claimed a kind of jurisdictional control over all popular religion—particularly over all types of religious organization. The Buddhist monastery—an institution brought into the cultural realm from without—at first created a considerable problem for the jurisdictional claims of the Chinese state. Yet in time the institution was subsumed within the framework of the state. Except for periods of persecution, however, the institution enjoyed a high degree of actual autonomy and the state certainly did not intervene in the regulation of Buddhist philosphic discourse. The degree of interaction in the economic order, while varying over time, did not by any means prevent the emergence of a space for a market economy within a pre-modern economy. None of these regions of cultural or social life enjoyed legal autonomy and ad hoc state intervention for good or ill was always possible. This looseness of the jurisdictional net may have been due in part to technological constraints, in part to the fact that the ruling strata did not necessarily wholly identify their interests with those of the political center, and in part to the fact that the mainstream of Confucianism itself identified its spiritual-ethical claims with light government rather than with heavy intervention. There are many qualifications one could make to these gross generalizations. One might say that the account we have of the ancient Ch'in Revolution suggests something like a totalitarian aspiration. The Confucian imperial state proved effective over the course of time in mobilizing populations for various spectacular specific projects both civil and military such as the building of the Grand Canal, the Manchu campaigns of conquest in Central Asia, and even the organization of famine relief. It could also intervene with chilling effectiveness in crushing sectarian rebellions and carrying out mass purges such as the Ch'ien-lung emperor's "Literary Inquisition." Yet overall the meshes of this network of total jurisdiction remained wide. To be sure, hierarchy, status, and authority was also operative often at even intense pitch within lineages and nuclear families and in local society. Yet from another point of view, in later dynasties the authority conceded to lineages and local notables itself represented a limit to centralized power.

I would thus urge that the most totalitarian features of the exercise of authority in the People's Republic may owe more to the Marxist-Leninist heritage than to the traditional order and that Marxism-Leninism itself may draw on many Western roots. If the negation of hierarchy, status, and authority draws on one strain of the Enlightenment, it may well be that the Leninist development of Marxism draws on other strains. The Leninist party seems to fuse together into one effective unity the notion of the "social engineering" elite who thoroughly understand the science of society (in this case the Marxist science of social history) with the Jacobin notion of the virtuous vanguard which virtually embodies the general will of the people. Under this dispensation, present party leadership, whether it be one man (the Mao of the Cultural Revolution), or a collective leadership incarnates both the will of history and the will of the masses.

To the extent that there has been an uneven retreat since Mao's death from the aspiration to total aggressive control of all sectors of social and cultural life; to the extent that there are even vague hints that the present party leadership embodies neither the infallible science nor the virtue attributed to the party as an institution, what we may be witnessing is not so much an immediate movement to "democratization" on a Western model as something like a falling back within an entirely new setting, to the older, looser, and less absolutist habits of thought concerning the relations between the various sectors of social and cultural life and the structures of hierarchy, status, and authority. In this respect, the political order which has evolved on Taiwan during the last several decades may provide a more reliable example of the modern adaptation for good or ill of the traditional political heritage than a mainland which was in fact profoundly influenced during the period in question by the dogmas of a foreign ideology.

In speaking of further countervailing factors, one should again stress that the Confucian conception of hierarchy, status, and authority was compatible with a strong stress on the principle of meritocracy although it must be added that this principle is not carried as far within the Confucian tradition as in the rival ancient schools of Mohism and Legalism. To what degree the examination system (which was not purely Confucian in origin) of later ages produced extensive social class mobility in the society remains open to dispute, but the tradition of the worthy minister remains a live tradition down through the ages leading to a long history of Confucian martyrology. A strong notion of "careers open to talents" by no means stands in opposition to the continued stress on the need for hierarchy, status, and authority.

It must be added, however, that there also continues to exist in Confucianism another more ambiguous attitude toward hereditary authority than many have been willing to admit. The Confucius of the Analects strongly defends the legitimate authority of the hereditary rulers of his time against usurpation. He continues to regard such usurpations not as harbingers of "a change of mandate" but as representing a further descent into anarchy and chaos. It is his follower Mencius, living in what he regarded as an even darker age, who dreams of the rise of a new dispensation. Yet even in late traditional China there remains a deliberate ideological stress on maintaining the continuity of notable lineages. Even on the level of ideas, a profound tension exists within Confucianism between the stress on meritocracy and the view of the family as the sacred paradigm of social order and a school of morality. Flourishing lineages which become the bearers of Confucian values—which enjoy "the fragrance of books" *(shuxiang)* should be encouraged to flourish and to persist. So long as they do not bring about their own demise through decline and corruption, they provide an ongoing source of strength for the society.

There are other well-known countervailing themes which might be mentioned in passing. There is the acute appreciation within normative Confucianism of the absolute priority of meeting fundamental economic needs of the masses and even the aspiration for the achievement of some degree of economic equality within the ranks of the peasant masses. How these themes relate to the actualities of Chinese history remains an enormous problem but they can by no means be dismissed as mere ideology.

Finally, however, in dealing with modern Western attitudes toward the role of hierarchy, status, and authority in Chinese society, I would like to shift attention from our image of China to our image of ourselves. Have the post-Enlightenment doctrines of liberalism and socialism totally eliminated or rendered innocuous the role of hierarchy, status, authority, and inequalities of power in our own societies? Has the Confucian assumption that they remain inescapable features of complex societies been thoroughly refuted?

There have, it is true, been some brilliant accomplishments in the political order in the development of strategies for limiting and rendering accountable the holders of political power and for the establishment of the notion of human rights grounded in law. This kind of "constitutional democracy," whatever its fallibilities, is based on the notion of a legal order which enjoys a certain autonomy from and even ascendancy over the political order. It represents a strain of Western thought which is probably older than the Enlightenment itself. Yet if constitutional democracy has had its triumphs in controlling, limiting, and rendering accountable the holders of political authority and power this does not represent the triumph of the

"Athenian ideal" of democracy as a government of participant citizens. Neither Montesquieu nor Rousseau believed that democracy in this sense was possible in a vast territorial state. And neither would have regarded the representative democracies of modern times, with their vast administrative bureaucracies, only ultimately and indirectly accountable, as "true democracies." Certainly hierarchy, status, and authority remain with us.

When we turn to the economic sector, the more mythical aspects of economic liberalism, which equate the corner grocery store with the vast macro-organizations of the financial and industrial world, on the ground that they are equivalent actors in the free market, seem almost designed to repress the enormous role of bureaucracy, hierarchy, status, and authority in this world.

It is interesting to note that ideologies as disparate as Marxism-Leninism and economic liberalism of the Friedman variety share the tendency to treat certain forms of authority and power as inherently innocuous and benign. To the Marxist-Leninist, the power of the party is inherently innocuous and benign because it simply incarnates and implements the will of the proletariat and in the end it will finally fade away. To the apostle of the free market and of economic man, the financial and corporate elites are totally constrained in their behavior by impersonal considerations of loss and profit. Their acquisition and loss of power is dependent wholly on their economic effectiveness.

It is at this point that the economic experience of the so-called "Five East Asian Dragons" becomes relevant to our discussion. In dealing with the industrial success of these societies it has become fashionable to invoke Max Weber's conception of the role of the Protestant ethic and to ask whether Confucian (or East Asian) culture did not after all provide a functional equivalent of the Protestant ethic. My own brief response to this question would be to maintain that Confucianism as a total outlook did not provide such an equivalent but that certain deeply ingrained attitudes and habits often associated with Confucianism did prove highly favorable to the enterprise of modernization once it was underway. I would, however, suggest that an even more relevant aspect of Weber's social analysis may be found in his treatment of developed industrial society as a "going concern." The very Weber who tends to emphasize the theory of the individual entrepreneur in dealing with the rise of industrial capitalism when he deals with a fully "rational-ized" industrial economy shifts the stress very much to the side of bureaucratic organization, hierarchy, status, authority, group disci-pline, and other non-individualistic aspects of advanced industrial societies.

One might say that the unblinking acceptance of hierarchy, status, and authority in traditional East Asian society has made it possible for these societies to confront these aspects of late industrialism with a much clearer vision than is to be found in societies which continue to speak of advanced industrial systems wholly in the language of in-dividualism. By the same token, these East Asian societies are pre-pared to see no unbridgeable gulf between the hierarchies of the po-litical and the economic systems and to treat the relations between the two in a much more flexible and nuanced way than is the case in societies transfixed by the dogma of the ideal centralized planned economy versus the ideal free market system.

I by no means intend to idealize these societies. Indeed, I remain sufficiently committed to the value of Western constitutionalism and the idea of legally grounded human rights to hope that in some form these strategies for limiting and controlling hierarchy, status, and au-thority may be assimilated by them.

Yet the fact remains that Confucius has by no means been totally disproven. One may reject the Foucaultian notion that post-Enlight-enment Western society has witnessed the actual expansion and deepening of societal domination in all sectors of society. Yet hierar-chy, status, authority, and inequalities of power remain and have by no means been rendered utterly innocuous and benign despite all the machinery of legal and social controls. Hence the Confucian ques-tion, "Is it possible to humanize and moralize the behavior of those who occupy positions of social power and authority?" may not be as naïve as it may seem even if one does not share what Metzger calls Confucian "epistemological optimism" in these matters.

This chapter represents the wrestlings of one Western individual with the positive acceptance of hierarchy, status, and authority as necessary aspects of "civilized" human society in a large part of Chi-nese high culture (and perhaps even in popular culture). Beyond this question, there looms the larger one of whether our attitudes toward all aspects of Chinese culture must be colored and conditioned by our attitudes to these socio-political questions. Hierarchy, status, and authority have, in different forms, been as much a fact of Western history and culture as of the culture and history of China. Many of us continue to cherish the works of Shakespeare, Dante, and others who also apparently accepted the naturalness of these aspects of society. We no doubt do so because of our sense that there are dimensions of human reality which may not directly relate to or even transcend these questions. The same may hold true for T'ang lyrical poetry, Sung painting, the poetic-mystical visions of Chuang-tzu, and even some of the observations of Confucius on the ethical life.

11

꙳

Review of *Disputers of the Tao*

One might have safely predicted that any general book by Angus Graham on ancient Chinese philosophy (here defined roughly as the period from 500 to 200 B.C.), a period in which in his own view "The main lines of Chinese thought were already laid down," would constitute a major contribution to current Western discourse on this crucial period. The book does indeed reflect all of those qualities of originality, suggestiveness, and immense erudition on matters both Chinese and Western which characterize so much of his corpus of writings on both philosophy and literature.[1] This corpus has long since confirmed his eminence as a leading thinker in the Chinese field. One may quarrel with his principles of organization—and I find that I do have quarrels with his categories of organization both in his pioneering masterpiece *The Later Mohist Logic* and in *Disputers of the Tao*. Yet I find that both of these books are an inexhaustible mine which one can open at random at almost any page and immediately be confronted with arresting ideas which force hard and sustained cogitation on matters about which one has never thought or thought only dimly. Indeed, I find that it will be impossible to treat the vast array of questions raised in this volume. What I shall attempt to do is focus on what seem to me to be certain overarching central theses which appear to underlie and bring together otherwise disparate themes.

I shall not dwell at length on matters on which I find myself in agreement with the author, although some of the passages involved bring entirely fresh and persuasive arguments to bear on all these matters. Thus, in Appendix 2 (pp. 389–428) on the question of language, I find wonderfully concrete and decisive some of his arguments against what I would call the excesses of linguistic determinism—particularly his case against the notion that classical Chinese cannot frame statements about truth and falsity or statements about counterfactuality. On the question of the relationship between the being/nonbeing dichotomy in the West and the *yu/wu* dichotomy in classical Chinese, he continues to feel that differences in thought are deeply rooted in differences in the very nature of the structure of ancient Greek and classical Chinese. Yet even here his highly nuanced discussion greatly reduces the sense of linguistically conditioned incommensurability suggested by some of his previous discussions of this matter.

In his review of my own book on ancient Chinese thought, Graham sets up a broad distinction between: (1) students of foreign cultures who tend to stress universally shared human concerns which underlie all human cultures and are therefore highly prone when reading the texts of these cultures to believe in their ultimate comparability in all areas of human thought—perilous as such comparisons may be—and (2) those who are constantly oriented to the irreducible and incommensurable otherness of other cultures. Graham assigns my own book—not with total approval—to the camp of the universalizers. Presumably one of the main pitfalls of this camp is a naïvely unconscious "culture-boundedness" which leads it to identify as universal some of the most culture-specific aspects of its own culture. Certainly one can hardly deny that this mode of culture-boundedness exists. On the other hand, if a faith in universally shared concerns is based on an acute awareness of the deep difference between cultures (and even within cultures) in the responses to these common concerns; if it is based on a realization that the abstract terms which deal with matters which we call philosophical, religious, ethical, and political, in all cultures are highly indeterminate in their ranges of meaning and thus rarely lend themselves to exact lexical equivalents; if one is even prepared to admit that even within one culture the kind of coherence of meanings which holds together a term may be nothing more than Wittgenstein's "family resemblance," this does not dogmatically preclude the possibility that such terms may still point to areas of common concern. Those deconstructionists who believe that such terms are signifiers which do not signify, or that the indeterminancy of terms and texts is so boundless that one cannot talk of common concerns within the text itself, feel no need to step beyond the boundaries of their own cultures to arrive at such conclusions.

A case can in fact be made for the culture-boundedness of many modes of cultural relativism. The dogma which absolutely denies that terms such as the Western "being" and the Chinese *yu* may sharply diverge from each other at certain points while coinciding at others, tends to encourage the belief that the meanings of both terms within their respective cultures are somehow clear and unambiguous. Indeed the very idea of a culture as a self-contained, clearly integrated whole constituting an incommensurable and irreducible "other" represents an absolutization of the concept of culture which has itself emerged only recently within the West. There is also the well-known yet paradoxical fact that many of the supporters of the notion of the incommensurable other continue to use Western concepts to "explain" the otherness.

It may be urged that whenever we present an account of universally shared human concerns, such an account is itself inevitably culture-bound. One may, in fact, feel as I do that in all our accounts of basic human concerns, both within and across cultures, there is a residue of the enigmatic and mysterious concerning the human animal which may not have been fully plumbed by any of our existing cultures. I would nevertheless maintain that the actual study of the experiences of foreign cultures has in fact supported the case for a range of shared human concerns, and for the notion that cross-cultural differences are, more often than not, comparable and commensurable differences about which it is possible to communicate.

My reading of *Disputers of the Tao* when considered as a total text has led me to the view that Graham leans in the same direction. When, in dealing with the question of "being" and *yu,* he puts forth a very central thesis—namely that "One may see '*yu*' as illustrating the Chinese tendency to divide down from a wider whole—'is' and 'exists' our own tendency to start from the thing itself" (p. 411). I would suggest that this generalization about the dominant tendencies of both cultures is presented as a generalization which can be understood by both Chinese and Westerners—that we have here a problematic which can be communicated across the cultural divide. In fact, Graham makes it quite clear that this dominant tendency was challenged within the Chinese cultural sphere by the much less successful countertendency of late Mohist thought which advocated a pluralist view consciously focused on "concrete and particular" things (p. 140). He would probably not deny that when one thinks of Spinoza, Jakob Boehme, or even Hegel, one finds a counter-tendency in the West very much oriented to "wider wholes." It would indeed be intriguing to test out this generalization within the sphere of Indian culture.

While presuming to claim Graham as an ally on this question, there are nevertheless matters concerning which I may perhaps contribute most by raising questions. One is a subject on which Graham and I have already exchanged views—namely Herbert Fingarette's interpretation of the Confucian Analects. I shall dwell on this matter not in order to reiterate past exchanges, but because I find that Graham's emphasis on Fingarette's interpretations relates to many issues discussed in this volume, not the least being the interpretation of the Analects itself. I found myself somewhat surprised by the degree to which his reading of the Analects as a whole is shaped by Fingarette, leading, it seems to me, to a somewhat impoverished reading of that many-sided text.

Fingarette's book *Confucius, the Secular as Sacred* has been a remarkably provocative stimulus in the field of Confucian studies. There can be no doubt that he has contributed a good deal to an understanding of the vital importance of *li* as sacred rite and ceremony within the vision of the Analects. When rites and ceremonies function as they are meant to function, the sacred magical power associated with them immediately comes alive; their spirit then ideally permeates the networks of social and status roles which hold together a society in peace, harmony, and social decorum. Thus far Fingarette's interpretation enriches our understanding of a major theme in the Analects. His contribution, however, is accompanied by an entire litany of dogmatic negations. A candid first reading of the Analects suggests that the text discusses a host of other matters quite apart from the question of *li*. Most of the "ethical" discussion of the text involves references to moral attitudes and dispositions considered quite apart from the *li*, often in terms or relations to each other rather than in terms of their relations to *li*. Indeed, a candid reading of the text suggests that it is basically not about a society in which the *li* is functioning as it should, but precisely about a society in which the *li*, even when formally observed, do not function as they should. In such a world where the "Way does not exist," one might almost say that the Analects is, among other things, an inquiry into why ceremony does not function as it should. It may be true that moral attitudes and virtuous dispositions must manifest themselves in society through proper forms of ritual behavior, but the "magic and sacred aura" of the *li* comes alive only when linked to proper attitudes and dispositions. There is no hint that these attitudes find their only ultimate source in the repeated and even skilled performance of the forms of *li*.

In his discussion of the central virtues, which have often been translated as "loyalty and reciprocity" *(chung-shu)*, Graham remarks that "Western readers of Confucius often try to detach his moral thinking from its bedding in ceremony" (p. 18). While ceremony is certainly an integral part of Confucius's moral thinking, the plain fact is that the text constantly discusses moral attitudes and dispositions in complete detachment from their relations to ceremony. One is indeed tempted to say that in answering the question: "Why do the ceremonies not fulfill their spiritual-moral function in our society?" The Analects suggests that what is required are certain preconditions, which are separate from the body of *li* as a body of social conventions. On the individual level, these preconditions seem to involve an education which requires both the study of "*li* and music" and the unattached and direct discussion of moral dispositions in their relations to each other. On the societal level, it again seems to involve a wide-ranging discussion of matters, in an area we would roughly call "political," which do not seem to relate directly to ceremony. Thus, when Graham insists like Fingarette that "all government can be reduced to ceremonial," he again refers to the ideal society where the Way prevails, while the Confucius of the Analects is acutely conscious of the fact that in his society the Way does not prevail. Graham himself admits in passing that "Confucius protests at excessive taxation and recognizes the need to enrich the people before expecting them to respond to teaching" (p. 14). He does not insist that these matters of policy can be realized in his world simply through the skillful performance of *li*. On the contrary, these are preconditions for the effective actualization of *li* in the life of the people.

The text includes many references to matters of what we would call domestic and foreign policy and statecraft in general. Later ver-

sions of Confucianism which stress technical problems of statecraft
and policy have not necessarily distorted the Analects when they
seek the authority for their interest in the Analects. On the other
hand, Fingarette and Graham do indeed call our attention to the fact
that the proper practice of ceremony remains a central concern of
"state Confucianism" to the very end.

Now it is quite clear that Fingarette's resounding negations are
very much related to an interpretation based on certain very definite
ideas of modern British analytic philosophy—particularly the ideas
of Ryle and Austin. Since most Western interpreters of Chinese
thought derive many of their own assumptions, either implicitly or
explicitly, from Western thought, we cannot fault Fingarette for
doing likewise. Graham, in fact, is deeply impressed by the fact that
Fingarette is able to relate the Analects to certain exciting tendencies
of twentieth-century "serious philosophy" which have turned their
back on traditional Western "conceptual schemes." Confucius, we
are told, "can be relevant to contemporary 'professional' philosophy." The central operative principles here seem to be Gilbert Ryle's
views on the mind/body problem and Austin's analysis of the role of
language as "performative utterance."

Before relating to these issues themselves, we note here the presence of the much larger issue concerning the question of culture-
boundedness. In his use of terms such as "serious," "professional,"
and "twentieth-century Western philosophy," one almost has the
uneasy impression that Graham is invoking a new principle of authority. The practice of validating Chinese thought by invoking re-
semblances to certain Western philosophies such as Kant or Hegel
without further discussion of the Western thinkers themselves has
often in the past been recognized as a kind of culture-bound approach. It is not the comparison itself that is culture-bound but the
assumption that one side of the comparison represents unquestioned
authority.

In dealing with what might be called the authority of the "latest
word" from the West, Graham is, of course, not unique. There are
many modern Chinese and Western scholars of Chinese thought
who also invoke the latest word in postmodern Western philosophy
as a source of validation but who find this word in the continental
philosophy of Heidegger or Derrida rather than in British analytic
philosophy.

These remarks are not based on any a priori view that ancient Chinese thought cannot be meaningfully compared to Ryle or Wittgenstein or Heidegger. It may well be that late twentieth-century Western thought may in some of its tendencies be closer to ancient Chinese thought than to Plato. I would nevertheless submit that in order to validate the Analects by references to Austin one must critically examine the claims of Austin himself and even examine what critics of Austin in the West have had to say about him. What if it should prove that some Chinese thinkers such as Chu Hsi have more affinities to Spinoza than to the "latest word" in twentieth-century Western thought, whether British or continental? Does the fact that both may dismiss Spinoza as "metaphysical" automatically invalidate Chu Hsi? Any scholar who sincerely respects the views of both would simply have to defend what has been called "metaphysics" against its modern detractors.[2]

Much of Fingarette's critique of those who defend the notion of an inner morality in the Analects is based on what Ryle and others call the Western mind/body opposition. In Graham's words, they believe in "a contrast between mind and body as inner and outer compartments of oneself" (p. 26). Is this indeed the heart of the issue?

The fact is that the radically paradoxical dualism of the mind/body as the "ghost in the machine" is post-Cartesian in the West and is as foreign to much Western thought as it may be to China. It can certainly not be found in ancient Hebrew thought or in pre-philosophic Greek literature. The tendency to link affective–mental traits with specific organs of the body is as prevalent in this thought as in ancient China. I would suggest that the roots of a radical dualism in ancient Greek philosophy arise in those modes of thought which speak not of individuated mind and body but of matter and a disembodied spiritual or mental substance. While this idea greatly influenced later Platonic philosophy, the Aristotelianism which dominated so much of medieval thought was based on a moderately dualistic and even organic view of the mind/body relationship. While the mind/body problem was not "solved," one even finds a notion of the person as an entity in which mind and body are inextricably bound into one complex. Much the same can be said, I would submit, of the Analects' view of the person as a source of inner morality. The inner and outer aspects of the Analects refer not to mind and body, as conceived of by Descartes, but to the person (as a fusion of

both mind and body) as the inner locus of moral attitudes and dispositions (the "heart/mind" is both mental and physical), and to the
pattern of behavioral rules, conventions, institutions, and so forth as
the outer which constitute what might be called the objective, normative socio-cultural order. In the Analects, the two realms are very
much interrelated, but neither is dissolved into the other. The person
in the Analects is not simply the "initial point-source and the terminal point on which a force impinges" (a force "operating in actions
in a public space and time").[3] The person is not a contentless initial
point but a richly complex entity. I would also submit that the term
te as applied to people refers to a "potency" residing within people
and by no means is necessarily "inherent in the spontaneity of ritualized relations" (p. 25). Without the "potency" which resides in people, the "sacred" which resides in the "ritualized relations" may be
unable to manifest itself.

The notion of force deriving wholly from ritualized relations is
closely linked in Fingarette to Austin's discussion of the performative
utterance as opposed to constative utterances or statements which
describe what objectively is. Austin no doubt deserves great credit
for focusing attention on this aspect of language. A performative utterance rooted in social convention is an act in itself, an act which
possesses as it were an indwelling force itself capable of producing
effects on all persons involved in the interchange. Here, of course,
lies the similarity to nonverbal conventions such as ritual acts. A
speech act such as "with this ring I thee wed" is an act in itself and
an act which produces its own magical effect.

The fact remains that such utterances do not arise in a vacuum.
They derive their meaning from an entire preexistent universe of culture and states of affairs which cannot be discussed wholly in the
language of performative utterance. "With this ring I thee wed" presupposes the institution of marriage and the rules which govern this
institution, which can only be described in the language of constative
utterances. The statement of a ritual rule is itself not a performative
utterance. It is a description of a pattern of behavior. The authority
of the officiant at the ceremony may express his authority in performative utterances but the authority itself has other sources. The
human entities who accept the magic of the utterance are entities
who are much more than a stream of conventional utterances and
acts. Thus the "magic" embedded in these acts derives from a myr-

iad of sources and is not simply embedded in the spontaneous, conventional nature of the act itself. One of the weightiest messages of the Analects is the message about how easily the performative act can lose its "magic."

In his suggestive essay "Performatif/Constatif," Austin at one point discusses the "unhappy" conditions under which performative utterances may actually become "null and void." One of these conditions is "that if it is issued *insincerely*. If I say 'I promise to . . .' without in the least intending to carry out the promised action, perhaps even not believing that it is in my power to carry it out, the promise is hollow."[4] Austin does not imply anywhere that "sincere intent" is something which has simply been "internalized" in the speaker by a long life of performative utterances. The Confucius of the Analects is keenly aware that people may engage in all sorts of performative utterances and acts performed over a lifetime without a sincere intent. As in the case of Confucius, Austin does not here speak of "skill in performance" but uses the language of moral dispositions.

Thus, not only may Austin's own writings bear further scrutiny, but in dealing with him ought we not to consider the critiques by others such as Strawson, who in his "Intention and Convention in Speech Acts"[5] denies that all utterances which have "illocutionary force" must be "conventional" (based on long, sustained, and unreflective habit or custom). One might even consider Derrida's critique of Austin.

In the case of Graham, I would venture to speculate that one of the great attractions of Fingarette's concept of "performative speech and act" is its relation to the concept of the "effortless and spontaneous," which relates, it seems to me, to his central category of "spontaneous awareness." In the Confucius of the Analects we do indeed find a strain leading to a concept of the ideal sage whose moral behavior (which involves much more than the observance of *li*) flows effortlessly from his spontaneous synoptic awareness of the ultimate order of things. This is the sage who fulfills Confucius's aspiration not to feel obliged to "speak." It is indeed a strain in the Analects which points toward what is later called Taoism, and, unlike Fingarette, who tends to take a dim view of all later thought in China which does not conform to his vision of the Analects (including later Confucian thought), Graham is fascinated with the idea of "spontaneous awareness" even where it becomes completely detached from "sacred ritual."

Graham is, however, also deeply attracted to Fingarette's view that Confucius is not concerned with the Western conceptions of ethics as basically involving a "choice between alternatives." Again, it is argued that the lexical equivalent of this phrase does not occur in the Analects.

Again, the notion that ethical discourse in the West has always been overwhelmingly concerned with "choice between alternatives" is itself questionable. Much of it over the centuries has been concerned with the inculcation of ethical precepts which allow for no acceptable alternatives and even with the depiction of what we would now call positive and negative "role models." Much of Judeo-Christian ethical discourse involves not a choice between arguably optional values, but, very much as in the case of Confucius, the implicit choice between following the Way and straying from it.

While it is clear that the Confucius of the Analects has no doubt that there is only one Way—only one true value system—does he really believe that this system provides automatic, preestablished answers in all the myriad situations which arise in life or even that the corpus of the sacred rites *(li)* cover all such situations, precluding the need for discrete concrete judgments which may even involve deep perplexities? Here again we note the astonishing absence in Fingarette of any reference to the central idea of *li,* which in one of its meanings seems to refer to right judgments in concrete situations.

While Graham, like Fingarette, may be right in considering the Analects as probably the most reliable source we have for the early Confucius, we are aware that in ancient China (as early as Mencius), Confucius, at least on one side of his thought, was very much linked to the tradition of the *Spring and Autumn Annals.* While one is conscious of all questions which have been raised about the texts associated with that tradition, the notion that Confucius was linked to this tradition is highly plausible. One of the major aspects of this tradition is precisely its interest in the examination of moral (and political) "choices among alternatives" in the complex history of the "Spring and Autumn" period.

One of the key terms in these texts is, in fact, the term *ch'üan,* which may be plausibly translated as "weighing alternatives." In the commentaries, we are constantly presented with narratives concerning highly complex situations requiring the weighing of alternative possible courses of behavior. This term is found in a passage of the Analects itself: "There are those with whom one can study, but with whom one can not progress to the Way; there are those with whom one progresses to the Way, but with whom one can not stand fast; there are those with whom one can stand fast, but with whom one can not engage in weighing alternatives."[6] It is interesting that in this passage the ability to weigh alternatives seems to represent the acme of spiritual progress.

As in the case of the question of the "performative" it is my feeling that Graham is also attracted to the notion of "no choice" in Fingarette because both themes seem very much linked to his own theme of "spontaneous awareness." Nevertheless, I would suggest that the word "awareness" in Graham's central theme of spontaneous awareness points to a significant difference of emphasis between Fingarette and Graham. The word "awareness" suggests a mode of knowing—a kind of epistemology. In Fingarette, the fundamental base of the Way is the pattern of sacred practice called the *li*. Again, it is not that Fingarette is a behaviorist in any crude sense, but it is the constant immersion in the practice of *li* which "ultimately internalizes the sacred and magical" essence of this practice into the human individual being who begins as "a raw stuff and raw material."[7] Learning and knowledge are instrumental to the educative process, but the ultimate goal is the "flowering of humanity in the ceremonial acts of men"[8] (and this is certainly one goal of the Analects). In Graham, however, spontaneous awareness as a form of ultimate knowledge seems to be very central even in his view of Confucius. "The overriding imperative is to learn and arrive at knowledge; once you know, orientation towards action may be left to take care of itself as confused inclinations sort themselves out" (p. 28).

I would heartily agree with Graham that to the extent that one can perceive in the Analects the vision of a kind of synoptic intuitive knowledge which, once attained as by the ideal sages of yore, spontaneously leads humans to act appropriately in all life situations and in all their ritual acts, one can say that the Analects "anticipates Taoism," (p. 18). Unlike Fingarette, who seems to be massively indifferent to everything in Chinese thought which lies outside of the visions of the Analects as he conceives of it, Graham pursues the idea of "spontaneous awareness" into every avenue of later Chinese thought totally detaching it from any necessary connection to Confucian *li*. While spontaneity is wholly associated with ceremony in Fingarette, when one surveys *Disputers of the Tao* as a whole, it becomes clear that the idea of "spontaneous awareness" as a mode of knowledge for Graham represents a dominant shared orientation of Chinese high culture. In Appendix 1, he goes so far as to make the surprising claim that "spontaneous awareness" as a mode of knowledge underlies all modes of thought in ancient China to the extent that these modes of thought share a notion of an ideal sage who is the living embodiment of an all-embracing spontaneous awareness. Even the Mohist sage has achieved a stage of grace where his knowledge and understanding of the world is spontaneous and a priori. The sage in a state of grace sees every issue "in awareness from all viewpoints—spatial, temporal and personal of everything relevant to the issue" (p. 383). Whether sagehood is inborn or achieved, the sage has an immediate, intuitive grasp of the whole landscape of reality whether this reality is represented by the wordless reality of Chuang-tzu and Lao-tzu or the ethical reality of Confucius. "The ideal sage will for all Chinese schools be the man perfectly aware from all viewpoints, with spontaneous desire and ability to benefit all by orderly government" (p. 384).

I would not challenge the view that this notion of the "sage" and sageliness does represent a shared ideal aspiration of much of the high culture. From my own point of view, I would stress that it is an orientation closely linked by an implicit logic to the orientations toward holism and all-embracing order stressed in my book on ancient Chinese thought.

The question remains whether these "ideal" preferential orientations can be used to provide us with an adequate account of the entire content of Chinese thought. I would continue to adhere to the view expressed in my *World of Thought in Ancient China* that these "shared cultural assumptions—like shared cultural assumptions elsewhere—create not finished solutions but vast *problematiques*."[9]

The Analects is not a work written for ideal sages, and Confucius himself does not even identify himself as a sage "who had it from birth." Graham very much stresses that in his statement of his own moral progress (Analects 2.4) Confucius triumphantly proclaims that after the age of seventy he could "follow the heart's desire without transgressing rules" (p. 384). The point may very well be that he cannot do so *until* the age of seventy. Otherwise, his praise of "learning and practice" throughout the book seems to refer to cumulative, incremental knowledge of discrete items of empirical knowledge, to self-examination and constant cogitation and renewed efforts of will and even, pace Fingarette, to periods of puzzlement and perplexity. There may be flashes of illumination and "spontaneous awareness," but the Lao-tzu and Chuang-tzu texts are entirely correct in viewing the contemporary Confucian concept of "learning" as being essentially *yu wei* (based on deliberate, purpose-oriented effort) rather than *wu wei*. Graham himself remarks: "Until you have yourself achieved this awareness you have to control spontaneity and obey the instructions of those who know better" (p. 384).

It may be argued that much Chinese high cultural ethical thought is closer to the pole of moral optimism than to the pole of moral pessimism because of reasons mentioned by Graham: (1) the possibility of the leap from the realm of unremitting moral and intellectual learning to the realm of an all-embracing intuitive awareness which spontaneously leads all human inclinations in the correct direction; and (2) the fact that this higher knowledge embraces not only what we call the world of fact, but also the world of value. It embraces a cosmos in which the "ought" inevitably flows from the "is." To the extent that one lacks this total awareness, one's inclinations will necessarily remain precarious. While this knowledge differs radically from the deductive-analytic knowledge ascribed to Socrates, it shares the view often attributed to Socrates that true knowledge necessarily leads to goodness.

The question of how this higher knowledge operates in the ethical sphere remains a problem both for Graham and for the entire subsequent history of Confucianism, which must contend with the fact that the bulk of humankind including even those Confucians called noble men *(chün-tzu)* are not "ideal sages." Neither are they "born sages" nor do they necessarily attain perfect sagehood. Thus what Graham calls his "quasi-syllogism" concerning this matter begins with the major premise that perfect spontaneous awareness will necessarily lead to correct behavior in all circumstances. The minor premise is that those who lack this all-encompassing awareness will be controlled by their one-sided incorrect inclinations. The conclusion of the quasi-syllogism is, however, not a constative statement such as "when one is aware of everything relevant to the issue, one's inclination will move into the correct direction," but a prescriptive injunction, "be aware of everything relevant to the issue." It is thus only by a deliberative act of will and through a knowledge acquired by a non-spontaneous learning process that the non-sage can advance toward the ultimate ideal of sagehood.

In fact, when one reads the Analects as a whole, one has the impression that the Master by no means despises a learning process based on a consciously pursued incremental acquisition of knowledge and on deliberate efforts of will. There may be moments of illumination in which one has a synoptic intuition of the whole, but "non-spontaneous" study and thought must go on. While there is a strand in the Analects which may point to Taoism, there is another opposing strand which, as has often been noted by Chinese commentators, may well have encouraged the Mohist emphasis on *yu wei* reasoning. Even Mencius, who represents that pole of later Confucianism which stressed that knowledge of the good and inclination toward the good grow organically out of human nature, stresses—perhaps in the face of the Taoist tendencies already present in his time—that this intuitive awareness is easily clouded over and that the "noble man" can only maintain his contact with that which is spontaneous in himself by unremitting, deliberate cumulative acts of righteousness. The question of the relationship of "spontaneous awareness" to non-spontaneous knowledge and deliberate acts of the will remains a central problem of the entire subsequent history of Confucian thought.

I would finally agree with Graham that the sharp disjuncture of fact/value and ought/is in post-Cartesian Western "scientific" philosophy which necessarily banishes "value" and "oughtness" from a cosmos which is defined wholly in terms of a reductionist scientism and assigns these categories wholly to the human sphere—to human subjectivity or human culture, and so forth—is absent in China. In most Chinese thought "oughtness" and "value" still somehow have a cosmic source. Yet Graham's statement that the texts of correlative cosmology tell us not "what man ought to do but what he is stimulated to do when the cosmic interactions are orderly" (p. 385), is in my view mistaken. I would submit that while the sense of oughtness may have its source in a "heavenly" reality, man (particularly the ruler) has the perverse human power to remain "unstimulated" even when the cosmic interactions run their proper course.

To the extent that Chinese thought deals with mysteries of the human ethical life, it faces dilemmas common in all cultures. Similar explanations of what is considered to be "moral evil" are to be found in all cultures. The notion that true knowledge (however this knowledge is conceived) necessarily leads to the realization of values (however much the content of these values may vary from culture to culture) can be found in India and the West as well as in China. The same is true of explanations in terms of "weakness of the will."

I have discussed what seem to be some major theses of this enormously complex book, but have by no means exhausted the richness of its insights.

12

❦

Chinese Visions and American Policies

Washington is, of course, aware of Peking's hopes for the future; one is tempted to add, only too well aware. What might be called Mao Tse-tung's optimum global vision has only recently been called to our attention once more in Lin Piao's widely publicized article, "Long Live the Victory of People's Wars." Here we find Asia, Africa, and Latin America enveloped by "wars of national liberation" strictly modeled on the classical pattern of the Chinese revolution. The ingredients of this classical model can be clearly enumerated. The war must first of all be led by a genuine Marxist-Leninist party (which now means a party oriented to Peking); the party must rely primarily on peasant support and establish rural base areas; the peasant-based people's armies must fight a type of guerilla war which draws its basic inspiration from Mao's maxims on this subject; the people's war must also be supported by a broad united front of "all those with whom one can unite" which will, however, remain firmly under Communist control. In this way the main enemy will be effectively isolated. In spite of Peking's continuing denunciations of Moscow's effort to "wave the baton" in the Communist world, one need not doubt that the Chinese themselves dream of waving the baton decisively in a world Communist movement reconstituted through the Maoist strategy and now centered on Peking.

❦

In the face of assertions that Lin Piao's statement represents a newly-proclaimed Chinese *Mein Kampf*, and in the interest of historical perspective, it is important to point out that all the essential features of this statement were contained in Liu Shao-ch'i's famous speech in 1949 to the meeting of the Asian and Australian wing of the World Federation of Trade Unions (WFTU). At the time, the message was delivered within the limits imposed by a seemingly monolithic international Communist movement led by Moscow. Liu could deliver the speech only because the Kremlin was for the moment itself lending a certain hesitant and suspicious support to the notion—rendered plausible by certain developments then current in Vietnam, Indonesia, India, and Malaya—of the applicability of the Chinese model of revolution to other areas of the non-Western world. It was made entirely clear, however, that the center of world Communist authority lay in Moscow. Since then, the inhibitions have been removed, and Peking has been able to proclaim its vision in all its imposing amplitude.

Nevertheless, that vision was probably more unambiguously plausible in 1949 than it has been since. The rapid retreat of the Western empire had just begun and by no means seemed inevitable (from the Communist perspective least of all). The isolated cases of Indian and Philippine independence could easily be dismissed by both Moscow and Peking as a bourgeois sham, and the hope that rising nationalism would everywhere come under Communist leadership was vivid and reasonable. Ho Chi Minh was even then the paradigm of the popular nationalist leader who was also a convinced Marxist-Leninist.

The rise within the next few years of new states under non-Communist auspices and the failure of various Communist efforts in Asia subsequently led both Moscow and Peking to adjust their sights to a world which neither had foreseen. Out of this experience, there emerged the famous Bandung policy of cultivating Asian, African, and Latin American states already in being, whatever the nature of their internal polity. Bandung is often depicted as a triumph of Chou En-lai's suave diplomacy. If it was a triumph, however, it was a triumph of massive adjustment to an unlooked-for situation—hardly a triumph of the vision projected by Liu in 1949. Since Bandung, Peking's policies toward the third world have oscillated within the range of possibilities lying between the optimum vision and the Bandung line, while certain particular policies toward particular states can be explained quite satisfactorily in terms of the most conventional power politics. No doubt, the optimum vision remains the "esoteric" doctrine closest to Mao's heart. Yet there have been considerable stretches of time when the vision has been discreetly thrust into the background for the very solid reason that it is difficult to cultivate the existing states of Asia, Africa, and Latin America while simultaneously calling for their overthrow by "genuine" Marxist-Leninist wars of liberation.

⁂

In the Lin Piao statement the optimum vision reemerges in full clarity—perhaps to encourage patience in Hanoi by stressing the "protracted" nature of the classical people's war; perhaps because at a time when the Bandung approach is generally not flourishing, a reaffirmation of the faith seems necessary; perhaps, again, because of the continuing need to distinguish Peking's "pure" line from the adulterations of Moscow. But whatever the real motive behind the restatement of the original vision at this time, a careful scrutiny of Lin Piao's article reveals the odd fact that, side-by-side with the optimum projection, ambiguities and ambivalences can be found which leave the doors wide open to alternative approaches. For example, having asserted that "national democratic" revolutions must be led by genuine "proletarian parties," having declared that genuine independence can be wrung from the imperialists only by "people's wars," and having contemptuously dismissed the socialist claims of all states not ruled by genuine Communist parties, Lin Piao avoids drawing any concrete conclusions. That is, he sedulously refrains from assigning the existing states of Africa, Asia (with the exception of India), and Latin America to the ranks of the "lackeys of imperialism"; nor is he likely to do so, as long as Peking continues to cherish hopes of a Bandung-type conference in which it would play a leading role.

   The Lin Piao document simultaneously gives expression to the optimum vision and to diluted versions of it. The original united-front doctrine—the doctrine of "uniting with whom one can unite"—was meant to apply *within* given societies. In the diluted version, entire established nation-states are brought into the doctrine. Thus, the theme of the class struggle between rich and poor has been extended to "rich nations" and "poor nations." Very recently, even this conception was diluted by Mao's further extension of the doctrine to the not-so-poor nations of the "second intermediary zone" (Western Europe, Canada, etc.) which might conceivably be included in a vast united front against the main enemy—the United States.

While all this may appear to represent an enormously clever extrapolation of Mao's maxims, uniting with "poor nations" is not the same thing as uniting with the poor. The genius of the Maoist united-front strategy lay in its ability to combine absolute discipline and clarity of purpose in the core organization—the Chinese Communist party—with a maximum of maneuverability vis-à-vis other social and political groups which it could effectively control. The notion that the established states of Africa, Asia, and Latin America—no matter how poor—are as subject to direction from Peking as were the peasants of North China or the "Democratic League" during the late 1940s is based on a false analogy between incomparable entities. On its immediate periphery China may, of course, exert the same types of coercive pressure which other great powers exert toward their weaker neighbors. This does nothing, however, to demonstrate the demonic effectiveness of the Maoist strategy. Indeed, in dealing with the whole "first intermediate zone," Peking has already discovered that a simple appeal to common poverty and to a colonial past will not automatically lead existing states with their own concrete conceptions of national interest, their own specific histories and preoccupations, and their own sensitive pride, to accept Peking's "hegemony" in any international united front. Nor will it be at all easy to convince states which have had little experience with the United States in the past, to think of it as Chinese patriots thought of Japan in the 1930s and 1940s.

The ambiguities created by such dilutions pervade the Lin Piao document. Does the sensational assertion that North America and Europe now constitute—"in a sense"—"the cities of the world," while Asia, Latin America, and Africa constitute the "rural areas," refer only to the vast peasant masses of those latter regions, or does it also refer to the established regimes there? The answer is left in what is probably an intentional haze. No doubt, any regime willing to accept Peking's slogans will at least provisionally be included in the category of "rural areas" even if its polity be that of a feudal monarchy.

Even the concept of a "war of national liberation" is subjected to dilution by Lin Piao. After stating flatly that people's wars must be led by the "proletariat," Lin Piao concedes, in passing, that "various classes [that is, a non-Communist political elite] may lead people's wars against imperialism." Thus, in his list of countries which have undergone genuine "people's wars," Lin Piao is able to include Algeria and Indonesia (the Indonesia of the period before the most recent coup), despite the fact that neither of these cases fits the classical model outlined elsewhere in the same article. In Algeria, it is true, the elements of armed revolution, guerrilla warfare, and base areas were present, but the most vital ingredient of all—the leading role of a "Marxist-Leninist party"—was missing, as it certainly was also in the case of Indonesia.

"War of national liberation" has become, then, one of those accordion-like terms which can be given either a strict or broad construction. Even states which have achieved independence by the most innocuous and pacific means may qualify as members of the anti-imperialist camp so long as they express the correct attitudes toward U.S. imperialism. A fortiori, Peking is likely to apply the term "war of national liberation" to almost any revolution or rebellion anywhere in the third world on the assumption that any violent disturbance can only propel the Chinese wave of the future and weaken the United States. It is one of the great triumphs of Peking's propaganda that Washington has come to agree with this view. If Washington had been in the same frame of mind with respect to "wars of national liberation" during the Algerian revolt, the United States would no doubt have thrown its full support behind the French policy of suppression.

In sum, then, the Lin Piao article simultaneously restates Peking's maximum hopes and reflects all the adjustments which Peking has had to make to a world which—with the notable exception of Vietnam—has so far failed to shape itself to Chinese expectations.

But what of the future? The idea that the whole third world will easily succumb to China's infallible strategies has won ready acceptance among a large assortment of C.I.A. operatives, Pentagon strategists, professional Communist experts, games-theoreticians, political scientists, and others. Only yesterday, we had an enormous literature designed to show that the Soviet model and Soviet strategies would prove irresistible in the third world. It having since been discovered that Moscow must cope with a world as unpredictable and refractory to its own purposes as it is to ours, the same style of thought has now been transferred to China.

It would, of course, be utterly presumptuous to predict that the Chinese optimum strategy may not succeed in this place or that. The pressing question at the moment, however, is: which is the more dangerous—to predicate American policy on the fear that the whole third world is ripe for a Chinese takeover via the Maoist strategy, or to base it on the assumption that the third world is likely to develop in ways infinitely more varied and complex than anything dreamt of in Mao's philosophy? One would, at the very least, expect that arguments weighing against the Chinese projection would be given equal weight with arguments tending to support it. The great receptivity to the Chinese projection seems to rest, at least in part, on a theory which many of us share with the Chinese themselves—namely that the third world (whether it be described as "the rural areas" or the "underdeveloped" ones) is so homogeneous in its essential features that any political strategy which succeeds in one sector of this world may be expected to succeed in another. What is true of one underdeveloped, agrarian society is true of any other.

The features which all these societies have in common may indeed be of overriding importance. It is, however, extremely doubtful that the political destiny of any one of them can simply be deduced from the characteristics shared by all. The success of the Maoist strategy in China was made possible by certain very specific conditions existing in China during the 1930s and 1940s—primary among them the failure of the Nationalist government to achieve firm military control within its own territory. This special feature of the Chinese political landscape, which helped to create and shape the Maoist strategy (as Mao himself has often admitted), is by no means universally present in the states of the "underdeveloped" world. Whatever may be their failures in other areas, many of these states (India for one) have proven quite capable of creating fairly unified and disciplined national armies. Apart from this, China, particularly North China, was subject during the 1940s to the Japanese invasion and Japanese military power was subsequently dispersed in many directions. Mao Tse-tung and his group not only developed their strategy, but were also superb implementers of it. The very combination of Marxism-Leninism and nationalism that characterized Mao and his group was itself a product of certain peculiarities of Chinese history during the 1920s and 1930s.

The Vietnamese case offers little real basis for generalizing, for the striking thing about Vietnam is that it has, to a unique degree, shared some of the characteristics of the Chinese situation. While the proximity to China must be given its own due weight in the history of Vietnam since 1945, the decisive point was the emergence of a shrewd, able, and ruthless Vietnamese Communist group which succeeded in gaining fairly effective control of a genuine Vietnamese nationalist movement. Even in 1949, Ho Chi Minh's movement represented the only Communist operation in existence which closely approximated Liu Shao-ch'i's model. This movement continued to find support in certain segments of the population of the South who identified with it out of nationalist motives. Above all, it was able to apply its strategies against a regime which suffered from some of the same weaknesses as the Nationalist government in China. There was vast rural discontent, which Diem proved incapable of handling; there was his inability to unify and control his own military elite; and there were bitter communal divisions within the society which, while not resembling anything which had existed in China, produced effects similar to the regional fragmentation of power there.

But what of the other countries of Southeast Asia? They are all within geographical proximity of China, and none can afford to ignore the Chinese reality or the possibility of direct Chinese military intervention. To the extent that China's hopes in this area still rely on the efficacy of the Maoist strategy, is it inevitable that Thailand—to take one case—must follow the path of Vietnam? In recent months there have been many reports suggesting that Peking is now "turning on" its strategy in Thailand. Behind all such reporting, of course, lies the assumption that the success or failure of the strategy depends on buttons pressed in Peking, even though we have little evidence to show that the spectacular rise of the Vietcong during the last few years has, in fact, had anything to do with immediate direction from Peking, however welcome it may have been to the Chinese. In assessing the potentialities of the strategy in Thailand, therefore, it is the following questions which have to be examined. Does the Thai government effectively control its own armed forces and are these forces reasonably cohesive? Is there acute discontent in the countryside (outside of the much-discussed Northeast)? Is the direction of the incipient "people's war" in the hands of Thai leaders, or are Laotians, Vietnamese, and Chinese (in the South) playing a dominant role? These are the relevant questions, whatever the Chinese may wish and however the war in Vietnam may go.

⚎

It may, of course, be argued that even if the Chinese are not able to export Communism by exclusive reliance on their own revolutionary strategy, they will prove flexible enough to use other methods to achieve the same end. To do this, however, they will need more than those few precariously pro-Peking Communist groupings now in existence; a whole host of new Marxist-Leninist movements under effective Chinese control in places where they do not now exist will have to be created. The view that they will easily be able to create such a vast movement rests again on an unflagging belief in an ongoing entity called "world Communism" or "international Communism" which somehow has a life of its own over and above the sum total of actual Communist states and parties, and which remains unaffected by the vicissitudes of its constituent "detachments."

Involved in all this is a refusal to take the crisis which has erupted in the Communist world in recent years with real seriousness. Only yesterday, the phrase "world Communism" was generally used to describe an ostensibly monolithic power system centered on Moscow and based on the unquestioned authority of the Kremlin; the phrase referred not to a disembodied set of ideas, but to an organized movement. Now, however, one often encounters among those who speak of "world Communism" a view which conceives of Communism as a kind of homogeneous unchanging substance which is subject to shattering but whose inner essence remains unchanged even after fragmentation. Since the substance remains the same the shattered parts may again be reassembled and resolidified at any moment (this time, presumably, under the leadership of Peking). Furthermore, the expansive capacity of the substance also remains unaffected by the experience of fragmentation. (It is no accident, incidentally, that many who argue most strongly for this particular view of "world Communism" were among those who most strongly insisted in the past that the system was monolithic and unbreakable.) However much they may come to differ, we are told, all Communist states share the aim of achieving Communism.

But what is Communism? Theoretically, the power to define what it is remains the exclusive prerogative of the Communist party. In Communist ideology, the party is not merely a political organization: it is the embodiment of all those transcendental qualities which Marx attributed to the industrial proletariat. Whatever the good society may be, it can only be attained by the Communist party, for it is the Communist party which alone has access to the inner secrets of history and which can therefore apply infallibly correct solutions to the unfolding problems of history. As the embodiment of the general will of the proletariat, the party should be trans-national and immune to inner conflicts of interest. These attributes of infallibility, universality, and unanimity have been the inner essence of the Communist party as the ultimate mystery of Marxism-Leninism. Can one say that this mystery has remained unaffected by the recent crisis in the Communist world?

The Chinese, to be sure, have found a comforting precedent for the crisis in the history of Communism. Lenin, they say, often found himself in the minority within the Russian Social-Democratic movement. He did not hesitate to break with the majority when the majority was wrong, and in the end his truth prevailed. Here again we find ourselves in the realm of false analogies. Can the relationships among vast Communist nation-states be compared with those of the warring factions among Russia's Marxist intelligentsia? Will China be able to deal with the USSR and its ideological claims in the manner in which Lenin disposed of the Mensheviks after October 1917? Will China be able, in any foreseeable future, to suppress the claims to Communist legitimacy of the Yugoslavs, the Poles, the Romanians, or the Italian Communist party? The hard fact is that for all its pretensions (some quite spurious) to a purer Marxist-Leninist doctrine, Peking is doing quite as much as Moscow to undermine the transcendental status of the world Communist movement. The famous doctrine that the decisions of any given Communist party (i.e., that of the USSR) are not universally binding on other Communist parties subverts not only Moscow's claims of central authority but *all* future claims of other potential centers of world Communism. It need hardly be pointed out that the slavish obedience to Moscow's line by foreign parties during Stalin's lifetime was not based on reasoned judgments that Stalin was always right, but precisely on the doctrine of the infallible authority of the Kremlin. Even if the Chi-

nese do manage to create new pro-Peking Communist movements in
Africa and Latin America, can they ever expect to exercise the type
of authority over these groups which the Kremlin formerly exercised
over the Communist world?

What is actually happening behind all the polemics is that the
nation-state is asserting its primacy over the trans-national claims of
Marxism-Leninism while the very concept of an ultimate authority
decays. To be sure, this still leaves open the possibility of the elabo-
ration of national varieties of Communism. The Maoist vision of the
good society is one such variety; the day has passed, however, when
one variety of national Communism is accepted without question as
the mandatory image of the future even by "Marxist-Leninist"
groupings.

The question of whether there can any longer exist an ultimate
seat of authority in the Communist world and who—if anyone—will
occupy this seat has now become the very essence of the Sino-Soviet
conflict. It is probably not a question which can be resolved by com-
promises and agreements on the substantive issues which occupy the
foreground of the polemics. But could it be resolved—as some have
argued—by a reversal for the United States in Vietnam, which would
prove the Chinese contention that the U.S. is "a paper tiger" unable
to cope with local "people's wars," disprove the Soviet position that
American power must be respected even in this area, and convert the
whole of world Communism to China's outlook? Even this is highly
doubtful. For if it means that Moscow will itself be converted to
Peking's outlook, it must be stressed that Moscow's ideological position on "wars of national liberation" has by no means been as consistently "revisionist" as Peking would have us believe. Even now
there is some question as to whether Moscow is or is not willing to
lend support to Cuban-sponsored wars of national liberation in
Latin America. In the improbable event that Moscow were to acknowledge Peking's correctness on this issue, Peking has guaranteed
itself against the necessity of reconciliation by imposing on Moscow
a whole catalogue of impossible conditions on other issues. East-
European Communist states and the Communist parties of Western
Europe have adopted a generally "anti-Chinese" stance. They have
done so for solid political reasons of their own, and they are not

likely to be swayed into the "Chinese camp" by debaters' points. Finally, Peking's ability to create strong new Chinese-oriented Communist parties throughout the third world will continue to depend on local conditions within that world and not merely on the "demonstration" effect of Vietnam.

In sum, the Sino-Soviet conflict has—to use a term employed in the polemic—become a "hegemonistic" conflict. The two principal actors have grown more concerned with the question of who shall prevail than the question of who is right. But this does not mean that either one or the other must prevail, for both the Communist states and the Communist parties lying between the two are probably less and less interested in having an ultimate source of infallible authority anywhere.

In emphasizing the enormity of the present crisis in the Communist world, I have no intention of implying that the world is "going our way," if by "our way" we mean the imminent universal enthronement of American-style liberal democracy or European social democracy. The retreat of empire has produced neither the Communist floodtide nor the "Western" or "American" century. The major drift has been in the direction of what might be called, for lack of a better term, populist-nationalist dictatorships. Whether their power rests on a single party or on the armed forces, the leaders of such states invariably claim to incarnate the will of the "people-nation." On many issues, no doubt, they are closer to the Communist world than to ours. They generally profess adherence to socialism, their anti-colonialism often draws on the Leninist vocabulary, and they often find it expedient to denigrate the mere "machinery" of political democracy in favor of "organic" theories of representation.

One need not conclude, however, that this development is in any sense inevitable. Some societies may avoid it. All one can say is that circumstances in many areas have been favorable to it. Nor need one gratuitously idealize it as do some elements of the "New Left," on the grounds that it is revolutionary and "socialist": some of these states may prove abominably corrupt, exploitative, and ineffective; others may be fairly effective in important areas and reasonably decent. Nor, again, need one be led by a dogmatic liberalism to assign them all to the Communist camp and refuse to coexist with them.

The same development might well have occurred if Marx and Lenin had never lived, since the basic fund of ideas on which these leaders draw was, in fact, fully available in certain Left Jacobin–nationalist tendencies emerging out of the French Revolution. Ultimately, indeed, these ideas may turn out to be hardier than the more spectacular hybrid, Marxism-Leninism. Given the infinitely less intense and less transcendental nature of the ideologies governing the new states, there is a good chance that they may not go the whole way to totalitarianism, that they will prove more relativistic and technical-pragmatic in their economic approaches, and that some may also perhaps prove open in the long run to demands for personal freedom. Above all, one must remember that the overruling passion of these leaders is the passion to remain masters in their own households. This involves the refusal to accept any claims to hegemony—including spiritual claims—from outside. Since we, on our side, are presumably unburdened by an official philosophy which imposes on us the duty to universalize our own system by force, one would think that it would be a great deal easier for us than it would be for either Moscow or Peking to live with this passion for national autonomy.

※

It has, of course, been argued that all these regimes are simply halfway houses to Communism, and that the Chinese need but wait a little longer before an unstable third world—faced with enormous economic, demographic, and social problems—succumbs to Maoist strategies. No doubt, a minimum requirement for the survival of these states is that they show some movement in the direction of solving their problems, but it is far from certain that they must "solve" all of them immediately in order to remain viable. As a minimal sine qua non, they must demonstrate their power to maintain basic political and military control of the areas under their jurisdiction. But even where a given regime is overthrown, there is no reason to think that its successor will be less passionately concerned to maintain its own independence and autonomy. The notion that the Communist world possesses simple formulae for solving economic, demographic, and social problems which will prove irresistible in the third world is daily confounded by the growing diversity of models within the Communist world. The Chinese model (itself in a state of flux) no longer follows the Soviet model and does not resemble ei-

ther the Yugoslav or even the Polish model. Fidel Castro, in spite of
his adherence to Marxism-Leninism, has yet to find anywhere in the
Communist world a ready-made model adequate to the concrete
problems which confront him. Furthermore, while it continues to be
represented as an ultimate and inevitable apocalypse or nemesis, the
very nature of Communism has become highly problematic. Marxism-
Leninism itself is proving a kind of halfway house to types of national socialism which oddly approximate some of the tendencies in
the third world. Future spiritual and social movements capable of
bursting through the tough integuments of the nation-state framework may arise, but it is doubtful whether Communism as we have
known it will be one of these movements.

I would suggest, then, that it is mistaken and dangerous to base
American policy on the expectation that the whole third world is
about to behave in a manner corresponding to Peking's optimum
hopes for the future. It must be stressed again that these hopes are
grounded not on the exportability of Chinese soldiers, but on the exportability of Chinese revolutionary strategy. Peking may staff its
embassies with huge contingents of experts in "people's war" who
will try to manipulate the "natives," but it has yet to be shown that
the embassy staffs are quite that clever, or that the natives are quite
that manipulable. Even in Southeast Asia where the Chinese can, and
may yet, intervene with troops, Peking still fervently wishes to rely
on the salability of its strategy. In Vietnam the strategy has, with
adaptations, been quite effective—not because of buttons pressed in
Peking or because of huge embassy staffs, but because of the very
particular political history of Vietnam. Its effectiveness in other
countries of Southeast Asia remains a function of internal situations
in those countries, particularly if we assume the ongoing presence of
American and Soviet power in the area.

Is Peking capable of adjusting to a world which does not correspond to its maximum hopes? Granted that in the mind of Mao and
those closest to him the hopes are still active and real, the fact is that
the process of adjustment has long since begun. The Bandung line of
1955 represented a major retreat from Liu Shao-ch'i's line of 1949.
The current effort to cultivate commercial and even political relations with states of the Western world and with Japan can only be
squeezed into Maoist categories by stretching these categories to the
breaking point. Even the extraordinary concession which Peking has

felt obliged to make to the principle of national independence and autonomy within the Communist world in the course of its polemics with Moscow, constitutes an unacknowledged adjustment. In the eyes of Mao, these adjustments may represent temporary expedients which will soon be rendered unnecessary by the true wave of the future. There is, however, no need for us to accept Peking's assessment of their significance.

It nevertheless remains true that a minimum condition for Peking's adjustment to a world recalcitrant to her most grandiose ambitions is the recognition of China's status as one of the great world powers: a willingness to move as far as we can to involve and enmesh China, however harsh and unaccommodating its behavior may be, in whatever precarious structure of world order we have.

There is a reasonable possibility that, as a recognized great power, China would in the end come to accept its position in a world of nation-states large and small. To some, it may seem foolhardy to predicate foreign policy on "reasonable possibility" rather than on "policy science." I would simply urge that what we have on the other side is not science but unthinking extrapolation of the Chinese maximum vision, and a host of ill-considered clichés and stereotypes (put forth by people on various sides of the policy debate). We have, for example, the notion that whereas the Russians are "Western" (although they were once considered "Oriental"), the Chinese are occultly Oriental, or Asiatic. What conclusions one is expected to draw from this distinction, I do not know. A candid survey of the span of Chinese history leads to no firm conclusions on the question of whether the Chinese are more or less belligerent or more or less fanatical than Westerners: certainly, the imperial state was not more aggressive than the Czarist empire. We have the further stereotype that with its vast population, China must of necessity achieve world hegemony. From this, some have drawn the conclusion that we ought to recognize Chinese hegemony as quickly as possible, while others have called for the immediate dispatch of a few well-placed missiles. Then we have the notion that "Asia" must inevitably form part of a Chinese empire either because China controlled "Asia" in the past (which is false), or because Asians are all alike culturally or peculiarly prone to submit to those of superior strength. While China will undoubtedly play a leading role in Asian, and indeed world, politics, Asia is not a po-

litical, and certainly not a cultural, entity: there are many states in
Asia as little anxious to form part of a Chinese empire as states on
other continents and probably as resourceful in avoiding this fate
as others.

⁂

Finally, there is the more serious argument that the Chinese leaders
still think of China as the center of civilization in a world of barbarians. Here I would point out that the cosmology of Chinese universal
kingship on which this faith was founded has collapsed along with
the world which made it plausible; that while Peking does regard itself as the center of an international faith, it is not the same faith
which animated "sinocentrism" in the past (many of its tenets are
not even Chinese); and that the China of the present finds itself in a
world which will continue to reject its "sinocentric" claims. These
are all considerations, it seems to me, which may be quite sufficient
to overcome the pull of mental habits inherited from the past.

I have not here attempted to put forth solutions to our Vietnamese
dilemmas. Obviously, whether we regard Vietnam as the first "test
case" in a chain reaction leading to a realization of the Chinese optimum vision, or whether we accept the reasonable possibilities suggested above, is a question which bears very strongly on the price—
military, political, and moral—we are willing to pay to maintain our
present position in that unhappy land.

13

❧

The Reign of Virtue: Leader and Party in the Cultural Revolution

"When societies first come to birth" says Montesquieu "it is the leader who produces the institutions. Later it is the institutions which produce the leaders."

Whoever would undertake to give institutions to a people must work with full consciousness that he has set himself to change, as it were, the very stuff of human nature, to transform each individual who, in isolation, is a complete but solitary whole, into a part of something greater than himself, from which, in a sense, he derives his life and his being, to substitute a communal and moral existence for a purely physical and independent life with which we are all of us endowed by nature.

—J. J. Rousseau, *The Social Contract*, Book II, Chapter VII

One of the most arresting aspects of the Great Proletarian Cultural Revolution has been the confrontation between Mao Tse-tung (or the Maoist group) and the Chinese Communist party. There is, to be sure, an area of vagueness and uncertainty concerning this whole matter. Have the Maoists attacked the party as such? What indeed is the party as such? The party may be conceived of as the sum total of its actual members—of its human composition. It may be conceived of in terms of its organizational structure—its "constitution," rules, and established mechanisms. To any genuine Marxist-Leninist, it is more than its cells and anatomy. It is a metaphysical organism which is more than the sum of its parts. The "soul" of this collective entity incarnates all those intellectual and moral capacities which Marx had attributed to the industrial proletariat.

Now there can be no doubt whatsoever that the Maoists have carried out a frontal assault on the human apparatus at all levels of party organization, at least in urban areas. There is also considerable evidence that party structures and mechanisms are in a shambles and that even where they survive, as in the rump Central Committee and army party branches, they have ceased to be an important vehicle of decision making. The whole discussion of "party building" which was a prominent theme at the end of 1967 and the early part of 1968 indicates the degree of party wrecking which has been going on. The area of uncertainty is the third miasmic area of the party as an ontological category—as a whole which may persist whatever the fate of its parts. In this area, it does not appear likely that the Maoist group is prepared to jettison the sacred label.

It is interesting to note that in another sector of what is still vaguely called the Communist world, the possibility of eliminating the role of the party as such has emerged. In Regis Debray's book *Revolution in the Revolution?*, which is now regarded as a textbook of Castro ideology, we find the following striking assertions: "Fidel says simply that there is no revolution without a vanguard but that this vanguard is not necessarily the Marxist-Leninist Party."[1] "The effective leadership of an armed revolutionary struggle requires a new style of leadership, a new method or organization."[2] "Parties are never anything but instruments of class struggle. Where the instrument no longer serves its purpose should the class struggle come to a halt or should new instruments be forged?"[3] Debray suggests that "an end be put to the plethora of commissions, secretariats, congresses, conferences, plenary sessions, meetings and assemblies at all levels—provincial, regional and local. Faced with a state of emergency and a militarily organized enemy such a mechanism is paralyzed at best, catastrophic at worst."[4] "There is no exclusive ownership of the revolution."[5] "Eventually the future People's Army will beget the party of which it is to be theoretically the instrument. Essentially the party is the army."[6]

Debray, to be sure, is discussing the period of revolutionary struggle and his doctrine is not incompatible with the view that after the victory a party of the Communist type may be established. Debray's assertions seem most applicable to China's Cultural Revolution. The Maoists insist that China is in a permanent state of revolutionary class struggle and that the party both in terms of its human composition and as a structure has gone radically astray. Is it not possible that the Maoists are also ready to eliminate the party's role in history as an instrument which "no longer serves its purpose?"

Against this possibility, however, one must note the fact that the concept of the Communist party is now part of Chinese Communist sacred history, and that in pressing their own canonized revolutionary experience as the exclusive model for the third world, the Chinese must inevitably stress the role of the party in the revolutionary struggle. In Latin America, this brings them into direct collision with the Castro-Debray line which tends to express a studied contempt for the "pro-Chinese" groups in Latin America. The Maoists are constrained by their own history to reject Debray's elimination of the party in the revolutionary struggle.

There is also the need to refute the current Soviet line on events in China. The Soviets have flatly asserted in their polemics that the "Maoist group" is bent on the destruction of the Chinese Communist party.[7] The Chinese party has always been defective, we are told, given its woefully weak proletarian base, but it was born under the inspiration of the October Revolution and for many years was guided by the directives of the Comintern. Even after 1949 it received much sound guidance from Moscow. Unfortunately the petty bourgeois Maoist group was able to establish its ascendancy and is now bent on destroying it. One may still hope, however, that the bulk of party leaders now in opposition will ultimately be able to restore the party to its legitimate role and also recognize Moscow's spiritual hegemony. In their discussion of the Cultural Revolution they have also dwelt at great length on the Maoist violation of party constitutionality.

In the face of these Soviet efforts to identify themselves with the "legitimate" CCP heritage, the Maoists must deny Moscow's claims. In a statement attributed to a "Stalin group"—a revolutionary organization in the Soviet Union[8]—we find a condemnation of "Soviet revisionist calumnies that China's Great Proletarian Cultural Revolution is 'directed against the Chinese Communist party' . . . The fact that the broadest masses of the people are taking part in the Cultural Revolution together with the party does not in the least impair the prestige of the CCP."

Unlike Castro and Debray, the Maoist group (including such people as Ch'en Po-ta and K'ang Sheng) cannot but be profoundly conscious of the weight of the concept of the "Communist party" in the history of Marxism-Leninism since 1917. Far from being a dispensable element, it lies at the very heart of Leninism. It was Lenin who insisted after 1917 that only Marxist-Leninist parties could act as the vanguard of the proletariat. It was Lenin who insisted that the party structure be imposed on all vanguards abroad. It was Lenin who insisted that no revolution could be called socialist unless led by Communist parties and it was during Lenin's lifetime that the ultimate authority of the international Communist movement became lodged in one center on the basis of a logic inherent in Communist party organization. The Maoist group in China is still bent on capturing for itself this transnational Marxist-Leninist authority and it is most difficult to see how it can do so if it abandons the very concept of the Marxist-Leninist party.

And yet, the uncertainty of the Maoist attitude toward party organization in China can be most graphically illustrated by the uncertainty of Peking's relations to its own Maoist followers in Belgium and France. In Belgium, the so-called "Rittenberg case" has thrown a glaring light on some of the issues involved. Sidney Rittenberg, an American Maoist of long standing residing in Peking, wrote a pamphlet in the summer of 1967 excoriating Jacques Grippa, the recognized leader of the Belgian Maoists, for his defense of Liu Shao-ch'i's "How to be a Good Communist." Grippa, in turn, vehemently attacked Rittenberg and whoever stood behind him for attacking the Leninist principles of party organization in the name of a "cult or idolatry with regard to a leader."[9] Grippa (a former Stalinist) is committed to the party not only as a moral entity but as a Leninist structure. He is able to cull many telling citations from Lenin stressing the importance which Lenin attached to organizational principles and party rules. The essence of those quotations is that the forms of party organization are part of the very essence of what the party is. One would gather that Grippa's standing in Peking is now very much under a cloud.

In France there are at least three Maoist groups, only one of which has constituted itself as a Marxist-Leninist party of the conventional type, while at least one of the other groups has refused to acknowledge that the older party structure is still valid. It is apparently unclear whether any of these groups has as yet obtained Peking's official sanction. In all this, however, the issue is not necessarily whether the term "party" is to remain in use but whether the old structure is to survive or indeed whether structure as such is to play a central role in a Maoist political universe.

When we turn our attention to recent developments in China as they are refracted through the murky media of the Cultural Revolution, one notes that at the end of 1967 and at the beginning of 1968 there were many references in the literature to "party building." It is significant that even this literature hints that the party will somehow be restructured. We also note some discussion of the convening of the Ninth Party Congress, an act which would presumably once again place the seal of party legality on whatever state of affairs would prevail at the time of its meeting. Chou En-lai is alleged to have asked a delegation of proletarian revolutionaries from Canton on 11 November: "Haven't you discussed the subject of the Ninth Party Congress set for next year?"[10] This question would indicate, as one might suspect, that Chou at least is strongly committed to a return to as much organizational normalcy as possible under the prevailing conditions.

It is entirely possible that the Maoist group itself is interested in rebuilding the party in some form or other[11] but by no means as interested as others in restoring power to the bulk of the former membership or in rebuilding the entire former machinery or even in restoring its position of centrality in the polity. The question would thus not be one of whether the party should be rebuilt but how it should be rebuilt.

One may, of course, assume that the question of how the party should be built was by no means entirely theoretical. Undoubtedly it was intertwined with the most ferocious power struggle. Former cadres would be most insistent on "party legality" and the sacred character of party structure and the Maoists would be infinitely less committed to the "institutional charisma" of the party. The very *Red Flag* editorial of 9 July 1967[12] which attempts to refute the charge that the Maoists do not "desire the leadership of the party" makes it clear that whatever charisma the party may possess derives solely from the person and thought of Mao Tse-tung. It is made painfully clear that the party derives its legitimacy from Mao Tse-tung and not vice versa. Any notion that Mao Tse-tung must legitimize his Cultural Revolution through established party procedures is, in my view, not based on a correct reading of Cultural Revolutionary doctrine. Mao himself is the source of legitimacy and so long as his group remains more or less at the helm, he can legitimize any structure.

174 CHINA AND OTHER MATTERS

In 1968 the discussion of party building had again receded. Instead of discussions of party building there has been a resurgence of attacks on the "right"—on those nefariously attempting to "reverse verdicts." The "revolutionary committees" formerly treated as a provisional device seem to be emerging more and more (whatever they may be in actuality) as Mao's chosen vehicle of "proletarian dictatorship." If present trends continue they may themselves become the constituent units of any rebuilt party. Concretely this would mean that the People's Liberation Army (PLA) and proven non-party "proletarian revolutionaries" would play a dominant role at the heart of any reconstituted party.

The crux of the matter is not whether the party survives in some form but whether it can ever recover its central sacred character. The whole thrust of the Cultural Revolution has been to devalue and diminish its significance. The phrase "dictatorship of the proletariat" has never been used more obsessively and yet it is made crystal clear that the "dictatorship of the proletariat" and the Communist party are by no means interchangeable terms. Just as the phrase "dictatorship of the proletariat" has long since been sundered from any actual reference to industrial workers, the Cultural Revolution has now demonstrated that the particular "general will" which it represents is quite detachable from the particular organization known as the Communist party. For almost two years now we have been told that the dictatorship of the proletariat has been borne by the "Red Guards," by the PLA (the "main pillar of the dictatorship") and a whole assortment of non-party "proletarian revolutionaries." We have even been told that the battle between the "dictatorship of the proletariat" and the "dictatorship of the bourgeoisie" takes place within the arena of each individual soul. Far from possessing those self-purgative and self-regenerative powers which had always been attributed to it in the past, we find that the party must be "reproletarianized" from without—by Mao Tse-tung standing above it and by the "revolutionary masses" standing below.

The fact that the PLA has become the main pillar of the dictatorship of the proletariat can, of course, be explained in quite mundane terms. In turning on the party Mao and his supporters have been forced to fall back on the army. It is by no means clear, however, that the army as a whole is as solid a pillar as Mao would like it to be nor as thoroughly imbued with proletarian virtue. Assertions about the proletarian virtue of the army like many statements of this type reflect not so much the complex actuality as the normative reality—the way things ought to be and will in good time become. Whatever its actual power role, the faith in the army as the bearer of proletarian virtue certainly antedates the Cultural Revolution. In the early 1960s, an effort was made to turn the army into a model of Maoist behavior. Indeed, the army has played a central role in the whole history of the party since the early 1930s. From the vantage point of the late 1960s, one is tempted to observe that Mao may have always implicitly regarded the PLA as bearing as much proletarian virtue as the party itself. The isolated guerrilla fighter sacrificing his very life for the people has always been as much the epitome of higher virtue as the hard-working cadre.

It is entirely possible that with the demise of Mao or a reversal in the fortunes of the Maoist group, there will be an effort to restore the party to its central position in Chinese life and to re-establish all its sanctified organizational forms. As already indicated, men such as Chou En-lai are probably deeply conscious of the role of the party in Marxist-Leninist Communism. The fact remains that the Cultural Revolution has unmasked many truths which will not be easily forgotten, particularly by the young who have participated in recent events. The party may not have engaged in all the heinous bureaucratic crimes attributed to it in Red Guard newspapers, but its profane nature as simply another bureaucratic organization devoid of any inbuilt proletarian grace or powers of self-redemption now stands revealed. The institutional charisma will not easily be restored.

Some Historic Perspectives—Western and Chinese

Can the notions which lie behind the Maoist attack on the CCP and behind the Cultural Revolution in general be related to certain larger perspectives and contexts of ideas? If we are dealing with what many take to be a kind of madness, is this madness unique to Mao or does it relate in any way to a larger history of ideas—Western or Chinese? Is it indeed Western or Chinese or may it be said to feed on both cultural traditions?

In focusing on ideas and their genealogy there is no intention of implying that the Cultural Revolution or the conflict between the party and the leader is solely a result of ideas in the head of Mao or to deny the role of power struggles, psychological motives, or "objective factors." Mao's retreat to the "second line" of power since 1959 may have been voluntary or involuntary or partially voluntary. Even if it was essentially voluntary (and I lean to the view that it was), the fact that the "first line" leaders of the party were moving in a direction which the leader regarded as radically mistaken was not only an offense to his own vision of China's future but also to an enormous swollen sense of self-esteem which had become indissolubly tied up with this vision. The vision may be only one ingredient in the total complex. It is, however, an essential ingredient.

Mao Tse-tung found that the CCP, both in its human composition and as an organizational structure, failed at least for a time to embody the qualities of the "dictatorship of the proletariat." The latter phrase presumably designates the "social bearer" of certain social virtues and capacities but in current Maoist usage it often seems to refer to the assemblage of the virtues themselves—selflessness in the "service of the people," lack of self-interest, austerity, singularity of purpose, and implacable hostility to the forces of evil. The question of who the actual bearers of this "general will" are has become a crucial problem of the Cultural Revolution.

In seeking out the provenance of these notions I shall concentrate in the first instance on the possible Western origins precisely because of the tendency among Western "pragmatic" academics to see something peculiarly Chinese in Mao's highly moralistic rhetoric. Furthermore, in dealing with Western sources, it will no longer suffice to confine our attention to the specificities of Marxist-Leninist ideology. As the Marxist-Leninist ideology moves into a period of advanced disintegration one becomes more and more conscious of some of the more general notions which lie behind Marxism-Leninism, notions which have become embodied in specific ways within the Marxist-Leninist complex (as well as in other ideologies) but whose origins go back at least as far as the Enlightenment. These general notions have proved more enduring than the specific ideologies within which they have found a lodging. Our particular quest here leads us to Jean-Jacques Rousseau and the Jacobin effort to apply the doctrine of that fruitful but ambiguous thinker.

It is not at all a question of whether Mao Tse-tung was ever a profound student of Rousseau or Jacobinism. There can be little doubt that in his youth he read about both but one need not argue any intimate contact. The significance of Rousseau here is that he gives a highly vivid expression to more general tendencies which can make their way without any intimate contact with the great thinker himself. In the case of Mao, one can indeed maintain that Marxism-Leninism itself has been a bearer of the strains of thinking with which we are concerned.

Turning back to Rousseau we find that, as Burke states, "Rousseau is nothing if not a moralist." As opposed to many of his contemporaries such as Turgot, d'Alembert, Voltaire, and Diderot who were overwhelmingly concerned with the progress of the "arts and sciences," and who regarded moral progress as a concomitant of the accumulation of human knowledge, he was overwhelmingly concerned, in the first instance, with the question of how to make society virtuous and just. Amid the sophisticated and hedonistic libertines of the enlightened aristocracy and the new intelligentsia, he felt that he represented the essential innocence of a man of the people and the sturdy virtues of a citizen of Geneva. The others were social engineers concerned with how arts and sciences could be mobilized to render society felicitous. He was overwhelmingly concerned with society's moral progress; he had actually found in his "Discourses in the Arts and Sciences" and "Discourses on the Origins of Human Inequality" that the arts and sciences of his time had actually run counter to moral progress and contributed to all the corruptions of society. His own "civic morality" was not a "new morality" but a morality based on a kind of Plutarchian exaltation of ancient Roman and Spartan virtues. His good society would be peopled by men who would abnegate their private interests for the public good, men constantly inspired by a sense of duty to the fatherland, men who would sacrifice themselves without stint, and men who would live simple and austere lives. It is interesting to note that as the spiritual father of modern nationalism (although again, the "antique" example is here of overwhelming importance) Rousseau exalts the martial virtues and even praises hatred of the national enemy as a unifying cement of the sovereign people's will.

What makes Rousseau's ethic modern and revolutionary is, however, his lack of belief in the power of the individual to realize his potentiality for virtue through his own efforts and his consequent tendency to link ethics indissolubly to politics. In his own individual life he had discerned how impossible it is for a good man to realize his moral potentialities within a bad society. "I saw," he stated in his *Confessions*, "that everything depended basically on political science, and that no matter how one views the problem every people is just what its government makes it. What form of government is most suited to produce a nation which is virtuous, enlightened and wise—in short, in the highest sense of the word, as perfect as possible?"[13] The individual can realize his moral potential only by submerging himself in that larger "moral entity," the people. The people as a collectivity is not only the source of all sovereignty but also of all virtue. It is only when the individual will somehow becomes fused with the general will that the individual's own moral potential can be realized. The question of how—in concrete political terms—the general will comes to be internalized in the individual is, of course, one of the central enigmas of Rousseau's political thought and has been the subject of a vast literature. While related to the modern sociological view that the individual derives his "values" from "society," it is much more activist and political. What it asserts is that in some fashion the state is or should be the moralizing agency of human society. Its meaning is relatively clear when applied to an idealized ancient Rome and Sparta where citizens presumably expressed their general will in face-to-face primary assemblies and where the decisions of majorities were, in Rousseau's view, actually inspired by virtue. Even here he was forced to introduce a transcendent element in the form of that eighteenth-century device, the all-wise "legislator." It was Lycurgus who created an all-wise constitution and system of law which shaped the Spartans to virtue. "Of itself," we are told, "the people wishes the good; of itself it does not always see it."[14] Many enigmas emerge when this notion is applied to the modern nation-state. The question of how the virtue of the people is achieved in these vast societies is dealt with most cursorily by Rousseau and indeed he often expresses doubt whether social virtue is attainable in societies of this size.

   In spite of its imprecision, the concept of a society in which the organized people would be able to crush all selfish factional interests and infuse its individual members with public virtue was to prove most powerful. The attempt to realize this ideal within the framework of the modern nation-state was, of course, to fall to Robespierre, St. Just, and Babeuf who found that the mere elimination of established vested interests and privileges as embodied in the old order did not automatically actualize the general will. Furthermore, as legislators of the general will they soon found that Rousseau's sharp distinction between the legislator who creates the general laws of the good state but who does not attempt to implement them and the "executive power" which applies them was to prove completely inapplicable in practice. Before one could even begin to create good laws, it was necessary to eliminate the manifestation of individual, group, and factional egotism as well as the cynical sophistries of vain intellectuals which interfered with the establishment of good laws.

In essence, Robespierre himself becomes the embodiment of the general will not only as a "legislator" but also as a "magistrate." It is Robespierre who plays this role and not the Jacobin society which itself turns out to be susceptible to selfish factionalism. It is, after all, no accident that the transcendental factor in Rousseau's "Social Contract" is not an institution but an individual—the "legislator" who by dint of his god-like "great soul" is able to embody the indivisible public spirit. Institutions, made up as they are of many individuals, are hardly indivisible and may easily become the embodiment of "partial interests." Rousseau was not yet attuned to the notion of the dynamics of social history which endow institutions with a kind of dynamic historic life of their own. He must accept Montesquieu's view that "leaders produce institutions." The Jacobin clubs were never to develop the distinctive personality later to be attributed to the Communist party and Robespierre continually stressed that his Committee of Public Safety enjoyed its authority because of the purity and incorruptibility of its members rather than as an organizational entity.

The reign of virtue, as we know, was not established by the French Revolution and the question of why it was not established was to agitate a whole new generation of young thinkers including both the young Hegel and the young Marx. Both Hegel and Marx concluded that the "people" as a collective entity did not, in fact, embody the indivisible general virtue which Rousseau had attributed to it. It had turned out to be an agglomeration of all kinds of egoistic individual and group interests. Hegel was ultimately to find the realization of man's higher social virtue in the modern state while Marx was to find the social bearer of general virtue to be a particular segment of modern society, the industrial proletariat. It was, in the first instance, the economic origins of the proletariat which were to turn Marx's attention to the whole historic economic process which lay behind the rise of this redemptive class. However, Marx's growing interest in technico-economic progress during the 1840s was not wholly due to the necessity to explain the preconditions of the existence of the proletariat. His ideal of good society was no longer simply Rousseau's ideal of civic virtue. He had developed a genuine appreciation of the values of material progress which in his good society would be a precondition of cultural richness. His new man would be socially virtuous but would also live in material comfort and appreciate his Shakespeare and Homer. The proletariat was not only the heir of Rousseau's public virtue but as a stratum deeply immersed in technical life, it would also fulfil the role of Saint Simon's industrial-scientific elite. Thus Marx's concept of the mode of production fuses together the concepts of technico-economic and moral progress in an unstable complex.

There is, of course, implicit in Marx's class conception something like the Rousseauist conception of a class "general will." He was not, however, inclined to go into the question of how the proletarian general will would find its realization. Unlike Rousseau, he was able to invoke a new dynamic principle, the impersonal forces of history. The unfolding mechanisms of the capitalist mode of production would themselves lead the proletariat to fulfill its historic role, to actualize both its moral and technico-economic tasks. It is in this way that the later Marx avoids the problem of class organization, the problem of politics itself.

With Lenin, however, who devoutly accepted Marx's conception of the historic mission of the proletariat, the problem of politics comes back to center stage. The problem of how the general will of the proletariat is to be actualized becomes an immediate problem of political action. In Lenin's view, the virtues and capacities of the proletariat both in Russia and abroad had proven potential rather than actual and the impersonal forces of history had proven extraordinarily sluggish in carrying the proletariat along its destined path. The proletariat also required its "legislator" or its legislative vanguard to lead it on its destined path. Lenin probably never regarded himself as the living incarnation of the proletarian will. Indeed, he was quite sincere in his effort to create an organization which would play this role. Unlike the Jacobin clubs, the Bolshevik party[15] was to be a highly articulated organization with a distinct corporate life of its own. Grippa is quite right. To Lenin, the secret of his party lay not only in the virtues of its members but also in the efficacy of its organization. When one now scrutinizes the writings of Lenin on party organization, one is struck by his vehement defense of the importance of organizational forms and well-formulated rules against all detractors of "formalism."[16] One is further struck by the fact that while Lenin's "professional revolutionaries" certainly should embody all the proletarian virtues, Lenin dwells not so much on their virtues as on their professionalism, their organizational expertise. They are trained first in the science of revolution, and then after the revolution as the technico-administrative elite of the post-revolutionary society. Lenin has shifted from "spontaneity" to "consciousness" but, as in the case of Marx, Rousseau and Saint-Simon are both present in his outlook.

Yet while Lenin was most intent on creating a party institution with its own institutional charisma, the fact remains that during his lifetime it was Lenin rather than the party who embodied the proletarian general will. Again and again he turned on his own party and found it wanting. The institution had hardly replaced the leader.

When we turn to Stalin we find that he rose to power through a manipulation of the party administrative apparatus. He thus seems to provide an instance of the "institution producing the leader." Yet the fact remains that the relationship between the leader and the party remains as problematic as ever. In the case of Stalin and his jealous greed for power, one is tempted to see a particular instance of the universal struggle between the despot and his own bureaucracy. Yet within the Marxist-Leninist context, this also involved an extreme reluctance to share with any individual or any group the enormous indivisible moral and intellectual claims attributed to the party.

In retrospect, one is tempted to add that Stalin's de facto downgrading of the party organization was due not only to his own power greed and mistrust, but also to the party's inability to fulfill the tasks which Stalin felt that the times required. The "building of socialism," with its enormous emphasis on technocratic capacities, naturally led Stalin to emphasize the "social engineering" aspect of the party function rather than its moral virtues. In fact, the party bureaucracy proved incompetent to perform in this capacity. If Mao was to find the party insufficiently red, Stalin found it insufficiently expert.

Nevertheless, while Stalin shrunk the role of the party into that of a personal machine, on the conceptual level he never veered in the slightest from the Leninist conception of the centrality of the party. He claimed to the end to derive his legitimacy from the party constitution, however much he may have flouted it in practice. What is more, he left the formal lines of party organization intact. Like Lenin, he insisted that it was the institution rather than the leader which embodied the proletarian general will. Unlike Rousseau's legislator who provides a static body of good laws for all eternity, Lenin's party is required to act within the stream of history, to provide ever fresh yet infallible guidance through all the shoals and eddies of a changing world. To admit that the party's transcendental capacities are totally dependent on the haphazard emergence of great leaders is to render its claims precarious indeed. This was appreciated by both Stalin and Lenin.

Turning finally to the Mao Tse-tung of the Cultural Revolution period, we find first that the problem of leader and institution assumes entirely new proportions, and second that the Rousseauist ethical emphasis again achieves a clear ascendancy.

The institution of the Marxist-Leninist party (as a world movement) has been in existence well over half a century. Yet in China it is now reiterated ad nauseam that the Chinese Communist party is wholly dependent for whatever proletarian charisma it may have on the leader and his thought. What is more, the qualities of the proletarian dictatorship which find their fountainhead in Mao Tse-tung may be shared by groups, institutions, and individuals which lie outside the party. Indeed the party as such, when considered apart from Mao Tse-tung and his thought, may wholly degenerate and become another "partial interest" in the Rousseauist sense. The future of Communism is not guaranteed by the existence of the party but by the "Thought of Mao Tse-tung." It is the internalization of his thought which will realize general virtue and not the existence of the party.

When we turn to Mao Tse-tung's thought itself (in its Cultural Revolutionary interpretation) we are struck by the overwhelming predominance of social-ethical elements. When viewed in a Western perspective, one must say that the Rousseauist element has pushed the Saint-Simonian technocratic element well into the background. The aged Mao is bent on achieving the reign of virtue as he understands virtue and remains unprepared to accept any progress of the arts and sciences which is not based on virtue. This does not mean that Mao is against modernization. On the contrary, during the Great Leap Forward he fervently hoped that the energy of organized virtue would itself spur economic development. Maoist virtue was to play the role of a kind of collectivistic Protestant ethic. There is, however, no reason to believe that this ethic was regarded either then or now as only a means to modernization any more than Weber's Calvinists regarded their own ethic as simply a means to economic ends.

However prominent the Rousseauist-Jacobin component in latter-day Maoism, key elements of the language remain Marxist-Leninist. "Proletariat," "bourgeoisie," "class struggle," and "dictatorship of the proletariat" are terms which occur in maddening iteration. The Maoist virtue remains "proletarian" and does not stem simply from the people or the masses. However capable the masses may be of proletarianization, however necessary it is for "proletarian revolutionaries" to be in contact with the masses, the source of proletarian virtue lies above and beyond the masses just as the word "bourgeoisie" refers to forces of egotism on a world scale. The word "proletariat" still refers to some ill-defined, trans-national, transcendental historic force and it is as the embodiment of this force that Mao confronts both his own people and the world. The Maoist dream of reconstituting a new world Communist movement centered in Peking remains indissolubly tied to this vocabulary.

We have spoken of Maoism within a Western perspective. It may well be suggested at this point that many of the dominant notions of the Cultural Revolution seem to suggest the greater cogency of a Chinese cultural perspective (in spite of the explicitly anti-traditional stance of the Maoist group). If we choose to personify ideas, may not Mencius be more relevant than Rousseau?

In early Meiji Japan as well as in early twentieth-century China, affinities were often noted between Mencius and Rousseau. Is it possible to make meaningful comparisons between the eighteenth-century political philosopher and the ancient Chinese sage? Much of the prevailing historicist and social scientific dogma would reject this possibility. Yet it seems to me that it is possible to compare the two.

To inquire why would carry us very far afield. It might simply be noted, in passing, that the ancient Chou thinkers and the eighteenth-century philosopher do, oddly enough, confront the human situation from a similar perspective, the perspective of vicarious statesmen who have prescriptions for "society" as a whole.

One is immediately struck by certain similarities in the relationship of ethics to the political realm. As in the case of Rousseau, the majority of men in Mencius are potentially good (they possess the roots [*tuan*] of goodness) but seem incapable of realizing their goodness through their own efforts. In both cases the unfavorable social environment negates the possibility of such realization. In both cases the people's ethical potentialities can be realized only through political mediation. Yet Mencius manages to avoid many of the enigmas surrounding Rousseau's abstract conception of the general will of the people. The moralizing agency of his society is clearly an ethical elite and the superiority of this elite resides in the moral superiority of its individual members who are somehow able to actualize through individual self-effort their own potential virtue and wisdom.[17] Unlike the mass of mankind, these *chün-tzu* are able to realize their own potentialities by "following that part of themselves which is great."[18] They are able to transcend their environment and are thus also able to transform the people below them through the power of example, education and proper policy. Thus Mencius accepts the principle of hierarchy gladly and without hesitation.

Rousseau, on the other hand, sets out from a rejection of hierarchy. His ideal society is one in which all citizens fully participate as "free" and equal citizens on the idealized ancient Roman model. The attainment of the ideal is immediately cast into doubt, however, by all sorts of tragic dilemmas. There is not only the dilemma raised in the question, "How can the multitude which often does not know what it wants because only rarely does it know what is for its own good undertake an enterprise so extensive and so difficult as the formulation of a system of laws?"[19] Mencius himself might have recognized this dilemma. There is also, however, Rousseau's clear realization that princes, magistrates, and all those who govern (the "executive power") are made of the same clay as the people. Rousseau can solve his dilemmas only by introducing the deus ex machina of the transcendent legislator, that rare genius of unaccountable "greatness of soul" who is able to create a system of general laws which educates the people to virtue.[20] Rousseau is, after all, an heir to Western legalism and ultimately seems to believe in the rule of law. It is the law itself which plays a determining role in forming the general will.[21]

With the Jacobins, however, this sharp distinction between the legislative and executive breaks down and Robespierre must represent the general will as both legislator and magistrate. In Leninism it survives in the feeble guise of party constitutionality and legality. Here, however, we perceive the enormous contradiction between Rousseau's intentions and the unintended uses to which his doctrines have lent themselves.

When we turn to Mencius's account of the famous sage-rulers Yao, Shun, and Yü, we find that the distinction between legislator and prince does not exist. These mythic figures are in a sense "legislators" in that they create or make manifest the sacred institutional framework of society, but they are also the active rulers of society who stand high above the institutions which they have formed. The institutions are simply the channels through which they spread their spiritual-ethical influence. The Confucian tradition even in its Mencian interpretation is hardly anti-formalistic. Even to Mencius, the virtues of rulers and of the *chün-tzu* must be channelled through an institutional setting and find their objective expression in the rules of propriety. Yet in Mencius it is not the institutions which mold the sage-rulers and the men of virtue; it is the sage-rulers and *chün-tzu* who irradiate their ethical power through the institutions.

When one examines the idiom of the Cultural Revolution one somehow feels that the untroubled image of Mao as the fountainhead of all morality, standing high above all laws and institutions, may owe more to certain Chinese cultural perspectives than to any Western source of inspiration. One feels this also in the tremendous emphasis on the power of example attributed to such paragons as Lei Feng and Men Ho, who may be men of the people but who are nevertheless capable of heroic acts of ethical self-transcendence. Again, they are capable of these acts only because they draw inspiration from the ruler-sage himself.

One is further tempted to speculate that even the aged Mao's anti-formalism and anti-institutionalism may have their indigenous roots in the heterodox strains of the Chinese heroic *(yu-hsia)* tradition so vividly expressed in the epic novels which were his favorite childhood reading. Here we find the heroic bands of blood-brothers fighting for the right under leaders recognized by all for their natural qualities of leadership. The ties which bind here are not the institutional forms of the corrupt traditional establishment but the moral cement of shared sentiments. These literary images must blend easily in the leader's mind with the actual experience of the Hunan-Kiangsi and Yenan days.

In all of this the Chinese perspective may explain much which cannot be explained in terms of a purely Western perspective. There are, however, areas in which the particular Chinese perspectives and the particular Western perspectives, far from being mutually exclusive, prove to be mutually reinforcing. There are also areas where only the Western perspective can adequately account for a new reality. The concept of the masses as active and total participants in the whole politic process (whatever may be the actual situation) has, of course, become an essential part of the "Thought of Mao Tse-tung." As in the case of Rousseau, Mao Tse-tung's masses are the masses not necessarily as they are but as they "ought to be" and there can be no doubt of the leader's aspiration to make them what they ought to be. They are to be made public-spirited and their virtue is no longer to be passive and negative, but active and dynamic. It is to be a moral energy consolidated in the service of the nation. What is more, this moral energy is to be unified in a positive aggressive struggle against all the forces of evil. Here both the nationalist motif of Rousseau and transnational image of Marxism-Leninism are united into one.

One could go on in this scrutiny of Western and Chinese perspectives. Perhaps of more pertinence than the question of cultural origin is the fact that we are here dealing with issues that have now assumed a transcultural significance. Some Westerners profess to find in the Mao of the Cultural Revolution (by a painfully selective interpretation) answers to their own discontents pointing to this transcultural dimension. On the one hand they respond to the Maoist anti-institutionalism and anti-formalism. On the other, they respond to the Rousseauist emphasis on morality in reaction to the preponderantly technocratic version of the theory of progress. In responding to their version of Mao, they are thus drawing upon elements of their own cultural past.

14

A Personal View of Some Thoughts of Mao Tse-tung

*D*uring the turbulent years that have just passed, many of those involved in the study of contemporary China have been challenged to reveal whether they are for or against the "Chinese Revolution" and have been summoned to abandon forthwith the sham posture of "objectivity." The challenge was, of course, a reflection of the more general attack on the notions of objectivity and neutrality in the fields of human and social studies.

It seems to me that certain "social scientific" conceptions of objectivity are indeed vulnerable to this attack. There are still those on the academic scene who continue to believe that they approach experience with an assumptionless tabula rasa. When they employ "hypothetical models," they would have us believe that their choice of model has nothing to do with previously held tacit assumptions or general perspectives. Yet such models are never chosen at random out of the infinite realm of possibility: they are chosen because they seem promising, and they generally seem promising because they conform to previously held views of how the world hangs together. Humans of any degree of intelligence do not approach a vast area of human experience such as contemporary China with the Lockean blank sheet. They bring to their work their accumulated perspectives, both conscious and unconscious; and these perspectives certainly do not all derive directly and strictly from conclusions based on precise empirical evidence, but from a variety of sources and a total life experience. This is hardly the place to plunge into the bottomless pit of genetic sociological or psychological theories of life-views, and it will suffice simply to note that all of us without exception have such assumptions, perspectives, and orientations. Indeed, they must exist if thought is to take place.

I would nevertheless maintain that none of this precludes the legitimacy of an aspiration to a certain definition of objectivity or to *Verstehen* in the Weberian sense. There are certain canons governing the validity of empirical evidence that can be accepted as norms by persons of the most varied assumptions and perspectives. One must thus accept the principles that assumptions may be undermined or seriously modified by empirical evidence and that empirical evidence contrary to one's assumptions must be accounted for. One may still aspire to consider all the empirical data that may be relevant to one's subject and to achieve an accurate understanding of contrary views concerning the same subject. One may also aspire to achieve an understanding of the orientations and life-views that are quite different from one's own.

Thus the type of interpretative writing that refrains from constant explicit reference to one's own premises and "value judgments" remains perfectly justified. The perceptive reader may discern the dialectic interplay between the author's perspectives and values and his treatment of the particular subject matter at hand. The fact that such assumptions have been discerned by no means invalidates the analysis. The reader must, in the end, judge whether the assumptions of the author have led to or inhibited fruitful understanding. In general, a straightforward analysis is much more worthwhile than a constant hammering on one's own "value judgments" concerning the experience at hand. And yet there may be occasions when the direct confrontation of one's own judgments may be an exercise in intellectual self-clarification.

I do not propose in this brief article to pass any blanket judgment on that vast unfinished human experience known as the "Chinese Revolution," since I remain utterly unconvinced that it is the kind of unitary entity which can be simply affirmed or negated. What we are dealing with are some twenty years of the history of mainland China. During this period the People's Republic has undergone many shifts and turns, experienced many crises and many upheavals in leadership. At times the leadership has itself harshly condemned previous lines of policy which have received the blanket endorsement of those abroad who believe that the "revolution" must invariably receive total approval at any given point in time. It is thus quite possible to acknowledge the undeniable accomplishments of the People's Republic in many areas without making a total commitment to the "Chinese Revolution" and particularly without accepting all of Mao Tse-tung's claims as a political and moral philosopher.

What I propose to deal with is not the Chinese Revolution but certain themes in the "Thought of Mao Tse-tung," particularly in their "Cultural Revolutionary" development. While these themes derive out of the matrix of his previous ideas, in their Cultural Revolutionary version they assume a particularly polarized form.

I shall not concern myself with the question of whether Mao is an "original" moral and political philosopher. It is probably quite true that if he had not achieved power, few of us would be interested in his metaphysical or moral-political philosophy. Yet the fact that those with political power are able to attempt to implement their ideas will always lend a peculiar interest to them. What is more, the ideas themselves concern issues fundamental not only to China but perhaps fundamental to all of us. In challenging the dogma that differences of culture and differences of "stages of development" preclude any sort of mutual relevance of thought or any kind of involvement in a common world of issues, Western admirers of Mao, whatever their limitations, have performed a distinct service.

Incidentally, the question of whether Mao's "Cultural Revolutionary" vision is relevant only to China's present condition (or, broadly speaking, to the condition of "underdeveloped societies") or raises more universal questions is one that divides the defenders of the Cultural Revolutionary vision as well as the skeptics. Among them one can distinguish what might be called the "tough-minded" and the true disciples. The true disciples believe that all of Mao's words are to be taken at face value; the "tough-minded" believe in an exoteric and esoteric Maoist doctrine. In the latter's view, Mao, like all sensible leaders, is interested mainly in "modernization" as this term is understood in the West. He is fundamentally a theorist of economic development. He realizes that in a woefully capital-poor country such as China one must lean heavily on labor intensivity and hence he appeals to selflessness, austerity, and infinite self-sacrifice—to "moral incentives"—as the only way to mobilize the masses. As a consummate social engineer Mao knows quite well that this morality of sacrifice and collectivity is an interim, instrumental morality, that

modernization will in the end lead to a society in which the dominant goals of life will be consumer pleasures and the pursuit of status; but he thinks of all these matters as a hard-headed strategist of
development. He is, as it were, self-consciously creating his own version of a Protestant ethic.

Yet it is precisely this parallel to the notion of the Protestant ethic
that leads one to ask questions about this whole approach. Neither
Calvin nor his successors were strategists of development. They sincerely believed that their ethic was tied to man's eternal salvation
and they were entirely unconcerned with the achievement of wealth
as a "spin-off" effect. Nothing could have been further from their vision than an interest in economic development. Indeed, if they had
believed in the supremacy of the goals of economic development,
they would have speedily abandoned their ethic of salvation. In his
own exposition of this doctrine, Max Weber argued that the economic benefits of the Protestant ethic were unintentional.

Mao's Cultural Revolutionary vision is explicitly committed to economic development and national power and even to the view that the
Maoist ethic will spur on such development. This, however, by no
means proves that Mao does not profoundly believe in his own image
of the Cultural Revolutionary ethic as an ultimate end in itself. In certain varieties of Western liberalism, it has been argued simultaneously
that individualism is good because it spurs economic enterprise and
that individualism is good as an end in itself. The same may be
equally true of Maoist collectivism. Thus in treating two themes of
Mao's thought I shall accept the interpretation of the true disciples,
who believe that Mao desires "modernization" but only the kind of
modernization that can be achieved within the context of his vision of
the good society. Finally, in dealing with these themes I shall not be
concerned with the motives of Mao's behavior in the Cultural Revolution nor with the question of what relationship his doctrines bear to
the actualities of Chinese politics in 1972, a time of a somewhat muf-
fled retreat from any of the doctrines here described.

The Maoist Conception of Science

What I here call the Maoist conception of science is an element of
the Cultural Revolutionary syndrome that goes back at least as far as
Yenan and perhaps has its roots in Mao's earliest contacts with the

concept of science in the writings of Yen Fu, Liang Ch'i-ch'ao, and popular tracts of the early twentieth century. At first approach, this concept of science seems to be based on an inductive-pragmatic view common in the Anglo-American world. It is essentially a Baconian concept which emphasizes the centrality of induction from the observation of concrete facts, as well as "learning by doing." This view of science is related by Mao to the simple epistemology which we find in "On Practice." Concepts are immediately derived from percepts in the course of man's social practice and then immediately applied in practice. Mao, of course, shares with other Marxist-Leninists the conviction that the word "science" is just as applicable to the "truths of Marxism-Leninism" as to the truths of natural science. Thus, the epistemology of science described in "On Practice" is apparently equally applicable to the social history of man and to the natural sciences, despite the considerable differences in the modalities of application in those two spheres. This conception of science harmonizes nicely with many other themes of both the Yenan and Cultural Revolutionary syndromes. Above all, it involves an element of populism. If science is basically a matter of learning from immediate practical experiences, it should be a kind of common sense accessible to all. Here one may even find similarities between Mao's linkage of science to populism and John Dewey's linkage of his experimental-pragmatic view of science to democracy.

On its negative side, this view of science becomes a weapon for attacking those intellectuals who believe in the possibility of separating conceptual reasoning from immediate reference to the perceptual. They believe in the possibility of arriving at truth through sustained abstract ratiocination divorced from immediate practical experience. They are also excessively addicted to book learning. Both the belief in the dynamic fruitfulness of abstract thought separated from immediate reference to concrete practice and the heavy reliance on past experience mediated through books involve the possibility that an intellectual cloistered in his study and divorced from political activity may independently arrive at truth.

Two questions face us at this point. To what extent is this view of science consistently maintained and to what extent is it valid? We will find that the first question is particularly relevant to Mao's view of the "science" of social history and to the supposedly populist implications of this view.

It might be illuminating at this point to compare Mao with
Dewey. As we know, in spite of Mao's insistence on deriving truth
from concrete situations, as in the case of Lenin and Stalin, "empiricism" is a bad word in his lexicon. Empiricism involves the failure to
place newly experienced concrete situations within the pre-established
framework of the "universal truths of Marxism-Leninism." (By now,
we can perhaps add the "universal truths of the thought of Mao Tse-
tung.") John Dewey also occasionally attacked the word "empiricism." What he meant by it was what he regarded as the "abstract"
empiricism of Locke and Hume,[1] which attempted to reduce experience to universal elements, namely, sensations. To Dewey, experience is made up of complex unique concrete situations. He objects to
a "logic of general notions under which specific situations are to be
brought" and is not prepared to admit the existence of any pre-
established universal truth which may not be upset or modified by
any new situation. All people, once equipped by education with scientific intelligence, will be able to solve the problems in their own situation in terms of those situations. They need not assume in advance
that any a priori universal truth necessarily applies. The conclusions
concerning the relations of general notions to specific situations will
be drawn by those involved.

In Marxism-Leninism (including Mao's version of Marxism-
Leninism), pre-established universal truths about the world as a
whole certainly do exist. In Mao's thought there are some truths that
are not only universal but even eternal, such as the famous "laws of
contradiction." Other truths concerning the "laws of history" are
not eternal but in principle universal during their period of application. Mao informs us that Marx himself arrived at his "universal
truths" from "detailed investigations and studies in the course of
practical struggle."[2] Leaving aside the fact that most of the investigations and studies involved in *Das Kapital* took place in the dusty
bookish archives of the British Museum at a time when Marx was
most minimally involved in "practical struggles" (other than his personal struggles to support his family), there remains the old philosophic problem of how universal, necessary truth can be derived inductively from what must always be partial and contingent empirical
data. In fact, some of the large universal categories of Marxism-
Leninism derive from Hegel, who firmly believed that his major categories were based on a general contemplation of the total nature of

the universe and not merely based on atomic empirical observations or "learning by doing."

Quite apart from the question of whether all the universal truths of Marxism-Leninism have been derived inductively, there is also the thorny question of who is authorized to relate pre-established universal truths to the specificities of new particular situations. The Leninist answer is that only the party has this authority, while Mao informs us that "our comrades who are engaged in practical work must realize that their knowledge is mostly perceptual and partial and that they lack rational and comprehensive knowledge."[3] It is thus quite obvious that those who gather perceptual knowledge are not necessarily the same persons as those who derive the new rational and comprehensive concepts from this knowledge. It must be borne in mind that in the cases of Lenin, Stalin, and Mao the application of universal truth to concrete new situations generally involves the modification and constriction of previously-held universal truths and hence a denial of their universality. Lenin and Stalin (however different they may have been from each other), no less than Mao, constantly spoke of "applying and extending" pre-established theory to new, unanticipated experience. In this sense they are all three "empiricists" and "pragmatists." Like Mao, both Lenin and Stalin applied the truths recorded in the canonical books to "life." Thus the party, or the current leadership of the party, or the Leader come to have the exclusive authority to interpret universal truths and to forge the linkage between the universal truth and the new lessons derived from new perceptual experience. What is involved is nothing less than the awesome authority to reinterpret preexisting universal propositions.

Thus at the heart of the Yenan *cheng-feng* (rectification) debates between Mao and those to whom he referred as "dogmatists" among the Communist intellectuals and cadres was not simply the question of whether truth is to be derived from pre-established truth and books or from direct, perceptual, "practical" experience. To the extent that Mao spoke of the universal truths of Marxism-Leninism he was referring to truths recorded in books. In essence he was placing the authority of the church to interpret the sacred scriptures above the scriptures themselves. He was by no means asserting that every man in the village has the right to interpret the scriptures in the light of his own "partial" reading of perceptual experience. It is

probably true that Mao's reading of Chinese political and social realities in the Yenan period may have been generally more accurate
than that of many of those whom he attacked, but embedded in his
remolding speeches was the claim that the task of "synthesizing the
experience of the masses into better articulated principles and methods" was the exclusive prerogative of the "correct" political leadership—correct not only because it could base its inductions on a
broad view of the experiential landscape from the mountaintop but
because it knew *how* to relate pre-established universal truths to new
experience.

It may be maintained that Mao's inductive-pragmatic view of science is far less ambiguous and problematic when applied to the natural sciences themselves.[4] Here one might say that the populist implications are unambiguously clear. The man in the village or factory is
unable to relate his own immediate "partial" experience to the total
sociopolitical world and to the course of social history, but he is,
after all, in immediate contact with physical nature. A worker or
group of workers in contact with a machine may indeed be able to
discover ways of improving it, and new inventions have been made
by artisans down through the ages through "empiric" methods. To
the extent that one identifies the history of science with the history of
technological progress before the scientific revolution (and even to
some extent after the scientific revolution), Mao's conception of
"science" remains cogent. Indeed, as Joseph Needham has insisted,
China may well have been in the vanguard for centuries in terms of
this empirical mode of technological advance.

A more fundamental question than any we have yet considered is
whether the Maoist conception is valid when applied to the science
that has emerged from the scientific revolution. A layman's reading
of many contemporary historians and philosophers of science such
as Alexandre Koyré, Karl Popper, Stephen Toulmin, and Thomas
Kuhn would suggest that the cutting edge of the scientific revolution
in the "hard sciences" was not first and foremost the inductive
method, accurate and exhaustive observation, or even experimentation as such, but the construction of fruitful deductive hypotheses of
a logico-mathematical nature. Observation, experiment, and "practice" are crucial to the process of verification but not, we are told, to
the process of discovery.

The ability of the human mind to abstract itself from immediate reference to concrete experience, its ability to conceptualize, and to engage in sustained reflection and ratiocination are crucial elements not only in science but in intellectual endeavor in general. Indeed, to the extent that Mao Tse-tung is inclined to treat literature as a kind of applied science of social engineering, one must add that it is also true of the creative imagination. Mathematics, having played an enormous role in the scientific revolution, furnishes us with the paradigm case. To be sure, the scientific discoverer must in his reflection constantly refer to a vast accumulation of acquired human experience, but much of this experience may well be mediated through memory and books. The plain fact is that an Einstein could accomplish most of what he did apart from immediate practical experience.

One can still make an argument for many of Mao's maxims concerning intellectuals on social ethical grounds, and such arguments have been made in many times and places. Intellection may become a self-contained scholasticism; people in the academy may lose the capacity to see the relationship between the printed word in books and the realities which they mediate. On the other hand, people involved in "social practice" may flatter themselves in the illusion that their social practice constantly reconfirms their general maxims when in fact it does nothing of the sort. Intellectuals may be enormously arrogant and may use the social advantage derived from their claims to knowledge to achieve special privilege. Whether they are more inclined to these infirmities of the flesh than "practical" revolutionary politicians whose social advantage derives from their positions in the political vanguard is, of course, questionable. Something may also be said for the view that in China in particular, with its long tradition of divorce of the literati from physical labor, some direct contact with physical labor may have some sort of wholesome effect; but whether it has all the intellectual and even moral effects attributed to it may well be questioned. It can also be argued that what a poor China requires of science is not so much theoretical discovery as practical application. Finally, the notion that in a vast and poverty-stricken country one should train large numbers of paraprofessional medical and technical personnel without insisting on a full mastery of the theoretical foundations of a given scientific discipline is a notion with considerable merit, even if it does not vindicate Mao's ideas concerning the foundations of modern science.

The main point at issue is whether truths concerning society and the cosmos can be discovered by people in libraries, and laboratories—people who do not occupy a position within or close to the present constellation of leadership. Viewing the whole matter from a somewhat negative perspective, the notion that truth can be discovered in this way challenges the leadership's monopoly of the privilege of "synthesizing the experiences of the masses into better articulated principles and methods." The present Maoist philosophy of education is designed to make education as strictly applied and practical as possible. While this again may be defended on the grounds of practical necessity, it also presumably reflects Mao's Baconian-pragmatic view of science. As for the synthetic universal principles required by the masses, they will, of course, be derived from the thought of Mao Tse-tung or whoever happens to be in a ruling position. The masses may thus be shielded against the corrupting effects of wrong "syntheses" derived from illegitimate sources.

On Bureaucracy and Domination

There is no element of Mao's Cultural Revolutionary vision that has had more appeal among many in the West than his attack on bureaucracy and on organizations in general. While the capitalist societies of the West have been a primary target, some of the most subversive implications of his doctrine apply not only to the Soviet Union as an ongoing society but also to pre-existent Marxist-Leninist doctrine in general. Mao has returned to a position long shared by liberals and anarchists—namely, that the kind of social power and privilege deriving from the occupation of positions within a political institution or bureaucracy can be as primary and as autonomous a source of oppression, domination, and exploitation as the social power and privilege deriving from the possession of private property. We are now told that the bureaucrat who sits in his office shuffling papers (as the intellectual sits in his study perusing books) may be as far removed from the interests of the masses as the Western owner of property. The current Chinese doctrine concerning the capture of the Soviet state by the "bourgeoisie" is the confirmation of this doctrine. It obviously does not rest on the assumption that there exists in the Soviet Union a large class of people whose power rests on the private ownership of the means of production. As in so much of Mao's use of Marxist vocabulary, words are emptied of their concrete socioeconomic meaning and given largely moral references. The potent word "bourgeois" now simply means exploitative, oppressive, selfish, and so forth. The new "bourgeoisie" of the Soviet Union has been able to achieve its position precisely through the control of the organizational levers provided by party and state.

If we look back to all the writings of Marx himself, the issue is never simple. There is actually one strain of Marxist thought that stresses the primacy and autonomy of political power—namely, the theory of Asian society. According to this theory, political organization—at least in Asia—was itself a primary class-forming agency of society. The question of what implications Marx drew from his theory of Asian society for the analysis of political power in the West remains a moot point. It seems to me that Marx simply did not think through the possible implications. It certainly did not prevent the predominance of a "vulgar Marxism" in which political power was treated as strictly "superstructural" and in which governments were treated as the "executive committees" of the ruling class. Again, the Marxist social democratic parties of the late nineteenth century, including the Mensheviks in Russia, insisted that their parties be organized along the lines of democratic constitutionalism. They by no means disdained the "machinery" of political democracy within their parties (despite the centralized, highly bureaucratic nature of the German Social Democratic party). No pre-established harmony was assumed between vanguard and rearguard such as would render superfluous the machinery of constitutional controls of leadership. It was, on the contrary, sincerely believed that because the party represented the harmonious general will of the industrial proletariat, it would be precisely within the social democratic party that political democracy would find its true realization. It was such Mensheviks as the early Trotsky and Martov who immediately suspected a tendency in Lenin to create a new bureaucratic elite, and it was probably their Russian environment that made it difficult for them to deprecate the social reality of bureaucratic power.

By the same token, it was precisely the Leninist strain within the Marxist movement that was most inclined to minimize the separate reality of political power and to emphasize its entirely "superstructural" nature, thereby invoking the vulgar Marxist notion that the state ruling power is merely the executive committee of the ruling classes. From this Stalin was later able to conclude that in any society, without the private ownership of the means of production, the existing state power—whatever its organization—necessarily represents the proletariat. Before his death Lenin had had some dark premonitions concerning the resurgence of bureaucratic power, but he seemingly allowed himself to be comforted by the thought that the proletariat occupied the heights of power and that the party continued to be the "virtual representative" organ of the proletariat.

Even under Stalin we find routine critiques of bureaucratism. But the attacks were directed mainly against the inertia and incompetence of party bureaucrats rather than their caste privileges and power to oppress; on the whole, the benign and "superstructural" nature of the new elite structure was stressed. Even the hounded Trotsky remained sufficiently imprisoned within his own post-October Leninism to refuse to admit the emergence of a "new class" in the Soviet Union.

Yet the Mao Tse-tung of the Cultural Revolution, like Milovan Djilas *(ceteris paribus),* seems to accept the notion of a possible new class. The kind of access to power and privilege that divides the occupants of party and government from the "masses" is by no means less real than the kind of access to power and privilege created by "relations of property." One may indeed use that most powerful epithet, "bourgeois," to describe both.

In the case of Djilas, this notion leads directly to a rehabilitation of all the tenets of constitutional democracy. If political power is a primary and formidable source of oppression and exploitation, the machinery created by constitutional democracy with the aim of checking political power and making it accountable resumes its full validity. If the machinery is defective and fallible, it should simply be improved and made more effective.

In the case of Mao, it need hardly be pointed out that constitutional democracy plays hardly any role in his mental universe—and probably less during the Cultural Revolution than ever before. The machinery of constitutional democracy is, after all, machinery, and the spirit of the Cultural Revolutionary vision is skeptical of institutional machinery of all types. In the discussions of party-building that have taken place in the last few years and in the documents of the Ninth Party Congress, we actually find a weakening of the electoral machinery that has survived as a kind of ghost of constitutionalism within the Soviet-type Communist Party. This has even led to

Soviet attacks on Maoist leadership for undermining the "norms of intra-party democracy" within the Leninist constitution of the party.

Anarchism is the other major modern response to the perception that political power and organization are themselves a social basis of class domination. Nineteenth-century anarchism, when it did not simply call for an apocalyptic annihilation of all authority, tended to advocate the destruction of the nation-state and the creation of a network of small communitarian societies in which direct democracy would prevail to the extent that political organization was required at all. One of the influences behind this variety of anarchism was the doctrine of Montesquieu and Rousseau that democracy in any true sense of the term was only possible in something on the scale of a city-state.

The Paris Commune, which has played a distinct role in the writings of Marx and Lenin and which was invoked in China during both the Great Leap Forward and the Cultural Revolution, was in many ways an embodiment of certain nineteenth-century anarchist ideas. The accidental fact that its government was confined to Paris was precisely what made its anarcho-communitarian character possible, although Proudhonians and other varieties of anarchists also played a role in it. The acid test of whether it would have remained anarchist would have been faced if the Paris Communal government had extended its sway over France as a whole—a test it would probably not have met. In summarizing Marx's complex attitude to the commune, one might say that his passing enthusiasm for it was largely based on what he regarded as its revelation that a revolution in Europe was still possible as well as on its similarities to his own vaguely articulated anarchistic utopia.[5] To Lenin, the Paris Commune had a narrow polemical meaning: it proved that there could be no peaceable transition from capitalism to socialism and that the "old state machine must be smashed." The question of whether there was anything in the commune that prefigured a centralized, bureaucratic organization like the Communist party is one he simply fails to consider.

In the case of the Maoist invocation of the Paris Commune, particularly at the time of the Great Leap Forward, one can perhaps discern a tendency to call upon some of its more anarchist implications. The communes of 1958 were depicted as being ideally autonomous cells of society which would carry on agricultural, industrial, cultural, and even military activities in a self-sufficient, highly autonomous way, thus greatly reducing the tasks of the central state organs. Their existence would lead to an enormous reduction in the size of the state bureaucratic apparatus, particularly in the agrarian sector. It must not be forgotten, however, that the centrifugal tendencies inherent in the image of the commune were to be quite effectively counterbalanced by the centripetal and unifying tendencies of the party organization; even in 1958 the party was ideally portrayed as being made up not of bureaucrats but of dedicated cadres. The unity of the party, unlike the unity of the state, was not to be simply a function of its bureaucratic organization but of the selfless discipline of its individual cadre members who would be effective local leaders while maintaining their unquestioning loyalty to the authority of the center. Nothing could have been further from Mao's mind than the disintegration of China as a unified national society. Indeed, the tasks of the party as an integrating nervous system would become heavier than ever.[6]

The Cultural Revolution goes much further. Here we seemingly have an attack not only on the state bureaucracy and organization but on the organic body of the party itself. In spite of all the remolding of the previous years, the party had, in Mao's eyes, proven itself susceptible to the same bureaucratic diseases as the state apparatus. Thus, the invocation of the Paris Commune under such circumstances would seem to have much more radically anarchist implications than during the Great Leap Forward. Indeed, some of the younger and more precipitous Cultural Revolutionaries leaped to the conclusion in 1967 that Mao was in effect calling for the abolition of the whole national apparatus of state and party and for the implementation of the anarcho-communitarian Paris Commune ideal. In fact, there is no reason to believe that Mao had ever accepted this idea or ever wavered in his belief that within the national society there should be a central, supreme authority—a "center"—with overwhelming decision-making power. One might say that in early 1967 he had, in his own person, become the living embodiment of this central authority, although even then he relied on the mobilization of his Cultural Revolutionary vanguard, the Red Guards, with the People's Revolutionary Army already lurking in the background. When the Red Guards proved susceptible to "anarchist" tendencies and the vicious "theory of many centers," he thus came to lean very heavily on that other crucial pillar of support of central authority, the People's Liberation Army.

Mao is, in fact, no anarchist. He has consistently followed his belief in vanguard leadership and political authority, both central and local. Since he obviously believes in the continued existence of China as a cohesive national society, he has never wavered in his conviction that the vanguard leadership must have a center of ultimate authority, just as in the Sino-Soviet polemics he always insisted that a Communist bloc ought to have a spiritual center. In all the discussions of the dissolution of the division of labor in human society, in all the aspirations for the development of a man who will be simultaneously peasant, worker, soldier, and intellectual, Mao has not questioned the need for the ongoing division of labor between leaders and led.[7] The attack on bureaucratic machinery and highly articulate hierarchic organization does not necessarily imply the rejection of a ruling elite. One may simply dream of a ruling elite whose authority is rooted in the moral and intellectual quality of its members rather than in their organizational positions and functions.

Mao Tse-tung, like others in the Chinese Communist leadership, has concerned himself more than Communist leaders elsewhere with the problem of the territorial distribution of power within the state, with those problems of central versus local government that constitute a staple concern of Western "bourgeois" political theory. Mao obviously dreams of a local leadership that will be creative, take initiatives, exercise independent judgment, and be close to the masses, even while maintaining a profound loyalty to the policies of the center. This concern with local grass-roots government may reflect many of the particularities of Chinese Communist history. It does not imply any anarchist proclivities. The rather unexpected praise that the Chairman recently expressed in his interview with Edgar Snow for American techniques of local government—however seriously meant—would indicate how far he is from a rejection of the nation-state structure.

If one recognizes the sinister potentialities of political power as such and yet rejects the liberal democratic and anarchist ways of dealing with those potentialities, how then does one cope with the corruptions of power? The answer provided by Mao is a very ancient one and one with a long Chinese past: one moralizes the holders of power. The very language used to describe the virtues one wishes to attain in the power-holder is itself very ancient. One wants leaders who will be servants rather than masters, who will sacrifice themselves for the collectivity, live austerely, be humble, constantly scrutinize their own behavior, and be open to criticism. Yet, if the answer is ancient, it is nevertheless true that some of the methods suggested to achieve these ends are indeed new.

Both Western liberals and anarchists would be inclined to reject out of hand the notion that the problem is one of moralizing the holders of power. The whole rhetoric of moral improvement is alien to their discourse. Indeed, as Djilas has shown, liberals would be more inclined to feel that the rediscovery of the autonomous malignancy of political power vindicates the long effort to create effective constitutional machinery designed to check political power and render it accountable. And yet, as we are well aware, Western liberalism has its own problems. Not only do there remain vast concentrations of private power which are hardly subject to effective accountability, but the needs of the nation-state have created vast and distant bureaucratic machinery and executive power which are accountable in only the most indirect and long-term way. While many who call themselves liberals have been quite impervious to the belief in a moral elite, they have not been equally impervious to the belief in a technocratic elite—that is, the belief that many of the problems of modern society must be handled by "scientific" experts. There is an easy acceptance of the notion that such experts are wholly dedicated to the imperatives of their science, as well as an easy acceptance of their competence as scientists. Since they are ultimately accountable, the question of their corruption and abuse of power does not arise. Relatively speaking, liberal democracy has probably been more successful in the area of civil liberties than in creating an iron-clad machinery for assuring the accountability of power. The devices of corruption and abuse of power have proven more ingenious than the machinery designed to control them. Thus the machinery of political democracy has by no means rendered irrelevant the ancient and tragic question of the corruptions of power and domination. Conversely, one might add that a recognition of the reality of the fateful problem of political power may also vindicate the ongoing efforts to control power by constitutional machinery.

We are by now fairly familiar with the Maoist methods of moralization. The holders of power must not be separated from the masses. They must be in constant *gemeinschaftlich* contact with them. Higher cadres must constantly be "sent down" from their offices to learn from the masses. There must be a constant and unremitting inculcation of the Maoist ethic of self-sacrifice, self-abnegation, and so forth, and words must be closely tied to practice and immediate application. Administration must be simplified as far as possible. The local cadre must be subject to constant scrutiny by others who are constantly judging his performance. "Participation in labor" is felt to have especially powerful moralizing effects. Finally, the masses, who will have been thoroughly imbued with a Maoist ethic, will themselves exercise a moral control over their leaders. Furthermore, the aim is not only moralization but also effectiveness, and here we see how the Maoist concept of science neatly meshes with his methods of moralization. The cadre, by being in constant touch with the immediate local practice, learns from actual experience how to apply the general line to local affairs.

One of the first questions that arises here is, how simple can administration be in a regime that aspires to become a "rich and powerful" nation-state? Has Mao disproven Weber on bureaucracy? To what extent can any state that aspires to exercise authority over vast territories eliminate the tendency to bureaucratic differentiation and the chain of command? This is by no means a new problem of "modernization." It is a problem inherent in the effort to exercise authority over long distances, and the tendency toward division of labor in government rises out of the same imperatives as the division of labor in general. Given the goal of extensive control over vast territories, the time and energy of men can be most effectively used by specializing their activities rather than by leaving them diffuse. This specialization also inevitably involves hierarchy and chain of command. Ever since bureaucratic government has existed, men have bewailed its pathologies—the Parkinson effect, the inertia, red tape, the Kafka-like distance of the administrator from the administered, and the more common abuses and corruptions of power. In China there is a vast heritage of literature on all these topics. Indeed, among many Confucian thinkers there was a recurring call for "simplification of administration," although not, of course, for "sending down" officials to the village. In the vast sector of Chinese society that remains agrarian, the local cadres may indeed continue to be closer to the ideal of "all-around men." It would, however, be quite

misleading to confuse the question of bureaucratic specialization
with the question of hierarchy and domination. So long as the ambition exists to maintain vast territorial control from the center, so
long as the modern ambition to extend the "wealth and power" of
the nation is added to the traditional aims of the maintenance of
peace and order, it will not prove possible to do without large-scale
organization or to ignore the fact that it is more effective to employ
the bulk of some individuals' energies and time in offices rather than
"in the field."

If we can believe Mao Tse-tung's recent remarks to Edgar Snow, it
is clear that he did not support either the extreme radicalization of
foreign policy or the attack on the apparatus of the foreign
policy–making machinery in 1967. The fact is that those leftist Cultural Revolutionaries who did opt for a radicalization of foreign policy had every reason to think that they were drawing the necessary
consequences of Mao's Cultural Revolutionary doctrine. The whole
existing international world system itself embodied all those vices of
bureaucratism that Mao had attacked. The diplomatic corps and
even the foreign policy specialists in Peking were that part of the bureaucracy most clearly out of touch with the masses and perhaps the
most vulnerable to "bourgeois" degeneration. If Mao himself believes that it is to the strategic advantage of the People's Republic of
China to maintain a dynamic and outgoing posture within the present framework of world politics, he must insist that China's foreign
policy specialists, diplomats, and trade officials spend a maximum
amount of their time and energies in exercising their taxing skills. He
clearly seems to accept the whole elaborate protocol of the present
system of international dealing, with its pomp, ceremonial airport re-
ceptions, limousine caravans, cocktail parties, and banquets. There
may still be some practice of *hsia-fang* (going down to the countryside) in the foreign policy organs of government, but no evidence
that the trend within these organs is toward the simplification of administration.

One suspects that if this is true of foreign policy organs, it is probably also true for other bureaucratic sectors. An anarchist might
point to the contradictions involved in an effort to enforce the
Maoist formulas for the moralization of power among the lower-
echelon cadres while neglecting such techniques on the highest level.

One might ask whether a more unstructured power operating in close proximity to the masses is necessarily more benign than the power of distant bureaucrats. There is here a tendency to confuse domination with bureaucratic organization. The leader of an unstructured gang may surely be as dominant as a bureaucrat in an office. The fact is that, in the broad sweep of human history, men have suffered as much—if not more—from the oppression and brutality of immediate overseers, foremen, and corvée heads as of the distant bureaucrats. On the other hand, it has often been pointed out that in China and elsewhere despots have been hostile to bureaucracy because of the constraints it places on the exercise of arbitrary power from above. Certainly, if the authority of the local power-holder is entirely dependent on the local community as envisaged in communitarian anarchism, he will be entirely beholden to the local community.

Yet, as we have seen, the central Maoist Cultural Revolutionary doctrine never abandoned the notion of the subordination of local powerholders to higher instances of authority and to decisions made from above. Indeed, the sins of "tailism" still exist. When Mao speaks of the infallible wisdom of the masses, he is referring to the masses as a kind of abstract totality and not as empirical groups and individuals making up a whole. In spite of all the rhetoric about learning from the masses, there is always the proviso that one must not learn bad and incorrect things from the masses in the flesh. The wisdom of the masses finds its ultimate distillation and synthesis in the mind of Mao, but the masses in their plurality are quite capable of wandering from the true path. Their basic apprehension of experience remains one-sided and narrowly perceptual. Thus, even the Cultural Revolutionary cadre must not become an instrument of their errors and backwardness. When there is a tension between the errors of the masses and the general line, the good cadre must do everything possible to bring them to the truth, and therefore the dangers of commandism are always present. One may be driven to commandism in order to avoid the pitfalls of tailism and departmentalism.[8] Thus, the local cadre's interaction with the masses continually takes place in a context where basic policy and fundamental decisions are made at the center, and higher levels of authority—whether structured or unstructured—continue to exist. Whether the cadre's relationship with the masses is bureaucratic or *gemeinschaftlich* seems to have little effect on this basic fact.

Again, while it may be a sound idea in China as elsewhere for "higher cadres" to "go down" to see how policies work in practice as well as on paper and to "learn from the masses," even the most selfless servant of the public must be concerned not only with his own direct conclusions from "perceptual" observation but also with the relationship of these conclusions to the whole drift of the general line which has been "synthesized" above him. If his reading the "little red book" has not overcome his selfish tendencies, the "going down" may turn into an entirely routine affair.

As for "participation in labor," it may indeed do something to overcome the traditional mandarin disdain for physical labor; but whether it has all the redemptive qualities attributed to it remains questionable. In the United States, where the disdain for physical labor is not really part of the cultural tradition, many have gone through the experience in their youth without its visibly affecting their adult behavior in positions of authority, except as an occasion for boasts about the hardships of their own youth. There still remains the essential difference between those who possess the power to command and those who do not; there still remains the fact that the physical labor of cadres is intermittent. No doubt, the experience may create in some cadres a sense of solidarity with the masses (a sense of solidarity which may not always lead to enthusiasm for the current general line). To many others it may be an unpleasant ritual to be completed as soon as possible in the happy realization that it is not one's life vocation.

None of this means that in the vast ranks of China's cadres there are not those who fervently and sincerely attempt to realize the tenets of the Cultural Revolutionary faith. There may also be larger numbers who belong to what Shao Ch'üan-lin called the "middling" type—those who attempt to realize the ideal but fail not only because of their inner weakness but because of sheer inability to cope with all its complexities.[9] Unfortunately, it is still not clear whether the game can best be played by the sincere disciple or the agile opportunist. While some of these techniques have their merits, it is still doubtful whether Mao's methods will in the end be more successful than others in moralizing the average power-holder (leaving aside the question of whether the Maoist ethic is itself an adequate life ethic).

The fact that the Chairman himself has doubts is indicated by his remarkable doctrine of the permanent revolution. The struggle be-

tween bourgeois and proletarian tendencies will continue into the future. The unrelieved mutual scrutiny of groups, the supervision of
the masses, the "struggle-criticism-transformation" sessions about
which we know so little are all designed to maintain an unremitting
revival atmosphere. The devil can be exorcised only by maintaining
the battle at fever pitch. Whether the Chinese are willing to conceive
of life in terms of permanent unremitting struggle is, it seems, a moot
point. In any event, one can raise questions about the methods of
struggle themselves. The masses are exhorted to supervise the cadres
but only from a correct point of view, and the correct point of view
continues to be determined at the center. To the extent that the center is Mao, to the degree that one believes that Mao infallibly synthe-
sizes the wisdom of the masses, the believer may rest assured that all
is well. But what if the center ceases to be occupied by Mao or any
genuine adherent of the "Cultural Revolution Ethic"? Similarly, the
technique of struggle-criticism-transformation with its malleable
Maoist language can be used by all sorts of people for all sorts of
purposes. The left deviationists of 1967 who had reason to regard
themselves as the purest disciples of the Cultural Revolution were as
vulnerable as the "capitalist-roaders" themselves.

We have here considered two themes of Cultural Revolutionary
Maoism. There are many other themes that might be considered,
such as the question of self-interest and selflessness, the nature of
mass participation, and the relationship of the masses to high culture
and Cultural Revolutionary views on education. To the extent that
Mao Tse-tung is presented to the world as a social philosopher and
philosopher of science, his doctrines can hardly remain immune to
questioning. While he himself would no doubt strongly resist any effort to divide the philosopher from the king, we are free to do so and
in doing so we are not rendering any final and total judgment on that
momentous slice of history known as the "Chinese Revolution."

15

※⁙※

The Rousseau Strain in
the Contemporary World

I remember having been struck in my childhood by a rather simple spectacle and yet a spectacle whose impression has remained with me ever since in spite of the vicissitudes of time and the diversity of experience. The St. Gervais Regiment had completed its exercise and had dined together in companies as was its custom. Most of the men who made up the Regiment gathered after supper in the Place de St. Gervais and began dancing together—officers and men—around the fountain on the basin of which stood the drummers, fifers, and torchbearers . . . It was late, the women had gone to bed; they all got up again. The wives went to join their husbands, the servant girls brought wine . . . Even the children awakened by the noise ran down half-dressed to join their mothers and fathers . . . From all this there resulted a general feeling of mutual tenderness [*attendrissement*] which I really can't describe but a feeling which, in its general gaiety, one experiences quite naturally in the midst of all that which is dearest to us. My father, embracing me, was suddenly seized by a fit of trembling which I can still feel and share. "Jean-Jacques," he said, "love your country. Do you see these good Genevans; they're all friends, all brothers; joy and harmony dwells among them. You are a Genevan; you will see other people some day but when you will have traveled as much as your father you will never find their like."

—J. J. Rousseau, *Lettre à d'Alembert*

Few would deny that one of the central strains in that complex of strains which we call modernity is what might be called the technological or engineering approach to the human condition. The notion that the crucial problems of man can be solved in large part by redesigning the machinery of the social-economic-political order was, of course, to become a central theme of the eighteenth-century Enlightenment, although it already had its illustrious predecessors in Bacon, Hobbes, and others. As the textbooks point out, this tendency was much encouraged by the Cartesian-Newtonian mechanical model of nature. Just as the Newtonian method provided the promise of infinite advance in material technology, so would its application to the "second nature" of human society prove equally successful in the realm of social technology. Indeed, a proper design of the social machine would itself foster an accelerated advance of material technology. To be sure, the implicit realization that many of the problems of complex societies are problems of social technology is certainly as old as the history of the higher civilizations. From the days of Sumer, Egypt, and the Shang dynasty, mankind has produced an abundance of "social engineers" who have wrestled with problems of bureaucratic administration and military organization, financial and fiscal policies, urban organization, and so forth. What is new is that the engineering paradigm now becomes a highly conscious, central one. There is the growing conviction that the only real problems of men are precisely those amenable to an engineering approach.

The Cartesian model, applied to material technology, is clear and unambiguous. The technologist is the embodiment of the intellect—the "cogito"—and the world of extended matter supplies the raw material. When the model is applied to the second nature of society, matters become more puzzling. The raw material of society is human beings, and human beings are presumably *all* combinations of matter and intellect. Where then is the engineer and where is his material? The answer which seems to emerge (and it is an answer which has survived in modified forms into the contemporary world) is that the bulk of mankind belongs to the realm of matter. The sensationalist psychology provides the model of a passive individual with the simplest needs completely shaped by his material and social environment. Just as the engineer requires raw materials of simple, predictable properties appropriate to his purpose, so does the engineering approach to the human condition require a drastically simplified and predictable model of man (or of most men). The model stresses man's need for security and the satisfaction of his physical needs—the maximization of pleasure and minimization of pain. With this model the strange moralist view of the individual as a creature torn between the realms of what he "ought" to be and what he actually is simply disappears from view. The human unit is what he is, and the social engineer is able to work with his material as he finds it. The question remains, however: who is then the embodiment of intellect? One eighteenth-century answer seems to be that there is a vanguard group of human society which, by dint of its preternatural scientific intelligence, seems to embody the Cartesian cogito. These are the "educators" and "legislators" who are somehow capable of transcending their social environment. "Legislator" within this context signifies what we would call experts or social engineers. One might well ask whether the engineering analogy should be applied to those tendencies of eighteenth-century thought which culminate in classical economics. It may be urged that the economists call not for an active manipulation of the social machine, but for a removal of impediments to the free operation of a kind of self-running "natural" machine. Yet the fact is that the economists were themselves concerned with the construction of a proper legal-political environment within which the forces of a liberated economy could operate. Engineers themselves, after all, are not simply potters who fashion inert clay, but people who know how to harness the dynamic laws governing the forces of nature. The liberated financiers, bankers, and manufacturers would themselves be the technicians of the new society.

One must, of course, not oversimplify the relationship of this engineering approach to other tendencies in eighteenth-century European society. One is thus struck by the quite different cultural contexts provided by French and Anglo-American societies. In his attack on the progress of the arts and sciences in his *Second Discourse,* Rousseau uses the word "art" not only in its broader ancient sense of the practical arts but also in its modern aesthetic sense. Voltaire, the encyclopedists and others who were in Rousseau's view the representatives of what I here call the engineering approach were, on the whole, also quite passionately devoted to the cultivation of the fine arts and belles lettres. Their conception of pleasure, while it may have included the grosser pleasures, also included the refined appreciation of the visual arts and of poetry, belles lettres, and the theater. They remained the heirs of the aristocratic literary culture of the seventeenth century. Their brilliant and witty conversations in aristocratic salons drew heavily on literary allusions as well as on scientific erudition, thus illustrating Rousseau's assertion that "the sciences, letters and arts . . . spread garlands of flowers over the iron chains with which men are burdened." It is not only that in his view the sciences and arts embellished and thus obscured the ugly reality in which men were morally sundered from each other, but that the arts were part of the problem. They helped to divert the rich and powerful while confirming them in their illusions of superiority. The *philosophes* themselves used them to project their own egos, thus blocking off any sincere, transparent relationship with other men.[1] The aesthetic values of this aristocratic culture were part of that overdifferentiated realm of the arts and sciences which not only underlay the sharp social cleavages of society but drew men away from the moral sources of their beings.

If we grant at least a certain validity to Max Weber's "Protestant Ethic" thesis as it applies to the Anglo-American world, we become aware that in that world the emerging technological approach to society was not necessarily as drastically disassociated from "virtue" as it appeared to Rousseau. Although Rousseau's own origins were in the artisanal class of Protestant Geneva, the argument that the sober Protestant virtues would themselves propel the advance of sciences and the practical arts is nowhere to be found in his writings. If confronted with it, he would no doubt have pointed to the paradoxical aspects of this notion pointed out by Weber himself. If the logical outcome of technological progress is the consumer society and the exaltation of comforts and luxury, how long could the sober and austere Protestant virtue survive? Yet the fact remains that even in contemporary America, however much Protestant theological foundations may have crumbled, the uninhibited pursuit of engineering solutions (whether these be economic, sociological, or psychological) to human problems has still not entirely lost its association with a kind of moral earnestness, at least on the part of the engineers themselves.

It would, of course, be quite wrong to say that this engineering approach, even in its French context, was not concerned with ethical ends. After all, the entire purpose of the legislator-engineer is to promote the welfare of mankind. Many of the encyclopedists shared Rousseau's devotion to liberty and equality as ultimate goals which would be an inevitable outcome of a well-designed society. Material progress would assure abundance. A well-designed polity would assure peace and security. Under such circumstances it would be easy to bring about the equal distribution of goods and services and to make it possible for individuals to pursue happiness in their own ways. As a utilitarian ethic of outcomes, the approach could, however, totally bypass the morality of motivations, the preoccupation with "being good." The means for achieving the desired ends are technicoscientific and the language in which they are discussed is the language of technical discourse, with its often cool, detached, and complacent pathos. This bears little resemblance to the pathos of anxiety and indignation, doubt and exaltation so often associated with moral discourse.

In its Enlightenment phase, the engineering strain was often marked by a deep sense of exasperation with the past history of mankind and its stupid distortions of man's true priorities. The energies of mankind had been diverted for ages by the extravagances of religion, myth, and superstition, by the futilities of speculative philosophy and other such follies from the pursuit of a felicity or at least a comparative well-being which might have been achieved by a systematic attention to material and social technology. In spite of this sense of exasperation, however, when we examine the writings of men such as Voltaire, Turgot, and Condorcet, we find that their condemnation of the history of mankind tends to be not as totalistic as that of Rousseau (who, of course, also made exceptions for Sparta, Rome, Geneva, and other models of civic virtue). The brighter side of the human story is to be discerned precisely in that slow but cumulative progress of the sciences and arts which in Rousseau's view was the fountainhead of evil. Looking to the future, when the progress of the sciences and arts might become the mainstream of historic development, one might anticipate a course of history which would finally dispense with the pathos of tears and anger.

Whatever the relations of the engineering approach to the ethical, when we turn to Rousseau we are immediately struck by the truth of Burke's observation that Rousseau is nothing if not a moralist. This was obvious to Burke even though he no doubt fully shared Samuel Johnson's belief that Rousseau was a thoroughly bad man and his morality a thoroughly perverse morality. In referring to him as a moralist, one points to a qualitative difference between his moralism and the utilitarian ethic of those whom he attacked as representatives of what has here been called the engineering approach. Morality does not refer in the first instance to desirable social outcomes which may ensue from technical means which are themselves morally neutral. It refers to the immediate moral quality of human beings and to the quality of the relationships among them. "Virtu-

ous" motives are crucial, not only because good social results can in
the end only be achieved in a society of virtuous human beings, but
also because what is most crucial to the achievement of social happiness is the immediate moral quality of human beings (and in
Rousseau's morality of sentiments, this quality manifests itself in the
pure and "transparent" sentiments of human beings in their immediate relationships). Liberty and equality as he conceived of them are
not ends in themselves but means to the creation of a society based
on virtuous binding sentiments. It has often been pointed out that he
did not entirely negate the sciences and arts and was willing to accommodate them to the extent that they might be compatible with a
moralized society. In the end, however, it is the moral quality of the
individual and his society which is central to the human condition.

It should, however, immediately be added that there is every reason to consider Rousseau a man of the Enlightenment and to speak
of his morality as a modern morality. In spite of the real and profound differences which divide him from his opponents among the
philosophes, in spite of the large gulf which divides the entire
Rousseau strain of modern thought from the technological strain,
there are, as I hope to indicate, shared premises which justify us in
subsuming both strains under the category of modernity.

In his preoccupation with the moral dimension, Rousseau is in
some sense more traditional than his opponents. A moral diagnosis
of the human condition was perhaps closer not only to the mainstream of Western tradition but also to the central traditions of the
great non-Western civilizations. Even when we look to the content of
his morality, we find that his catalogue of vices corresponds closely
to images of moral evil not only in the Judeo-Christian West, but in
non-Western civilizations as well. When one studies the moral orientations of non-Western civilizations, one ultimately finds that however much the moral systems of these civilizations may differ in their
positive commitments, they tend to be in astounding agreement concerning the manifestations of moral evil. Greed, pride, vanity, the desire for ascendancy and fame, uncontrolled sensual passions, calcu-
lating ambition—all of these would be readily recognized as vices by
Buddhists and Confucianists as well as by the mainstream of Western "traditional" ethics. These traditions may have quite divergent
views of the degree of tolerance to be accorded to the self-regarding
impulses, but in general the aggressive assertion of the ego is

negated. From this point of view, the legitimation of self-interest, of ambition, of love of material goods and sensual pleasure which we find in the newly emerging engineering approach marks a more radical break with traditional views of vice than anything we find in Rousseau. Rousseau was indeed quite conscious of this. In an attack on Melon (a French disciple of Mandeville) for his legitimation of luxury, he states, "It is true that until now luxury, while often prevalent, has been regarded by the world as the fatal source of an infinity of evils. It was reserved for Melon first to publicize this poisonous doctrine whose novelty will acquire for him more sectaries than the solidity of his reasons."[2] While Rousseau may be the father of modern social and political radicalism, it is his technocratic opponents who seem to be the more drastic transformers of values.

What then are the features which mark Rousseau as a man of the Enlightenment and which justify the claim that his morality is a modern morality? There is, first of all, his assertion that "tout tient à la politique" and his lifelong reiteration that the moral question and the political question are indissolubly linked. The word "political" as used by Rousseau tends to embrace the whole of what we would call the sociopolitical order. What is involved is the assertion that the behavior of the majority (leaving aside the quasi-transcendent educators and legislators) is determined by their sociopolitical environment. To be sure, Rousseau's "natural man" is not Locke's tabula rasa, even though he accepted a good deal of the prevailing sensationalist psychology. On the surface, natural man is a simple and harmless creature with limited instinctual needs, but one who enjoys a plenitude of being. Not only does he contain *in potentia* all the capacities which will emerge when he enters social life—both the capacity for the corruptions of an evil, unequal society and the capacity for higher social virtue—but even in a state of nature he possesses a profound sense of his own existence. That innocence at the core of his being already marks him as a moral being. In his later years, when Rousseau will take flight from an evil society to the solitude of an isolated existence, he will in his own mind return to that essential core of his being as a natural man. In the words of Starobinski, "In order to depict the original constitution of man it is to his own heart that he turns. He does not doubt that he is himself a 'natural man' or at least a man in whom the memory of nature has not been effaced."[3]

Yet we are struck by the fact that while Rousseau's natural man is not a flat surface, he is essentially as passive in relation to his social environment as the model of a man in the engineering approach. One of the accepted clichés concerning the nature of the modern age is that, for the first time, man is now confident of his ability to control his own destiny. Much depends, however, on what is the referent of the simple little word "man." If one is referring to the average individual, one is rather struck by the ascendancy of the notion of social determination. In Rousseau's case, he both deeply believes in man's essential innocence and in his incapacity to actualize his innocence in society. His own *Confessions* demonstrate the radical disjuncture between his inner innocence and his actual behavior, which reflected all the corruptions of a corrupt society. The innocence of his untroubled childhood reflected the wholesome social milieu of the artisan class in his native Geneva. His later misadventures in Savoy and France reflected the seductions of an evil society.

Although natural man may have had all the potentialities for the corruptions which arose when men became dependent on other men for the satisfaction of their newly created artificial needs, it is absolutely crucial for Rousseau to believe that the cause of this fall is external. "I assume for the sake of argument," he states in the *Social Contract,* "that a point was reached in the history of mankind when the obstacles to continuing in a state of nature were stronger than the forces which each individual could employ to the end of continuing in it."[4] The original fall into a corrupt civilization was caused by external forces of nature, the achievement of a virtuous society can also come only from "outside," through the "superior intelligence" and godlike charisma of great legislators. Having been misshapen by a vicious social environment, mankind "does not know what it wants because only rarely does it know what is for its own good."[5] Rousseau thus shares with his protagonists the belief in sociopolitical determinism and in the need for transcendant legislators and educators. Like his contemporaries, his mind is preoccupied not only with the relationship between the individual human mind and the world of nature but above all with the role of the "second nature" of the social, economic, and political world. Yet the conception of social environment and of the nature of legislators is markedly different in both cases. To the protagonists of the engineering approach, the passive human material made up of units composed of simple, calculable properties can be recombined into new, more effective social structures by legislators who are essentially social engineers. The environment is a material to be restructured. To Rousseau, the evil sociopolitical environment is—to use Starobinski's image—the "obstacle" which prevents human beings from relating to each other as transparent, innocent beings. In some sense, Rousseau's legislator is also an engineer, but one whose task is one of demolition. "People incessantly mended," we read in the *Second Discourse*, "whereas it would have been necessary to begin by clearing the area and setting aside all the old materials as Lycurgus did in Sparta in order to raise a good edifice afterwards."[6] The engineering image is further suggested by the language of the *Social Contract* when it stresses that the legislator must in a sense "denature" man. He "sets himself to change, as it were, the very stuff of human nature."[7] Yet the qualifier "as it were" is very important here. The fundamental constitution which the legislator ordains creates an environment in which it becomes possible for the core of natural goodness already present in all men to rise to the level of social virtue. Furthermore, the great legislator does not merely ordain laws. He communicates to the people something of his own greatness of soul. The public celebration in the Place de St. Gervais depicted in the passage cited as the epigraph to this article, with its mingled sentiments of martial comradeship, civic patriotism, and mutual tenderness seems highly spontaneous and natural. Yet it would not have been possible if Geneva had not received a noble constitution created long before by Calvin and others.[8] It was the constitution itself which made possible this effusive, seemingly spontaneous expression of the general will.

In a real sense, Rousseau is much more profoundly political than his opponents. It is not only that the highest moral potentialities of man can only be actualized by political means, but that his highest vision of human felicity is based on the image of "public happiness" which presupposes the "antique" ideal of political life. Rousseau's "individualistic" retreat into himself may provide him with a satisfactory refuge from an intolerable society, but it does not represent his summum bonum. The evils of a bad society may be mitigated by an escape into domestic bliss, as in *La Nouvelle Héloïse*, or by the ideal education of an individual, as in *Emile*, but in the end the evil "obstacle" can be eliminated—if at all—only by a total sociopolitical transformation, and the virtue of a good society could only be a political-communal virtue. Lycurgus in Sparta and the Roman leaders after the Tarquins were able to transform their societies totally because of a discontinuity created by a period of violence and civic strife.[9] The engineering approach, on the other hand, seemed committed to using political means to achieve nonpolitical ends of private happiness. What is more, the engineering metaphor encouraged the belief in piecemeal reconstruction, the belief that one could utilize parts of the present order to promote a better order. It was, in fact, the adherents of this approach who believed that one might use the institution of absolute monarchy as an instrument of enlightened despotism. The *philosophes* might, after all, persuade the monarchs that the reforms suggested by them were in their own best interests as well as in the interest of the society as a whole. However different these visions of society may be, what is shared is a common disbelief in the power of the average man to shape his own life destiny and the common belief in the overwhelming power of the sociopolitical environment.

At a deeper philosophic level, Rousseau is surely a man of the Enlightenment in his post-Cartesian anthropocentrism. In spite of his supposed religiosity, his gaze is fixed on man and his society. He is profoundly skeptical of philosophical and theological efforts to discern ultimate meaning in the nonhuman cosmos, and his certainties are subjective certainties. His own version of the "cogito" might read "I feel therefore I am," but the certitude of his sentiment of innate goodness is firmly rooted in his subjectivity. The great legislator, of course, embodies not only the certitude of feeling but also the certitude of an innate rationality.

When Rousseau speaks of religion, we are constantly aware that he is speaking of the affective side of religion and of the effects of religious feelings on man's individual and social life. In dealing with the role of traditional religion in the body politic he is as crudely pragmatic as Voltaire. The great legislators, we learn, attribute "to the Gods a wisdom that was really their own in order that the people . . . might freely obey and might bear with docility the yoke of public happiness."[10] At a deeper level, however, his true "civil religion" involves the concentration of religious sentiment onto the sociopolitical entity known as *la patrie* (or perhaps more accurately, *la peuple-patrie*). It is in this sense that Rousseau is an authentic father of nationalism as a religion. Indeed he is the father of all modern societal religions which direct religious sentiment toward some human collectivity and away from the notion of a meaningful cosmos.

When we turn to the more individualistic religiosity of the *sentiment de la nature,* there may be some justification for speaking of a kind of nature mysticism. Yet if religious sentiment in politics is the emotional cement of the general will, in the life of an isolated Rousseau turned in onto his own inner self, the beauties of the natural setting serve the function of enhancing his own "sentiment of existence." He had an infinitely more vivid sense than his opponents of the emotional needs served by religious sentiments, and he may indeed be the patron saint of all those in the modern world who define religion in terms of subjective states of consciousness, but in all of this he remains firmly embedded in the anthropocentric orientation of his contemporaries.

It may, of course, be urged that while all of this establishes Rousseau as a man of the Enlightenment, it does not establish the modernity—the contemporaneity—of his outlook. Leaving aside the distortions of a book like *Heavenly City,* in which Carl Becker sees an absolute opposition between the Enlightenment and his own view of modernity, there are those who would very much emphasize the transformations brought about by nineteenth- and twentieth-century thought in their definitions of the modernity. Although eighteenth-century thought may turn our attention to the "second nature" of social, economic, cultural, and political structures, it often tends to treat these as inert structures. Institutions and social structures may have an enormous power to shape the lives of men, just as the laws of Newtonian physics control the movements of matter, but they do not possess any inner dynamic principle of change. The sociopolitical order may be brought about by external cataclysms of nature or, in Rousseau's account, by the deus ex machina of the teacher or legislator. As "sociological" a thinker as Montesquieu states that "when societies first come to birth it is the leaders who produce the institutions. Later, it is the institutions which produce the leaders." The historicist and evolutionary thinkers of the nineteenth century all ridiculed this naive recourse to culture heroes. On the other hand, some eighteenth-century thinkers might have found the recourse to such entities as "historic evolution," "processes of development," and "sociohistoric forces" to represent the reintroduction of occult metaphysical categories into the explanation of human realities. To be sure, the beginnings of nineteenth-century historicist and "developmental" thinking can be found in Burke and even in Turgot, Condorcet, and others. Rousseau himself acknowledges a kind of cumulate progress of the "sciences and arts" which makes man's situation progressively worse.[11] Yet in projecting social change and social transformation, they could envision this only as the work of conscious human beings, however extraordinary these human beings might be. In Chinese political thought, there had also been the assumption that the normative good society could only be actualized by cultural sages, but in the Chinese cultural sphere the sages most often did derive their sagelike quality from a cosmic source. The cosmos remains the source of values. If they were not gods, they were certainly godlike. Rousseau would have his legislator be godlike, but the most he can ascribe to him is extraordinary genius and "greatness of soul." Thus Rousseau's attitude toward his legislator contains a certain reservation, which has much to do with his insistence that the legislator be the legislator and not the executor of the fundamental laws. As the executor of laws, he could never "avoid the danger that his views as man might detract from the sanctity of his work."[12] The legislator may both transcend and not transcend the effect of an evil environment. Yet whatever the ambiguities of the legislator's nature, Rousseau's hopes, such as they were, for the actualization of the good society were contingent on the existence of such legislators and on their ability to bring their greatness of soul to bear on social reality. It is no wonder that he has been called a pessimist in spite of his hopes for Corsica and his lukewarm constitution for Poland. It must be noted, however, that the hopes of his encyclopedist opponents for progress were also contingent on the hope that the enlightened vanguard would somehow be able to achieve positions of power.

With the strong emergence of the notion of an impersonal, progressive history after the French Revolution, one witnesses the transformation of both the Rousseau strain and the engineering strain in modern thought. They are, as it were, both "historicized." History itself, it was now proclaimed, would bridge the gap between the way things are and the way they ought to be. Yet both strains continue to find expression in quite different images of historic progress. Technology itself, instead of being a transaction between the technologist and the material on which he works, becomes "the process of technological development." "Industrialization," "economic forces," "technological development" become the dominant categories in what might be called the technicoeconomic version of inevitable human progress. Rousseau's influence, however, also finds its own transformation in those versions of history which treat history as primarily an ethical drama. Despite all of Hegel's reservations about Rousseau, his account of human history as a march to the realization of freedom as he understands that term is essentially an account of history as a spiritual-ethical drama. When one looks at the work of Marx from this perspective, one finds that what makes him so fascinating is that his later work seems to create an impressive synthesis of both strains. While sharing with Rousseau the view that the progress of the arts and sciences in its broadest sense as technicoeconomic history has been the occasion of enormous injustice and exploitation, he nevertheless finds it "objectively progressive." He is thus able to regard the progress of industry with both the somber indignation of a Rousseau and the complacent self-congratulation of those who marvel at man's technical genius. He would have us believe, as it were, that Satan himself may carry to completion the work of the Lord. His good society is, of course, not the same as Rousseau's Spartan utopia. Individuals in that society would reap the fruits of both the arts and the sciences even while embodying the social virtues dreamt of by Rousseau. These social virtues would furthermore no longer depend on the religion of *la patrie*.

However impressive this Marxist synthesis may be, I would urge that it has proven unstable among his followers. The question of how history as ethical drama relates to history as technicoeconomic development and as "rationalization" of society remains unresolved. Rousseau has not yet been fully reconciled with Saint-Simon.

It might also be added that the historicization of eighteenth-century thought has itself not been entirely successful. The need for legislators has not wholly vanished. The great nineteenth-century accounts of human progress had by the end of the nineteenth and early twentieth centuries become subject to serious doubts. There was the growing feeling that, in order to realize the hopes projected by these various schemes of historic progress, one would no longer be able to rely wholly on the operation of larger impersonal forces. Human intervention, whether by revolutionary vanguards or a social engineering elite, would be necessary to guide the historic processes along their proper channels. This may not have amounted to a full rehabilitation of the great legislator of the Enlightenment nor a full retreat from faith in the forces of history or "development," but it would indicate that the role played by the legislator in Enlightenment thought had not been rendered entirely superfluous.

Rousseau's vision was also to be transformed in other ways. It must first of all be noted that he was himself deadly serious about his commitment to the ideal of the small polity as exemplified by Sparta, republican Rome, and Geneva, however much he may have doubted the possibility of restoring this ideal and however much he accepted the notion of mitigating the evils of large societies. The size of these polities was a necessary if not sufficient condition of their ideality. We can fully grasp the meaning of the general will, one and indivisible, only when we think of a face-to-face assembly in a public place. It is only in this context that we can really think of a citizenry which directly represents itself, of a citizenry undivided by regional interests and wide divergences in the conditions of life, and of a government without the need of a complex bureaucracy. Patriotism in this situation is what a citizen feels when he surveys the entire city from the town acropolis. Here one clearly sees the love of *la patrie* as a collective symbolic entity and the love of the people as a community of equals, as two sides of the same coin. One might imagine something similar in peasant communities which could adjudicate their affairs under an oak tree or perhaps even in a territory as large as Corsica where conditions of life were simple and roughly equal. None of this, however, seems at all applicable to the large territorial state. The complex division of labor, the emerging of selfish interests whether of region or class, the need for vast bureaucracies and vain intelligentsias all relate to the size of societies. Rousseau himself might have rejected the possibility of the realization of his ideal in a society as large as France. Yet the attempt was to be made and the attempt was to have significant consequences. In the words of Habermas, "The pupils did not respect the limits of this model's applicability which the teacher himself had drawn; they wanted to bring about a republican constitution in a large state by revolution; or more precisely, to carry the revolution which had already broken out toward its goal in accordance with this plan."[13]

One aspect of the transformation may, however, be said to have succeeded. The religion of city-state patriotism had in fact been transformed into the religion of nationalism. It has proven possible to direct the religious sentiments of vast masses of humans toward national symbols, even in large territorial states. Men have been willing to die for their country, whatever the size and nature of its polity and social system. Men have been able to enjoy their moments of exaltation and glory, take pride in their sense of "identity" and sense of solidarity against the outer world (an integral aspect of Rousseauan patriotism) within the framework of vast nation-states as well as within the city-states of antiquity.

The ideal of the sovereign general will of the people has not made such an easy transition. One must suppose that Rousseau would hardly have accepted the Jacobin notion of a leader or a vanguard group which virtually embodies the general will of large societies even while obliterating the crucial distinction between the leader as legislator and the leader as administrator. He would no doubt have regarded this idea as a license for tyranny. Robespierre himself would probably have rejected such a notion of virtual representation before he attempted under the goad of circumstances to realize the reign of virtue in revolutionary France. Yet the idea of a general will of the people, one and indivisible in its common ideals and common interests, led by a vanguard absolutely incapable of doubting the purity of its own devotion to public virtue, was to have a considerable future. The idea takes on a particular potency when "people" and "nation" become coterminous in the confrontation with a surrounding world of enemies. In the Leninist transformation of Marxism, we also find the notion of the general will incarnate applied to the idea of class rather than to the idea of the territorially-based people-nation.

Representative democracy of the Anglo-American type has, on the whole, not drawn its theoretical justification from Rousseau, and Rousseau again would probably have rejected its claims not only because of his general rejection of the idea of representation but because he would never have conceded that a countervailing balance of "selfish" group and individual interests could ever constitute a general will. Like Hannah Arendt, who was not particularly kind to Rousseau but who thoroughly shared his antique civic ideals, he would never have conceded that a state devoted to the pursuit of individual happiness conceived of in hedonist "consumer" terms could ever realize his dream of social virtue and public happiness. Certainly the engineering approach to human problems has reached its very acme in American society. Yet the religion of nationalism and the blending of nationalism with a faith in the virtues of a people properly led has not completely disappeared as a strain even in contemporary American culture.

If it is true that Rousseau might not have accepted many of the subsequent transformations of the kind of thought he represented, are we at all justified in speaking of a "Rousseau strain" in the contemporary world? Judith Shklar in her *Men and Citizens* states: "Rousseau is not *rousseauisme*. The way in which philosophy may or may not become operative ideology is interesting enough but it is a part of social history not of political theory directly."[14] To this I would say that the great thinkers cannot be as completely dissociated from responsibility for the unexpected consequences of their thought as this would seem to imply. The fact that the followers are often so enthralled by the master's compelling vision that they do not, in the words of Habermas, respect the limits he has drawn would still imply that the vision plays some role in shaping their thought and behavior. The subsequent career of the master's ideas also leads to meditations on the limitations and blindspots of the master himself. Furthermore, having a somewhat less purist view of political theory, I would still see the later career of the ideas as part of the history of thought as well as of social history.

In spite of the overwhelming predominance of what I have here called the engineering approach to the human condition (modified by nineteenth-century historicism and evolutionism) in the modern Western world, the moralist strain of modernity represented by Rousseau has not disappeared. To be sure, the sense that some of our fundamental problems are inherently moral—or spiritual-moral—and that they will not readily yield to engineering solutions is by no means confined to the Rousseau strain. Yet by and large, the contemporary Western world continues to live within the framework of the premises of modernity established by the Enlightenment. The Rousseau strain continues to survive in the "New Left" kind of radical pathos. This derives its sustenance not only from the observation that the engineering approach has not solved all our socioeconomic problems, but from a belief in the importance of the immediate moral quality of human beings and of relations among human beings (the moral again is conceived of largely in terms of moral sentiments). The "New Left's" further belief is that the progress of the arts and sciences, far from advancing the morally meaningful life, has led to its deterioration. The radicals still remain fiercely committed to the view that everything depends on politics. Their hopes are still fixed on that redemptive act of revolution which will somehow bring about a reconciliation of modern technological society with the vision of the morally meaningful community. Revolution must play the role of the Great Legislator. Some have even convinced themselves that the revolution can be goaded into being in a recalcitrant society only by terror. While they may believe that their ultimate aim is to remove the "obstacle" which stands in the way of creating a society in which human beings will relate to each other in terms of utter transparency, their real sense of life's meaning probably derives from the fierce belief in their own righteousness and from the sense of shared adventure and common risk. This "revolutionary ethic" itself becomes the operative morality of some terrorist groups.

When we turn to the world outside the West, we find that the Rousseau strain, with all its later transformations, remains very much alive among the articulate intelligentsias and political leaders of this world. It is, of course, true that it was by its technological and sociotechnological ascendancy that the West first forced its attention on this world. It is also true that the "pragmatic" engineering approach has found its adherents in this world and may find even more adherents in the future. Yet contrary to the expectations of many American theorists of economic and political development, the intelligentsias and political elite of those societies have not always played their assigned role as strategists of modernization and "nation-building." The influence of modern Western thought still remains dominant among the elite, but the Rousseauan strain in this thought has not lost its attraction. The operative ideology (to the extent that one can speak of the presence of ideology) of many of the elite is based on the notion of the people-nation led by an ethical vanguard which effectively embodies the higher general will of the people and which leads the people to internalize ideals of socialism, justice, virtue, and devotion to *la patrie*. The vanguard may take on the form of a national single party or of a military elite, but in the forefront of its consciousness one often finds an overwhelming concern with fostering the religion of nationalism and with what it regards as the moral basis of a just society. There can be no doubt that Marxist-

Leninist Communism in both its Soviet and Chinese forms has been an important influence particularly in its conception of the vanguard party and its stress on a nationalized economy. What is more, it is quite clear that we are no longer dealing here with a sharp opposition between an antitechnological Rousseauan strain and a total reliance on the "progress of the arts and sciences." None of the elite are against modernization. As nationalists they certainly appreciate the relevance of technology to national strength, particularly in the form of modern weaponry. They probably genuinely believe that they are creating social structures which will in the long run be favorable to modernization. At the same time, they will not easily be diverted from what might be called their immediate religious-moral concerns (concerns which also relate very directly to the legitimation of their power) by arguments about technological and sociotechnological "rationality."

Although not particularly attracted by what I have here called the operative ideology of many countries in the non-Western world, I feel that something must be said about some of the deeper impulses which may lie behind it. In most of these nations there has by no means been a complete rupture with the traditions of the past. In most of these traditions—whether those of large civilizations or those of tribal cultures—the religious-moral diagnosis of the human condition has remained alive and as suggested previously, the Rousseauan strain of modernity is, in the end, more continuous with such traditions than the engineering approach. To the extent that tradition has decayed and to the extent that modern anthropocentrism has taken hold, nationalism as a religion comes to fill a vacuum in present religious-moral needs as well as to provide legitimation for authority. Nationalism is thus not simply instrumental to the ulterior goal of "modernization." To the extent that there has been a decline in older moral values among the people themselves, the effort on the part of an "ethical vanguard" to create a new social morality, a new general will, by political fiat is again not simply instrumental to modernization goals. It serves very urgent present needs. None of this is incompatible with the observation that the ideology may serve the power aspirations and hubris of the leaders themselves. One may also doubt whether the ideology is adequate to the problems it addresses. The problems themselves are, however, real enough.

As a "watcher" of contemporary China, it has been my impression that all the questions considered here have been highly relevant to the history of the People's Republic. To be sure, there is the presumption that China operates within the framework of an all-embracing unitary ideology. I would nevertheless suggest that the tension between the strains discussed above has been present within the envelope of China's Marxist-Leninist-Maoist ideology. Elsewhere I have explored the degree to which the Maoist doctrine of the Cultural Revolution might be understood in terms of the Rousseau strain as here defined.[15] In carrying on this exploration I was simultaneously struck by the degree to which Maoist Cultural Revolutionary themes also corresponded to certain particular features of traditional Chinese moral and political thought. Could it be that in some peculiar fashion the Rousseauan *problematic* resonated more with certain aspects of traditional moral-political thought in China (in spite of enormous real differences) than with the traditional moralities of many other societies? This is a subject well worth exploration, but the exploration will not be attempted here.

Since Mao's death there has been in China a noticeable turn in the direction of what I have called the engineering approach. Ultimately, however, the problems raised here remain unresolved for China as for all the rest of us.

16

Upheaval in China

What lies behind the "Great Proletarian Cultural Revolution" of 1966? The news out of China seems nothing less than fantastic: vast hordes of the young have suddenly been mobilized to carry out the spiritual transformation of Chinese society; a wholesale assault has been made upon the entire Chinese cultural heritage, as well as upon the "bourgeois" culture of the West, including everything from Bach to recent Soviet literature and modish hairstyles. This movement has been attended by a hysterical, unrelieved scream of adulation for the person and thought of Mao Tse-tung as the single source of all wisdom, and by the revelation of a titanic political struggle involving some of the CCP's most prominent leaders and extending deep into the whole institutional apparatus of Chinese society. The official Chinese media have themselves emphasized with monotonous insistence the unprecedented revolutionary nature of what is happening. Every effort is being made to suggest that the People's Republic is turning a fresh page in its eventful history.

Is all this nothing more than the surface reflection of an all-out conflict of power among individuals and groups eager to snatch the mantle of leadership from an enfeebled Mao? Is it a struggle between the army and the party? Does it represent an effort to achieve a maximum mobilization of the population in the face of what is felt to be the imminent possibility of war with the United States? Is it a response to a vast economic crisis hidden from our view? Or does the very phrase "Cultural Revolution" furnish some real clue to the nature of what is going on?

Before indulging in speculation over the long-term implications of the Cultural Revolution, we might remind ourselves that China has witnessed at least two such unpredicted shifts of course during the last decade. The Hundred Flowers campaign of 1956–57 suggested a new policy of liberalization and relaxation; it was followed in 1957–58 by the apocalyptic Great Leap Forward with its communes, backyard blast furnaces, and hints of total collectivization. Each of these departures was attended by unexpected consequences and sober reassessments. Together, they serve to warn us of the dangers that must accompany any attempt to assess the full impact of the Cultural Revolution on the vast masses of Chinese society, or its lasting effects.

We can, however, say something about its antecedents. For in spite of the emphasis on its novelty, many of its component themes may be traced to beginnings made in 1961–62, and beyond that to the Great Leap Forward of 1958.

In many ways, the Great Leap Forward probably represented in Mao Tse-tung's own view his "finest hour." This is not to discount the overwhelming victory of 1949, the successful application of Maoist methods to the vast tasks of political consolidation and organization, or the seemingly successful Maoist effort to "remold" the mental outlook of an entire population. Yet as the government turned its attention in the early 1950s to the tasks of modernization, there was always discernible a modest deference to "superior Soviet experience." Shortly after the takeover, Mao remarked soberly: "Things in which we were well versed will soon be needed no longer and we shall have to do things in which we are not well versed." In all these matters the Soviet Union played the role of teacher, not only because this was a condition of the alliance with Stalin, but also, no doubt, because of a genuine belief in Soviet experience. Thus, while the last decade of Chinese Communist history has been marked by erratic departures and sweeping experiments, the first seven years seemed to move steadily toward an ever-increasing Sovietization of Chinese life.

After 1955, however, it would appear that serious questions arose (in the more lenient atmosphere made possible in part by the death of Stalin) concerning the total applicability of Soviet methods to Chinese problems, particularly to Chinese economic problems. The new feeling was that Chinese methods had to be found for dealing with

Chinese difficulties. By the end of 1957—after the demise of the Hundred Flowers experiment—we find the gradual emergence of new approaches in the economic sphere, particularly in the area of rural economy. These approaches, which were ultimately to culminate in the spectacular commune experiment of 1958, were designed to cope with the very real and intractable problems of Chinese agriculture and China's huge population; they seemed, moreover, to involve the application of Maoist maxims and teachings to areas where Soviet wisdom had hitherto prevailed. Just as the Red Army had won its victories by depending on men rather than weapons, the peasants were now expected to win their war against the land by mobilizing vast human energies rather than by relying on material resources. Like the guerrillas of the past, who sacrificed their petty interests to the larger cause with little thought of remuneration, the peasant masses, in their devotion to the new state, could be induced to put forth their maximum energies without the promise of material incentives. Filled with ardor and enthusiasm, the peasant would exercise all his initiative and ingenuity to fulfill his production tasks. In this effort he would be directly led and inspired, as in the old Yenan days, by party cadres thoroughly imbued with a selfless Communist ethic, and capable of exercising leadership in the most diverse areas of economic, social, and cultural activity.

❈

It now seemed possible that the same Maoist maxims which had worked so well in the idyllic days of Yenan (at least, as viewed through the lenses of Mao's nostalgic idealization) and in the postwar period of consolidation would be equally effective in pushing forward China's economic development. This possibility in turn opened up utopian perspectives. It can be said that in 1958 Mao experienced what would be called his full beatific vision. The vast hinterlands of China would be organized into a gigantic network of communes, each one a self-sustaining economic, cultural, and even military cell. These cells would be held together and led forward by the monolithic hierarchy of the Communist party, whose members embodied both the highest Communist virtues and the greatest technical versatility. The collective solidarity of the masses would be further welded by a sense of militant solidarity against the enemy without.

Needless to say, this image of the society as an armed camp of comrades-in-arms, united in clear-cut conflict against the ubiquitous reactionary enemy, was an integral part of the total vision. Within such a society, the role of the professionals and of the academic and literary intelligentsia—a stratum which had demonstrated its essential unreliability during the Hundred Flowers campaign—would be reduced to a minimum. Professionals and academic experts were not only guilty of presuming to lay claim to autonomous areas of knowledge (which they used to place themselves outside of and above the party), but were also inclined to selfish careerism and personal vanity. Built into their outlook—according to the new "vision"—was an exaggerated emphasis on "objective" difficulties and a kind of antiseptic neutralism directly antagonistic to Mao's view of China and the world—a view which stressed the titanic struggle between the forces of good and the forces of evil. The individualistic vanity of intellectuals and literary men had led them to a constant pursuit of irony, ambiguity, and complexity—qualities which are the enemies of simplicity—and into a concern for their petty personal destinies. They represented much of what was most obnoxious in modern Western urban civilization. China must achieve wealth, national power, and Communism while at the same time restricting and bypassing such baleful influences.

It might be added that Mao himself has always been more complex than his vision. He has not been immune to all the joys of the flesh or the vanities of individual glory. A literary man of no small vanity, he has allowed himself to write traditional symbolic poetry in a style not permitted to others, and in his conversations with foreigners has often suggested that his apprehension of reality is somewhat more ironic than the grand simplicity of his vision would appear to indicate.

One important aspect of the Great Leap Forward was its innovations in the sphere of foreign policy. The period was marked by a new and basic consistency of spirit (a consistency which had not always existed) between domestic and foreign policy. Just as China was now expected to overcome all internal obstacles by a massive mobilization of "subjective" forces, so too on the global scene the Communist bloc was called upon to join forces in a policy of bold confrontation with imperialism. This posture was, of course, still based on a continuing (yet wavering) belief in the solidarity of the bloc and on the assumption of long-term cooperation between the Soviet Union and China.

As we know, the utopian hopes of the Great Leap were not realized, but rather gave way to the massive retreat and the severe economic crisis of 1959–1962. Given the soaring hopes of 1958, one cannot but feel that the retreat must have occasioned the profoundest chagrin on the part of Mao Tse-tung. Those who came under attack in 1959 were precisely the "Right opportunists" (the most prominent of them was P'eng Te-huai) who had been least enthusiastic about the Great Leap and who were now saying, "I told you so." Even now it would appear that the "Right opportunists" of 1959 remain one of the main targets of the proletarian Cultural Revolution.

By 1960, the retreat was well underway. In the economic sphere it involved a decentralization of the communes and a striking new emphasis on the primacy of agriculture over industry and on material incentives for peasants in the form of private plots and free markets. It was a sober and realistic response and quite originally Chinese. It certainly did not involve a return to the Soviet model. As with all such major shifts in the past, it also seemed to involve reversals of policy in other areas of social and cultural life. Students were now told to devote themselves to their studies, and to respect elderly professors. The stock of "expertise" rose, particularly in the economic and scientific spheres. Academic historians were again encouraged to treat the problems of Chinese history with a certain limited degree of freedom. We can only speculate on Mao Tse-tung's relationship to all this. In spite of his utopian visions, he had always been able to recognize intractable facts. One may surmise that in the economic sphere he acquiesced to the new policies while perhaps holding his silence in the cultural sphere.

It is important to note that even at the height of the period of retreat there were certain obvious areas of dissonance. It was during the 1960–1962 period that the Sino-Soviet crisis surfaced. Peking was rapidly moving from a rejection of Soviet policies to an assertion of its own authority as the bearer of true Marxism-Leninism. One of the peculiarities of the relationship between the Soviet Union and China lies in the fact that they still remain enmeshed through their conflicting claims to possessing the one truth. This means that internal domestic policies cannot be divorced from foreign relations. One need not doubt the sincerity of the Maoist leadership when it began to see a relationship between the errors of Soviet world policy and domestic Soviet "revisionism." The Soviets, for their part, attacked the Great Leap Forward and its utopian mystique not only because they regarded it as economically unsound, but also because they could not afford to ignore what they considered to be Mao Tse-tung's "petty bourgeois," distorted image of the good Communist society (just as Mao could not later ignore Khrushchev's "bour-geois" vision of Communism). The Soviet Union, in Mao's view, was sliding back into capitalism because it had placed all its reliance on institutional conditioning and had neglected the spiritual transfor-mation of the masses. If China had its own message for the world, it was one which called for more rather than less emphasis on the ideological—or, as it is now called, the "cultural"—factor; it was, in effect, the message of the Great Leap Forward.

We now know that the universalization of Mao's teachings in 1958 also embraced the military sphere. Here too, the Soviet model—with its emphasis on professionalism, technical proficiency, and basic con-trol by the officer corps—was to give way to party dominance ("pol-itics in command"), an emphasis on the spiritual training of the sol-dier, a downgrading of the officer corps, and participation by the army in all sorts of social activities. This reversion to the maxims of Yenan was, to be sure, balanced by the determination to achieve a nuclear capacity, and in 1958 still presupposed cooperation with the Soviet Union in the event of war. In this sphere, however, despite the general failure of the Great Leap Forward, there was to be no re-treat. As late as August 1959, P'eng Te-huai, Minister of Defense and defender of military professionalism (and professionalism in general), was overwhelmingly defeated. Neither the deterioration of relations with the Soviet Union, the termination of Soviet nuclear aid, nor the serious crisis of morale in the army from 1960 to 1961 was to lead to any departure from the Maoist line in the army. On the contrary, the failure of morale in the face of adversity was attrib-uted to the woeful neglect of the spiritual training of the average sol-dier; a new emphasis was required to place "politics in command."

The Maoist line in military affairs has implications both for mili-tary strategy and for internal policy. Unless one assumes that the Chinese expect to put their modest nuclear arsenal to use in the near future, one must suppose that their present nuclear development is an aspect more of political than of military strategy. It represents a defiance of the American-Soviet nuclear monopoly, and a demonstration of what China can do in the sphere of advanced technology. The Yenan concept of mass military organization also seems to involve a fundamentally defensive posture vis-à-vis a possible American attack. In the event of war, the Americans are to be drawn into the endless expanses of China and worn down in the course of a protracted people's war. This strategy does not preclude the use of Chinese arms abroad in situations where Chinese superiority is clear and great-power intervention unlikely—as in the case of the Chinese incursion in India. Nor does it imply that China may not intervene in Vietnam in the event of further escalation. It does, however, imply an effort to avoid rather than to seek a confrontation with American power.

Yet it must be stressed that the main significance of the Maoist military line may have lain in its application to internal affairs. Mao was determined not to retreat in the crucial military sector, and it was as the implementer of Mao's line in the army during the most critical period of 1959–1961 that Lin Piao was to lay the basis for his ascendancy. Army loyalty is, of course, crucial in any state, but behind Mao's concern with the military lay an even deeper conviction harking back, once again, to the Yenan days. The Yenan experience had shown that a well-indoctrinated People's Army provided an ideal school for inculcating Communist virtues. If the spirit built into the guerrilla enterprise—a spirit of self-sacrifice, collectivity, simplicity, fortitude, and initiative—could be fostered and brought to high consciousness by zealous party cadres, then the average soldier and the average military unit could also become models of individual and collective behavior for the society as a whole. This vehement emphasis on spiritual training in the army might itself indicate that Mao had not really accepted the retreat of 1960 even in the cultural sphere and was still dreaming of the possibility of turning the army into a model of Maoist conduct for the whole of Chinese society.

In fact, the entire period between 1961 and the present has been marked by a slow but steady accretion of all those themes and motifs which have now culminated in the Cultural Revolution. I am not suggesting here that there was a prearranged, unfolding plan. At least in part, the growing vehemence and shrillness of this "cultural" effort may be directly due to the massive resistance which these efforts have met from every quarter of society since the retreat from the Great Leap Forward. As early as 1961, however, attempts were made to diagnose the failure of the Great Leap Forward in a manner which, though acknowledging the role of natural disasters and local mismanagement, still placed major blame on the failure to have imbued the masses with a true Communist ethic. Mao himself, it seems, had overestimated the spiritual preparedness of his people. What was required now was a longer, more sustained effort to internalize his "proletarian" conception of man in the very souls of the masses. This effort began, as we have seen, in the military sector, but it was not until the Plenum of the Central Committee in September 1962 that the counterattack against "cultural" relaxation became plainly visible. (It may have been facilitated by the modest recovery brought about by the sober economic policies of the post-1960 period.) By 1963, we already have the slogan, "Learn from the People's Liberation Army." The work of Lin Piao's General Political Department in the army had been pronounced a success, and the army was now ready to play its role in the society at large. Men who had undergone a supposedly successful moral transformation while serving in the army were to be brought into every area of social life. The cultural department of the PLA was to play an increasingly important role in the arts.

※

The years 1963–64 also saw the emergence of two soldierly models of Communist virtue, Lei Feng and Wang Chieh, together with their conveniently available diaries. A perusal of these diaries and of the three works of Mao which are now stressed above all others (the "three much-read works"—"In Memory of Norman Bethune," "On Serving the People," and "On the Foolish Old Man who Removed the Mountains")—indicates that since 1962 the military, economic, and political doctrines of Mao Tse-tung have become less important than his sermons on the Communist moral transformation of the individual. Despite the inability of many Westerners—themselves profoundly habituated to thinking of human affairs in terms of institutional devices and social conditioning—to credit Mao's belief in the effectiveness of these moral sermons, it nevertheless appears that he has indeed committed himself to this program in a genuine and wholehearted manner.

Also in 1963, the campaign for "socialist education" in the countryside gained prominence. Mao's concern over the "spontaneous tendency to capitalism" inherent in the institution of private plots and free markets had probably been present from the outset. Indeed, there is evidence that in Mao's own province of Hunan, the effort to counteract this tendency had begun as early as 1960, and involved mobilizing those designated as "poor and lower-middle" peasants to attack all excessive commitments to private activities. It would appear that, in an adumbration of the later role of the "Red Guards," youngsters and schoolchildren were also employed in the work of ideological pressure. Although it is impossible to ascertain the precise nature and limits of this campaign, the institution of private plots—one which has played a crucial role in the Chinese economy—has still not been abolished, despite the sustained effort at moral condemnation.

The "counterattack" in the intellectual sphere was also well under way by 1963. Historians and philosophers began to be excoriated for manifold bourgeois errors. Needless to say, a dominant theme in this Maoist cultural effort was the theme of Soviet decadence. The Soviet Union had by "negative example" proved the remarkable thesis that an "advanced social system alone cannot accomplish much without a revolutionary change in man himself."[1] In short, one can say that all the assumptions and essential themes underlying the present Cultural Revolution were on the scene by the beginning of 1965.

Yet the economic policies inaugurated after 1959 remain essentially intact even now. Has this hesitation to interfere with prevailing economic policies been due solely to a powerful resistance to change within the hierarchies of the party or the government? Or has Mao himself, after the failures of 1958, hesitated to launch new experiments in the economic area? While the assertion that the "revolutionization of the masses" will release enormous productive energies has been repeated again and again during the last few years, Mao himself may have accepted the fact that China's general economic development will actually be slow, and may hence have decided to concentrate upon laying the "spiritual" foundations of a Maoist society while leaving the economy alone. Technical experts were exhorted to base all their efforts on the thought of Mao Tse-tung but to keep their minds steadily fixed on the actual task at hand. At any rate, the question of the relationship between "class struggle" in the cultural sphere and in economic practice is still unresolved.

In sum, then, I would suggest that the stage had already been set for recent developments by the beginning of 1965. Yet clearly there have been new developments since then. Are these new developments simply a spectacular culmination of the evolution described above, or has American large-scale intervention in Vietnam played a crucial role? While the possibility of a war with the United States has never been overlooked, the actual prospect of imminent conflict became real only with the arrival of large numbers of American troops in Vietnam. It was quite conceivably this new prospect which reactivated the hidden debate on military strategy. In spite of constant assertions about the total success of the Maoist line in military policy, professional military opposition was far from dead. Indeed, the statement made by Chief of Staff Lo Jui-ch'ing in May 1965, entitled "Commemorate the Victory over German Fascism!" seems in retrospect of considerable significance.

This article praised the performance of the Soviet Red Army (hardly an army run on Maoist lines) during World War II and laid particular stress on its capacity "to destroy the enemy at his starting point, to destroy him in his nest." The article therefore also appeared to suggest that China itself requires a military apparatus capable of taking the offensive against an American enemy rather than simply waiting to wear him down in the heartland of China. It might also have suggested the possibility that China is willing to entertain the notion of limited cooperation with the Soviet Union in modernizing China's army and in taking a united stand against the United States in Vietnam. (It should be added, however, that this particular variety of professionalism and possible "pro-Sovietism" need have no "moderate" implications whatsoever for future Chinese-American relations.)

In any event, if such a debate on military strategy did indeed occur in the Chinese government, and if it involved wide circles of the governing elite, it would certainly have called to Mao's attention the degree to which there continues to be resistance—at least in one sector—to his program of spiritual transformation. It is clear, however, that Vietnam did not change Mao's own perspectives by one iota. Therefore, while the possibility of war with the United States may have intensified and exacerbated certain previously existing debates, and revealed the extent of the opposition to the "Thought of Mao Tse-tung," it did not change the terms of the debate itself. At most, it may have driven Mao further into that sense of exasperation which culminated in the Cultural Revolution of 1966.

It is also possible that resistance to Mao in 1965 may have manifested itself in fields other than that of military policy. The fact that the third five-year plan was to be launched in 1966 must have turned attention to economic matters. Mao's insistence on "culture" may not have seriously affected ongoing economic practices, but it certainly involved an enormous diversion of emotional and mental energies from economic concerns. Thus, in the sphere of education, an area vital to the economy, the increased emphasis on labor and on spiritual training represented a diversion of energies from the vocational training of experts. It is interesting to note that while the start of the five-year plan was announced in January 1966, the amount of attention devoted to economics in the public media since then has been minimal. It is quite likely that strong resistance was felt in this sphere as well, and that a man like P'eng Chen, who was prepared to endorse the "revolutionization" of the Peking Opera, was less than enthusiastic about the even greater insistence on "Mao's Thought" in the spheres of economics and education.

From Mao's point of view, the most crucial area of all was the cultural arena. Here too, there had been considerable evidence of resistance and foot-dragging on the part of all those party organs (aside from the army) concerned with cultural affairs. "Mao's Thought" dominated the foreground, but the cultural "monsters and demons" who had revealed themselves during the 1960–1962 period of relaxation were still on the scene. Now, as in the past, Mao has tended to seek symptomatic evidence of the health of Chinese society as a whole in the area of its culture—particularly its literature. Thus, the continued resistance of "bourgeois" tendencies in Chinese life to Mao's vision made the leader more grimly determined than ever to push through his own ideas. Lin Piao's famous tract of September 1965, "Long Live the Victory of People's War," and the all-out attack on the writer Wu Han which began in November 1965 may both be considered as aspects of this more vehement counterattack. Lin Piao's article is mainly a Maoist analysis of world developments, but it must also be seen as a response to domestic critics. It consists of a grandiose application of the Yenan model to the world at large and projects a world situation favorable to the triumph of this model. Although uncompromising in spirit, it does not anticipate the export of Chinese armies to foster Maoist revolutions abroad. Rather, it assumes a third-world situation favorable to the spread of the Maoist model of revolution, or—on a more immediate level—the acceptance of Chinese leadership by established governments in many of the world's "poor countries." It emphasizes the importance of Vietnam as a test case of Maoist revolution but also stresses the need for Vietnamese self-reliance. Finally, it emphatically confirms the need to continue along Maoist military lines at home.

The attack on Wu Han was to be the direct antecedent of the Cultural Revolution. Historian, vice-mayor of Peking, and part-time littérateur, Wu Han had written a play in the dark days of 1960 (published in 1961) with a historical setting in the Ming dynasty; the play has since been interpreted (probably correctly) as an assault on the Great Leap Forward experiment. In November of 1965, a decision was taken to make of Wu Han and his play a "negative example" of all that was wrong in the cultural sphere. Wu Han himself, however, had been closely connected to cultural figures in the Peking Party Committee machine headed by P'eng Chen; the attack may therefore have been merely a surface manifestation of the larger power struggle already taking place behind the scene. Or, if we credit the official account, it may have been launched in all sincerity, and then aggravated by the fact that the leadership of the Peking Party Committee failed to join in the attack with the proper enthusiasm, thereby revealing its own bourgeois proclivities. There have, after all, been previous instances of the use of literary figures as "negative examples" (Hu Feng, Yü P'ing-po).

Whether it was the Wu Han affair which brought the leadership struggle to a head or whether the affair was a manifestation of a struggle already under way, it is clear that by the spring of 1966 the power struggle was already visible. The nature of that struggle, however, was not yet apparent. Was it a horizontal struggle among different individuals and groups—and has Mao therefore been merely an instrument of the struggle itself? Was it a sheer power struggle, unrelated to issues? Or could it be described as a struggle between institutional entities such as the army and the party? The notion of a horizontal struggle for succession is based on the assumption that Mao himself has not played a decisive role in current events, or that he is a figurehead. My entire argument, on the other hand, has been grounded on the premise that now, as in the past, Mao has played a decisive role. Although he may at times withdraw himself expediently from the forefront of affairs, as he did in the early 1960s, when he decides to bring his power to bear on any matter he does so with crushing weight. A sensational revelation from a Japanese source cites a statement, presumably by Mao, that his authority within the party had been usurped by Liu Shao-ch'i, Deng Xiaoping, and others ever since the famous Wuhan meeting of December 1958, at which time he resigned his position as chairman of the CCP. Because of the convulsive conflict now raging in Peking, we must treat Mao's own accounts with as much skepticism as those of all other participants. There seems to be little doubt that Mao played a dominant role in the attack on P'eng Te-huai and the "Right opportunists" in 1959, and there is every reason to believe that he brought his full authority to bear on military policy from 1960 to 1962. Mao's style of thinking is stamped upon the whole Sino-Soviet conflict. It may well be, however, that the end of the Great Leap Forward was indeed marked by a more vociferous opposition in high councils to Mao's policies than had hitherto been assumed, and that Mao has found it judicious on occasion to bow to his opposition on certain matters. The charge that Liu, Deng, and others wholly usurped his infallible authority constitutes another particularly heinous item in the list of charges being drawn up against them.

I would suggest therefore that Lin Piao occupies his present position because he has been promoted by Mao on the basis of his proved abilities as the implementer of the Maoist line in the army— not because he had recourse to a well-oiled political machine. Nor can Lin Piao's rise be considered part of the ascendancy of the army. He has made his fortune as the representative of the Maoist line, not as a representative of the army (that is, the officer corps), which, one gathers, is as internally divided as other institutional segments of society. Nor does Lin Piao represent the party. Indeed, the extent to which the whole "Red Guard" movement is being used as a weapon by Mao and Lin against the established institutions of society argues for the view that Lin did not have a pre-established power base of his own. I would further suggest that T'ao Chu, the chairman of the South Central Bureau of the party, has also risen because of his proved merits as a servant of Mao's cultural policies, particularly in the sphere of socialist education in the countryside. Now, however, we have the additional news that T'ao Chu himself is out of favor; with the mounting frenzy of the conflict, even those who have proved themselves worthy in the past may come to seem unreliable if they oppose the more extreme developments of their leader's Cultural Revolution. We are dealing with a situation in which it is quite possible to go astray by standing still.

As for those now in the opposition, all of them have been, at one time or another, faithful mouthpieces of Maoist policies. Cultural Commissar Chou Yang, for example, the scourge of China's writers since the early 1940s, was always considered the spokesman of Mao's most Stalinist ideas in the realm of literature. P'eng Chen, until recently, was a leading spokesman on both domestic and foreign policy. Lo Jui-ch'ing, former chief of the secret police, had helped Lin Piao implement the Maoist line in the army during the early 1960s. Needless to say, the past public statements of these men had always been designed to conform as closely as possible to the Communist convention of total unanimity.

It is true, however, that P'eng Chen, Lo Jui-ch'ing, and Chou Yang had become closely associated with certain particular constellations of interests—P'eng Chen with the Peking Party Committee (which plays an extraordinarily important role in culture and higher education), Lo Jui-ch'ing with the officer corps, and Chou Yang with the culture and propaganda apparatus. The danger here did not lie simply in the creation of what Mao calls "independent kingdoms." Certainly, P'eng Chen's ample powers were not wholly dependent on the Peking Committee. But the day-to-day association with "authorities" involved in professional tasks may have dampened whatever ardor these men originally had for the ever more vehement emphasis on the "Thought of Mao Tse-tung," and may have resulted in giving them a new sense of solidarity with their professional protégés. Whether or not P'eng Chen truly sympathized with the writings of Wu Han, Teng T'o, and others, he might well have questioned the need for a campaign against them. Here questions of policy become hopelessly intertwined with questions of power.

It is, to be sure, somewhat difficult to think of Chou Yang as a defender of the professional writer or artist. Yet these "cultural workers" have, in fact, constituted his "kingdom." He may be a literary Stalinist, but Mao's ideas on art and literature have gone well beyond the frontier of Stalinism. In spite of all his repressive measures, Stalin accepted the conventional "bourgeois" conception of the author and artist; Mao, of course, envisions a literature of "workers, peasants, and soldiers" written for immediate purposes. In practice, this means a kind of literature turned out by committees of trained propagandists. We know that in the last few years many theatrical and literary activities have been taken in hand by the Cultural Department of the General Political Department of the PLA, thus bypassing the jurisdiction of the conventional party cultural organs. It would seem plausible under these circumstances that even Chou Yang may have demonstrated something less than singlehearted dedication to Mao's Cultural Revolution. The main visible targets of the Cultural Revolution on the lower regional and provincial levels of party organization have been party functionaries concerned with cultural and propaganda affairs. Foot-dragging has been a characteristic of the whole party cultural apparatus from top to bottom. This would also indicate that the issue of "culture," as Mao understands it, is at the heart of the present convulsion.

⚙

Something must be said about the political survival of the durable Chou En-lai. Chou, it seems to me, continues to be an indispensable resource man. The Mao-Lin projection of the world's future may be based on profound faith in the verdict of history, but in the short run one must deal with the world situation as it is. One negotiates with Pakistan seeks trade with Japan and attempts to exercise as much influence as possible under prevailing circumstances. Chou En-lai has always performed a crucial role in this area. His continued presence may also indicate that the forces which are determined to keep the Cultural Revolution and the Red Guards within some bounds are still vastly powerful and resistant.

What is suggested, therefore, is that there has probably not been an aggressive effort on the part of an opposition to seize power, but that ever since the early 1960s there have been various forms and degrees of resistance to Mao's determined effort to place his vision of man and society at the forefront; that this resistance has manifested itself in all institutional sectors of Chinese society, including the party; that this ongoing resistance (which may even have increased in 1965) has confirmed the aging Mao in his profound suspicion of the inertial "bourgeois" tendencies latent in all existing institutions and in all those involved with institutional responsibilities. One need not doubt that men like Deng Xiaoping, Liu Shao-ch'i, and P'eng Chen—men who had reason to cherish the highest private ambitions—must have deeply resented Lin Piao's ascendancy, but it seems to me quite impossible to separate the struggle for power from the issues involved.

The events leading up to the emergence of the Red Guards seem to have followed the major high-level purges. A new effort was now exerted to transform the soul of China and arm it against the forces of inertia. In June 1966, the West became aware of struggles within Peking University and other institutions of higher learning against "revisionist" academic administrators and students, struggles mainly involving young people. It is evidently out of such struggles that the Red Guards emerged. Youth was to be rescued from the clutches of the revisionists—including those in control of the Communist Youth League—and made the bearer of the Cultural Revolution. Only youth—particularly the very young—remained fresh and untainted. In spite of the continuing rhetoric about the masses, it would appear that the older and middle generations of these masses had proved themselves as susceptible as the institutional elite to the corrupting pull of mankind's past.

If youth was to help revolutionize society, however, it had to undergo the actual experience of revolution. Here we note a theme which had emerged as early as 1964, when, in response to American assertions about the more reasonable, pragmatic nature of the coming generation in China, and to the ominous example of Soviet youth, a new set of slogans appeared: "Everything must be done to make the youth succeed to the revolutionary heritage of the past." "One can learn to swim only by swimming [a slogan which reminds us of Mao's symbolic swim in the Yangtze]; one can learn to be revolutionary only by making revolution." One might say that the ethos of revolution is itself the ethos of Communism. Thus, the activities of the Red Guards represent, among other things, an effort to create within a vastly different environment a substitute for the revolutionary experiences of Mao's generation. This entire movement is suffused with a rhetoric which abounds in nostalgic allusions to the difficult yet golden days of the 1930s and 1940s. Such phrases as "little general" and "Red Guards" themselves recall the charming waifs who were attached to the Red Army during the old guerrilla days and who served that army with selfless devotion.

※

The Red Guard movement thus serves many purposes. It is used as a lever of power by Mao and Lin Piao against the resistant elements which permeate all the institutions of society. The enthusiasm and intolerance of the young are to be used to convey to the society at large the purest and most exclusive image of Mao's vision of man and society. Finally, the Red Guard movement provides the young with an unforgettable revolutionary experience. One should not make too much of the notion that the Red Guards are the auxiliaries of Lin's thoroughly transformed People's Liberation Army. In fact, the army leadership continues to be as suspect a sector of the elite as any other, and there have been many reports of local army resistance to the Red Guards. For the moment, the Red Guards represent the only full incarnation of the "proletarian" spirit.

There seems little reason to believe that the conflicts occasioned by the Cultural Revolution have been resolved, nor is it by any means clear what its ultimate implications may be in the economic sphere. There are those who feel that Mao is once more preoccupied with mobilizing the people to "get the economy moving." But while there is no doubt that Mao ardently desires rapid economic development, I would suggest that even he learned in the course of 1958 that it is no easy matter to translate "Mao's Thought" into immediate economic results. It is thus not unlikely that his main immediate concern is not primarily with the economy, but rather with the saturation of his people's minds with his own vision of the good society, even if this does not lead to spectacular, immediate economic results. One need not expect Russian-type "Libermanism" in China, but neither is it yet clear that "Mao's Thought" must lead to a Great Leap type of economic experimentation in the immediate future although there are now more and more indications that the leader wants to carry the activities of the Red Guards into the countryside and factories.

In the sphere of world politics, Mao's vision, in spite of its radical nature, does not involve a more aggressive military posture. The world, to be sure, has not yet conformed to the Maoist projection, but the Yellow River has many bends. In the end, the Maoist model of revolution and of the good society will prove infectious in an unstable third world. Meanwhile, China must offer this world a model of the good society, clearly marked off from that of the corrupt West.

Will Mao's ideas ultimately prevail? It seems to me that his terribly simple and constricted view of the human situation will prove as inapplicable to the human reality of China as to that of any other society, and that the forces resistant to his more extravagant dreams (forces which may represent a wide diversity of outlooks) will in the end prevail. Mao may not be totally deluded in believing that a society with a vast peasant population and many of its own cultural propensities will have to find its own path into the future. The China of the future may be radically different from the United States and the Soviet Union. But it is also not very likely to resemble Mao's utopia.

17

On Filial Piety and Revolution

*R*ichard Solomon's *Mao's Revolution and the Chinese Political Culture* is a bold and challenging book. It aims at nothing less than an encompassing explanation of traditional Chinese "political culture" and of Mao Tse-tung's revolution against that political culture. It also does more to concretize the nebulous conception of political culture than anything I have seen under that heading. Solomon does not simply pose certain hypotheses, but makes every effort to test these hypotheses against two large bodies of empirical data. In dealing with the traditional culture, Solomon supports his theses with materials based on an extensive interviewing project conducted in Hong Kong and Taiwan. In dealing with Mao and Chinese politics since 1949, Solomon, who is one of our most experienced China watchers, relies on the interpretation of the same documentation available to other China watchers. Because of the wealth of illustrative material, every page provokes an active reaction of assent or dissent.[1]

I shall not attempt to challenge the research procedures used by Solomon in his interview project although there is ample room for further discussion. For example, one might raise many questions concerning his sampling methods, reliance on Rorschach and thematic apperception tests, the contexts within which the interviews were conducted, and the meaning of words in the questions posed. All I would suggest is that while one might conceivably accept the validity of Solomon's research procedures, one could also find himself in utter disagreement with many of the interpretations which

Solomon imposes upon the replies of his respondents. My own difficulties arise at the point where he attempts to relate these replies—
the final fruits of his research—to larger matters, such as the nature
of political authority or the nature of dependency.

Turning to the central theses, Solomon finds in traditional China a
political culture marked by the unquestioned sway of authoritarianism, the acceptance of hierarchy, and the universal prevalence of a
"dependency orientation" which has its roots deep in Confucian
child-rearing practices. This eager acceptance of authority is rooted
in an overwhelming fear of conflict and disorder and an obsessive
concern with peace and harmony. This "dependency orientation" is
linked to an ethic which stresses passivity, nonassertiveness, and the
repression of all aggressive impulses. When suppressed aggressions
do burst forth, they lead to the anarchic "uncontained" violence and
disorder *(luan)* which we find in periods of rebellion and dynastic decline. All of this is contrasted to Western civilization, which stresses
individual autonomy, self-reliance, self-assertion, the kind of controlled aggression and competitiveness which can lead to dynamic
positive accomplishments, the exaltation of dynamism and the rejection of passivity. If Chinese political culture finds its hidden roots in
the depths of the Chinese family, Western political culture may find
its "root experience" symbolized in the family situation depicted in
the Oedipal myth. The Chinese counterpart of the Oedipal myth is
to be sought in works such as the *Classic of Filial Piety* and the literature of morality stories on the theme of filial piety. We can, of
course, perceive how this stress on the psychological roots of the traditional political culture relates to the significance of Mao's revolt
against paternal authority within his own family.

One can hardly deny that there is validity in some of these propositions. It is true that "individual autonomy" has been a dominant
strand of Western civilization in many times and places. It is true
that the "Confucian political order was centered on the notion that
the family was the matrix of society's political relations."[2] It is true
that the modern West in particular has seen the rise of attitudes
which place a positive value on self-assertion, activism, competitiveness, and "channeled aggressiveness." It is true that Confucian culture placed a high value on the maintenance of peace and order and
the avoidance of conflict. Yet to assert that these are prominent features of both cultures is misleading. They do not constitute the roots

from which the entire plant of culture grows, attractive as this image may be, particularly to those who lust for simple keys to foreign cultures. Western and Chinese culture are not plants and do not have single roots. It is not simply that these truths are partial. In wrenching them from the total context of culture and history—a context in which they can be understood only in tension with all of the other manifold strands and tendencies which constitute the turbulent and by no means integrated reality which we subsume under the simple term "culture"—partiality verges on error.

The trouble, however, lies even deeper. Concepts such as "individual autonomy," "authoritarianism," and "Confucianism" do not refer to clearly perceived entities, but to areas of reality, each of which involves its own complex problematic. Libraries of books have been written in the West on the subjects of individual freedom and authority, and in China vast tomes have been written on the problems of filial piety. It will simply not do to relate "political culture" to quasi-Freudian psychology and to ignore its relationship to political theory so long as one continues to employ words which imply all of the problems raised in political theory.

What is individual autonomy? Is Socrates's individual autonomy the same as that of John Stuart Mill? How does Immanuel Kant's view of individual autonomy relate to that of Senator Barry Goldwater? Does the Oedipal myth really supply us with a symbolic account of the origins within the family of the value of individual autonomy? While the emphasis on Oedipus immediately suggests the work of Sigmund Freud, Solomon's interpretation of the myth seems to me remarkably un-Freudian, despite his assumption that the secrets of culture are to be sought in the bosom of the family. Sexuality and incest play no role in Solomon's account. It is "at first reading more a story of politics than of family life or individual tragedy."[3] The story of the abandonment of Oedipus by his parents as an infant and his act of revolt against his father are the devious and oblique ways our "root culture" in ancient Greece expressed the assumption that "the individual is the basic 'actor' of society and should be trained in childhood to make do on his own, to be self-disciplining and self-directing." Yet the Chinese solution of the "problem stemming from the dependent and unsocialized condition of humans at birth," as depicted in the *Classic of Filial Piety,* exalts dependency and the total suppression of all self-direction.[4] Solomon, of course, is aware that

Sophocles presents the Oedipus myth as a tale of horror and tragedy, while the *Classic of Filial Piety* is presented as an unproblematic work of moral inspiration:

> The twenty-four models of filial piety are, of course, an ideal of hope just as the tragedy of Oedipus is a myth of horror. Such stylized expressions of a culture's anxieties and aspirations are meaningful to the extent that they define, in an explicit if highly simplified manner, certain cultural values and conceptions of life role and social relations.[5]

Yet surely it makes a great difference if given cultural values are presented as the objects of anxiety or of aspiration! In fact, most of what has been written about the actual history of the family in the classical world would suggest that parental authority in the Greco-Roman world was formidable. In ancient Roman law, the power of the father was terrifying. This does not preclude the possibility that Greece (Athens) was one of the sources of Western conceptions of individual autonomy, but there is little reason to think that this had much to do with the actual patterns of authority and child-rearing within the family. The classical world tended to draw a sharp distinction between the private realm of the family, where patriarchal authority prevailed, and the public sphere, where adult male citizens faced each other as peers. This suggests that the relationship between patterns of child-rearing and the emergence of ideas of individual autonomy may be far more complex than anything suggested in this book. In fact, if one considers the broad sweep of Western civilization from ancient Greece and deep into the period of modern "individualism," one finds that parental authority maintained a firm and healthy grip. No doubt there were profound differences in degree and modality between various types of parental authority in the West and the typical Confucian family in China, but the West has known staunch adherents of individualism who ruled their children with an iron rod. The abnegation of parental authority is a very recent phenomenon, and its effects on the kind of individual autonomy described by Solomon are as yet quite unclear.

If Solomon's book does scant justice to the history of family authority and its precise relationship to individualism in the West, what about political and social authority and hierarchy? If the trend toward individual autonomy has been a marked feature of Western culture, it can be properly understood only in terms of its constant tension with the claims of authority and hierarchy. What do we mean by individual autonomy, even in the most liberal states of the modern West? We mean that authority and hierarchy have been subject to limits, checks, and procedures of accountability which create a space for individual autonomy. We certainly do not mean that power, authority, and hierarchy have been completely displaced by individual autonomy. There is a large body of literature not mentioned by Solomon (including the writings of Max Weber) which is highly pessimistic about the future of individual autonomy in the modern West. When Solomon's Chinese interview respondents speak of political authority in terms of security, material well-being, and social peace, when they show reluctance to challenge authority or to talk back to their bosses, there is nothing in their testimony which seems idiosyncratically Chinese unless it be in the matter of degree. The notion that political authority is accepted because men are "afraid of being eaten by others" immediately reminds us of Thomas Hobbes's maxim, "man is a wolf to man." Hobbes was not giving vent to his own philosophic crotchets, but expressing a sentiment arising out of the experience of Western civilization. To the modern Western liberal, the political realm may have associations which go beyond the sentiments expressed by Solomon's respondents (this is also true of the idealistic Confucian), but these do not detract from the universality of their observations. There is a singular failure on Solomon's part to distinguish that which may be universally human in his respondents' reactions from that which is peculiarly Chinese.

Finally, in dealing with the Western side of Solomon's analysis, one can raise serious questions concerning his own particular conception of individual autonomy. The notion that the Faustian values of activism, assertiveness, positive orientation to conflict, and aggressiveness are necessarily linked to individual autonomy, and that the opposite traits are necessarily linked to group subordination and authoritarianism, reflects a peculiarly Anglo-American version of individualism. The modern West has been rich in *positive* authoritarianisms which, far from suppressing the aggressive energies of the individual, have demanded a full output of assertiveness, aggressiveness, readiness for conflict, and individual initiative, all harnessed to collective purposes and all entirely compatible with a total abnegation of individual moral and intellectual autonomy.[6] The recent experience of Germany seems to be totally absent from the author's consciousness. We shall find that Solomon feels obliged to admit in passing that in Mao these Faustian values are quite unconnected with any orientation to "individual autonomy." Yet the general implication remains that somehow the two are indissolubly connected and that the only reason for Mao's attacks on "selfish individualism" is that "he must cope with the need for social order and political discipline in a society where traditions have not prepared people for a critical and participatory role in the affairs of state."[7]

When we turn to the Chinese side of the analysis, we find similar simplifications. Granting that filial piety plays a unique role in the Confucian concept of political culture and that Confucius, like Solomon and Freud, saw an intimate connection between patterns of authority in the family and in the political order, has Solomon provided us with an accurate account of the implications of filial piety? We are told repeatedly that filial piety implies a "dependency orientation." (The image presented is that of the dependent small child and parents still in their prime who are able to impose their wills by moral and even by physical force, if necessary.) Actually, most of the paradigmatic stories in the *Classic of Filial Piety* and other literature do not involve dependency, but infinite obligation. We are most often presented with aged, feeble parents and adult children, or else children who have reached the age of reason and who often manifest extraordinary vigor and initiative in fulfilling their obligations to their parents. Without denying the presence of the dependency motif, the dimension of obligation greatly complicates matters. Among the gentry, a filial son could most spectacularly fulfill his obligations to his parents by becoming a successful official. This often meant a lifetime spent away from the family hearth. Unlike the notion of dependency, the notion of obligation does not necessarily suggest passivity. The Confucian political order may have stressed peace, harmony, and stasis above more dynamic goals, but it is not clear that this was due entirely to the dominance of filial piety. Indeed, it was not unreasonable for certain thinkers in China at the dawn of the twentieth century to hope that the motive of family obligation might be harnessed to the service of the new goal of patriotism as, in their view, had proven to be the case in Meiji Japan. Some might conceivably fulfill their duty to their parents by becoming captains of industry, military officers, or university professors, as well as by rising in the bureaucracy. This was not to prove a viable option in China, but the emphasis on infinite obligation to the social other—divorced from its familial context—is, in fact, a major continuity between Mao's vision and the Chinese past, which may be as important as the elements of discontinuity.

I shall not dwell here on the non-Confucian elements of Chinese culture which profoundly influenced the course of Chinese political history, but I do feel obliged to point out that Solomon has not furnished us with anything like an adequate account of Confucianism, either in terms of its normative values or in terms of the way Confucianism actually functioned in reality. In addition to the simplification of the notion of filial piety, there is a notable failure to discuss the relationship of filial piety to other political values among those who wielded authority and made decisions.[8] Again the assertion that in Confucianism "morality is always conceived of as being shaped by external conditioning" and that there is no conception of inner self-direction is, I believe, mistaken if one is referring to the Analects of Confucius, to Mencius, or to the main line of Neo-Confucian thought, which almost obsessively stresses the notion that all moral behavior on the part of the *chün-tzu* has its springs in the inner disposition of the soul. To be sure, there is the whole Hsün-tzu school, which stresses external conditioning, and there is an age-long debate in China between moral "intuitionists" and "behaviorists" which oddly resembles the similar debate in the West. To link this to the whole matter of childrearing practices is again misleading. There have been many staunch believers in inner direction in Western culture who have believed just as strongly as the Chinese that the only way to foster "inner-directedness" in early childhood is to exert strong parental authority.

Solomon may contend that he is not primarily interested in Confucian values as conceived by the philosophers, but rather with the way that Confucianism actually functions in Chinese society. He thus grossly underestimates the capacity of the "Confucian" state to deal with the "un-Confucian" actualities of the world. The wielders of power in China were well aware that problems of aggression and conflict in society could not be solved by Confucian childrearing practices. Over the centuries a bureaucratic system had developed for managing conflict both through violent and non-violent methods. There is a vast Chinese literature of statecraft and strategy, official and unofficial, concerned with the control of conflict. It is in fact a literature to which Mao has always been extraordinarily addicted.

This points to a major lacuna in the concept of political culture put forth in this book. All of Solomon's respondents are presented as the objects of authority rather than as the wielders of authority. While the theoreticians of political culture may boast that they are more concerned with the political attitudes of the masses than with their rulers, it will not do for any discipline which calls itself political to ignore the behavior of those who wield authority. The analysis of bureaucratic behavior and politics in the Chinese state over the centuries has just begun in the West. It is a world hardly touched in this book.

Mao's Revolution

The great protagonist of China's present-day political culture as depicted by Solomon is, of course, Mao. I would tend to agree that Mao has played a decisive role in the history of China since 1949. I would also agree that the notion of the positive role of conflict in human affairs has been one of Mao's persistent obsessions. No doubt Mao's much advertised youthful hostility toward his father (a hostility which hardly operated, however, on an Oedipal level) created a negative "rebellious" disposition which may have conditioned his subsequent responses to new ideas. Yet to see Mao as the lonely St. George battling the dragon of traditional culture, in isolation from the intellectual and political milieu within which he lived, is to distort the whole modern history of China. It seems necessary to Solomon's plan to see in Mao the dialectic antithesis of all of the characteristic traits of Chinese political culture. He is, as it were, the antithesis made flesh. Solomon consigns all those who have ever differed with Mao to the opposite pole of traditional political culture. All of this leads to a particularly static, one-dimensional, and uncomplicated Mao, as well as to a fantastic diminution of the role of other intellectual and political leaders.

If Mao had been born a few decades earlier, his struggles with his father would probably not have led him to any of his new ideas or values. The new values and ideas which Mao acquired in his school days were already available in the Chinese intellectual world and had already been embraced by others with quite different childhood experiences. Although some in the past may have overstressed the impact of Marxist-Leninist ideas on Mao, Solomon's tendency is to ignore the powerful molding impact of these ideas upon him. This leads to some gross distortions. One would hardly guess from this book, for example, that a good deal of the vocabulary of the "mass-line" is derived directly from Lenin. Also ignored is the enormous impact of Mao's political experience. If Mao had always rigidly emphasized conflict and implacable hostility in his political career, he probably would have long since been wrecked on the rocks of political reality. One would hardly guess that Mao at times has shown great adroitness in compromise and in "uniting with those with whom one can unite."

However much it may suit Solomon's categories to see Mao wholly in terms of the affirmation of conflict and assertiveness and the rejection of dependency, passivity, and social harmony, the Maoist vision of reality does include other elements of equal importance. Solomon himself acknowledges that Mao rejects with even greater vehemence the "individualism" which in Solomon's view is at the heart of Western culture. What Mao advocates is not "individual autonomy" but "group autonomy" (presumably as opposed to bureaucratic authority from above). The implications of group self-reliance are quite different from the implications of individual self-reliance. The individual must recognize his subordination to the group. He must also accept his infinite obligation to it. Although one need not doubt that Mao has Rousseauist dreams of "authority generated from group life," he has never wavered in his belief that such groups must conform their behavior to correct lines of policy imposed by the correct vanguard leadership. Mao may be suspicious of bureaucratic mechanisms, but he has never repudiated "correct" authority or leadership. In his vision of reality, one of the main roots of incorrect authority is the "selfish individualism" which leads traditional mandarins, Soviet officials, and Western capitalists to isolate their individual wills from the general will of society.

This static and one-dimensional view of Mao leads to some erroneous interpretations of Mao's attitudes since 1949. The author would have us believe, for example, that before 1956 the other party leaders were prepared to depend entirely upon the Soviet model of economic development while Mao—the unfailing rebel against authority—rejected this model. I believe that there is no evidence for this view. Mao had often challenged Soviet authority in the past, but there is evidence that he deeply believed in the Soviet role as a "teacher" before the middle 1950s. His insistence on a speed-up of collectivization in 1955 did not indicate that he was calling for an emphasis on agriculture rather than on industry. On the contrary, the speed-up of collectivization was a necessary ingredient of the Stalinist model of development. Mao's assertion that certain comrades should not be allowed "to use the Soviet experience as a cover for the idea of moving at a snail's pace" does not support Solomon's thesis.[9] In fact, the comrades in question were pointing to the disastrous results of the Soviet example and pleading for an avoidance of it, while Mao was maintaining that similar disasters would not occur in China.

There are many other matters of interpretation on which one might linger, but I shall confine my attention to Solomon's treatment of the background of the Cultural Revolution of 1966.[10] In dealing with the conflict between Mao and the other party leaders, he places his whole emphasis on Mao's fear of the recrudescence of the "ghosts and demons" of the political culture of the past. The attack on the "four olds" (old customs, habits, culture, and thought) was but one theme of the Cultural Revolution. It hardly occupied anything like the prominence of the attack on "bourgeois revisionism." Comparatively more attention was paid to the danger of an insidious "peaceful evolution" toward a Soviet or Western style of modernization than to the danger of a relapse into the Chinese past. Much more rhetoric was devoted to the insidious "negative example" of current post-Stalinist Soviet realities than to the mandarin past. In Mao's Cultural Revolutionary perspective, China's old society, the "bourgeois" West, and the Soviet Union all share fundamental features. Given Solomon's view of the differences between Western and Chinese political culture, can he possibly share these perspectives? Does he believe that modern Western bureaucrats and Chinese mandarins of the past represent the same evils? Does he believe that selfish individualism is at the heart of the matter?

At the center of Solomon's argument is the view that what Mao feared above all was the relapse of the masses into the political culture of dependency and the passive acceptance of authority. By adopting a purely economic and technocratic view of China's difficulties after 1960, the party leaders were neglecting the overriding necessity of mass mobilization in the task of China's nation-building. Even if this were the whole story, does it prove that the other party leaders embodied the political culture of the past or that they had a different view of what was involved in the task of "modernization"? An argument could be made that it was precisely Mao's opponents who were prepared to grant the local villages more autonomy in making vital economic and social decisions after 1960 and precisely Mao who wished to assert more authority in order to stem the drift toward what he regarded as "capitalism in the countryside." It was not a case of the assertion of "traditional" authority by the party versus a renunciation of authority and a reliance on the "mass will" by Mao. It was a case of Mao's assertion of his own infallible authority against what he regarded as the wrong policies pursued by the established institutions of authority. The effort to rely on the army, the "poor and middle peasants," and the Red Guards was an effort to find alternate sources of support for Mao's own unquestioned authority. It could be associated with such themes as antibureaucratism, distrust of formal organizations (which are no more "Chinese" than modern), and mass spontaneity, but at the heart of it was a substantive issue of economic and social organization in the countryside. Mao was deeply and passionately committed to collectivism, and the nation which he wished to build would have borne no resemblance to what Western social scientists might regard as a fully "built" nation. The notion that all of those within the leadership who have differed with Mao represent a "throw-back" to the "political culture" of the past reveals the limited nature of Solomon's categories when confronted with the richness of reality.

The tone of these observations has been largely negative. It may be said that they do scant justice to the daring and challenging nature of Solomon's enterprise; that they do not give the author sufficient credit for courage and resourcefulness in providing us with copious empirical support for his hypotheses; that they do not do sufficient justice to the many valid insights which are scattered throughout the book.

I confess that I cannot approve of Solomon's ambition to find the "key" to Chinese culture and Mao's revolution. The notion that there ought to be some simple categorical scheme which will explain the vast experience of Chinese culture and revolution is one which the average Westerner is all too prone to accept. It comfortably conforms to his expectations concerning the fundamental homogeneity and simplicity of far-off cultures. In dealing with his own environment, he may be sensitive to nuances within nuances, but he will offer little resistance to the notion that the "key" to Chinese culture can be found in one or two simple dichotomies. It is not at all clear that "Chinese culture" or the "Chinese revolution" are unified realities which can be reduced to a single formula. It is thus the duty of those who are attempting to study Chinese history and culture in depth to subject to the most searching scrutiny any effort to reduce this vast experience in time and space to some simple explanation. Chinese political culture is not reducible to the "dependency orientation," nor Western culture to "individual autonomy." Mao is not to be explained as the simple antithesis of Chinese culture, and the whole complex history of modern China cannot be reduced to a duel between the two. Formulas which claim too much are not always fruitful. At times they obstruct further inquiry by creating the illusion of achieved knowledge.

18

On the New Turn in China

*T*his may hardly be the ideal moment for general reflections on the significance of the present tragic turn in Chinese affairs. The brutal repression in Tiananmen Square was a decisive event, but the shape of things to come is still not entirely clear even though the signs are increasingly ominous.

Before I deal with the recent events, something must be said about the episodic nature of the history of mainland China during the last forty years and its significance for the entire enterprise of what has come to be called "China watching." Without claiming any particular wisdom for the highly diverse group of academics and journalists who engage in this enterprise (their ability to predict specific events is certainly not greater than that of American economists), we can say that they have all been forced to relate themselves to the shifting turns of political history. Since these episodic shifts have generally been associated with the conscious political decisions of political actors, a good deal of attention has necessarily focused on what is considered by many in the academy to be the superficial and unfashionable discipline of political history. Much attention has been devoted to the decisions themselves, to the role of ideology, of personality, of factionalism, of political-interest conflicts, and so on. In the opinion of some, there has been a deplorable neglect of the "deep underlying" socioeconomic structures of the "system."

A contrast has often been drawn with the Soviet watchers, who during the sixty or more years in which the "Stalinist system" prevailed were able to provide us with ample accounts of the "deep structures" of Soviet political organization, the Soviet economic system, the system of police control, and the systems of ideological control. In earlier years there was some debate in Soviet studies over whether extreme state terror and gulags were a vital organic part of the system, but after Stalin's death, there seemed to be a general consensus that the system could survive without these more extreme phenomena. Khrushchev created some problems, but with his demise the essential features of the system remained in place. To the extent that one could continue to say "more of the same next year" one could say that the Soviet system was predictable. Finally, there was even the notion that the system possessed inbuilt mechanisms that precluded any possibility of change from within. It came to be accepted that the Stalinist system could persist without Stalin. The role that political conflict and political decisions had played in inaugurating the system during the twenties somehow faded into the background and it came to be treated as a kind of enduring geological formation.

※

Now it is by no means my contention that there have been no enduring constants in the forty-year history of the People's Republic, although I would prefer not to use the mischievous word "system" in the full and comprehensive sense of that term. The Communist party succeeded very quickly after 1949 in imposing a fairly efficacious political control of mainland China, and despite all the vicissitudes of the following years (some created by Mao himself), the political unity of China has been maintained for good and ill. It has certainly been sufficiently effective to raise to unprecedented heights China's standing as a nation in the international arena. The Leninist conception of the transcendental authority of something called "The Party" has, in one form or another, survived all vicissitudes, including the most recent threat to it (as perceived by Deng Xiaoping) in the spring of this year. When I refer to the Leninist conception of transcendental party authority, I am not necessarily referring to the party's formal organizational structure or even to the corporate apparatus of the party. During the Cultural Revolution this transcendental authority was presumably concentrated in the person of Chairman Mao himself as against the established organization and apparatus, and at present it resides in the group of Deng and his closest cohorts whatever their formal party positions. Also, for a large part of the history of the People's Republic (perhaps least marked in the last ten years) political functionaries of all ranks have played a highly obtrusive role in the lives of the entire population. No doubt other constants could be mentioned. Yet all these constants taken together have provided us with little predictive power in plotting the evolution of shifts in policy.

It may, of course, be argued that policy decisions belong to the superficial sphere of the "history of events" while the more or less enduring constants belong to the "deep structure." In fact, of course, the decisions were made by a Leninist leadership that took for granted its power to shape such "deep structural" factors as the fundamental organization of agriculture, the role of intellectuals, and even models of economic development. What, then, is the relationship of the "history of events" to the deep underlying forces? If one is confident of one's theory or model, one may simply dismiss policy decisions that move in another direction as evanescent wave patterns on the surface of the sea. At this very moment there may be adherents of the "totalitarian model" who feel thoroughly revindicated by the latest events in Beijing. On the other hand, some political happenings may be treated as volcanic eruptions that reveal deep shifts in the geological structures. Even the shifting decisions of leaders can come to be regarded as manifestations of well-rooted "social evolutionary" forces. Hegel, in coping with the problem of the "great man" in history, was prepared to see Napoleon as the World Spirit incarnate while Stalin has been regarded as the embodiment of a necessary stage in the laws of economic development in backward countries. Thus at the beginning of episodes such as the Hundred Flowers (1956–57) and the Great Leap Forward (1958–1960) in China—episodes in which Mao truly played a commanding role—foreign observers could never be sure whether shifts of policy were "superficial" political shifts or represented long-term shifts in the "underlying forces." China watchers, particularly if located in the social sciences departments of universities, were under unremitting pressure to come up with the "deep theory" or "model" that would explain the latest episode. Naturally the existence of such models implied the capacity to extrapolate the long-term consequences of the model into the distant future.

※

In the period 1952–1955, when China seemed to be slavishly internalizing the Stalinist system in every field of social and political life, and when the trajectory seemed to point to an ever closer approximation to that system, the "totalitarian model" enjoyed enormous prestige. Its plausibility was even enhanced by Karl Wittfogel's theory of "oriental despotism," which added a sociocultural dimension to the modern Western theory of totalitarianism. By the "totalitarian model," I refer not only to what might be called the "totalitarian aspiration" but to the notion of the actual achievement of the total control of every aspect of human life including the ability to transform the psyches of vast populations. In the case of China the millennial history of oriental despotism had perhaps made available exotic techniques of social-psychological control that were not available even in the West or the Soviet Union, leading to much research on the peculiar efficacy of thought control ("brainwashing"). The French journalist Robert Guillain, who traveled in China in the 1950s and who was able to elicit the same stereotyped responses to all questions wherever he went, reported that China had effectively been transformed into the kingdom of blue ants. Any argument that there may have been silent factors that ran counter to the total internalization of the Stalinist system tended to be dismissed. Even such a simple question as whether—given the demographic facts of Chinese life—China could long afford to indulge in the kind of neglect of the agricultural sector that was built into the Stalinist model received little attention. The question of whether "oriental despotism" provided an adequate "key" to the vast and complex sociopolitical history of China resounded all the more majestically in the vast cavern of ignorance of China's complex past.

Stirrings among the Flowers

In the years 1956–57, however, the Hundred Flowers movement emerged in which Mao and others played a considerable role. Even in terms of elemental political psychology one might have entertained the possibility that a Chinese leader who had developed his own ideas in Yenan before 1949 and who probably was deeply ambivalent about Stalin's claim to supreme authority might not have been forever bound to all the particulars of the Soviet system and might even have been open to new suggestions. It was indeed in the Hundred Flowers period that Mao found himself again as the effective political and ideological leader of China. It was in this new mental frame that he was prepared to entertain the idea that China needed to reassess the role of its intellectuals despite his continued suspicion of them. With this opening up of new spaces of discussion and experimentation in the economic and cultural spheres, the "totalitarian model," with its emphasis on stasis, suddenly became questionable and gave way to "developmental" and "modernization" models. In both the Soviet Union and China there had been impressive economic growth. Had these economies not begun to approach a level where one could begin to expect economic, cultural, and perhaps even political liberalization? Did Mao Tse-tung not comprehend the long-term implications of his new policies? By the summer of 1957, however, it became clear that he was to become much more obsessed with certain unanticipated short-term political consequences, particularly by what might be called the emergence of the student factor. A new generation of university students (undoubtedly influenced by some of the older intellectuals) who had been subject from early childhood to all the totalitarian techniques of thought control suddenly began to express devastating critiques of the party's claim to transcendental authority—to the obvious dismay of both foreign adherents of the totalitarian model and Chairman Mao himself. Like the Deng of 1989, Mao had not come to power to witness any challenge to the transcendent authority of the party.

With the abrupt shift to the antirightist campaign of 1957 and finally to the apocalyptic vision of the Great Leap Forward (1958–1960) there was an abrupt decline in the fortunes of a development theory that relied heavily on economic analysis and on Weberian notions of rationalization. The rise of the communes, the emphasis on the collective moral fervor of the peasant masses, and the combination of fervent faith in rapid development with an anti-economist view of the motive power of this development coalesced in a revival of the totalitarian model and of the notion of the peculiarly "Asian" nature of Chinese totalitarianism. After all, Stalin at his most totalitarian had never denied the role of material incentives and of technology. It was at this juncture that talk of a new "Asian Communism" came into vogue. Many members of the "New Left" of the 1960s, enthralled with the Mao of the Great Leap Forward and later of the Cultural Revolution, became convinced that he had indeed discovered a sovereign method to bypass all the evils of inequality, individual self-interest, and bureaucracy, even while pushing forward the modernization of the society as a whole. Mao was indeed the voice of the masses incarnate and thus no deep and painful inquiry was required into how his visions related to grim realities on the ground.

Although the "New Left" Maoists were to blend the visions of the Great Leap Forward and the Cultural Revolution into a new model, we now know that disastrous events unanticipated by Mao brought an end to the "great leap" and created a rift between himself and the bureaucracy which in the end rejected his anti-economistic bias. Thus when Mao retired to the background during the early 1960s, the bureaucracy returned to a more economically oriented "pragmatism." They were no longer enthralled with the Stalinist model, and there was even cautious revival of some of the intellectual openness of the Hundred Flowers period. Among China watchers in the West in search of a model, there was for a brief time a revival of the rational-development model—a revival soon aborted by the wrath of the aging Mao.

The Cultural Revolution of 1966 posed in a most acute form the problem of the role of the "great man" in history. One could truly say, "No Mao Tse-tung, no Cultural Revolution." Relying on the sheer potency of his own cult, Mao managed (with tacit support from at least some sections of the military) to override and humble the party bureaucracy, to concentrate in his own person the mystique of Leninist infallibility, and at least for a time to enchant and enthrall the student youth with his apocalyptic vision of a pure society. No doubt part of his initial appeal to them lay in his systematic desanctification of the party bureaucracy. What then could one say about the socio-economic and cultural causes of this episode? Chinese society of the 1960s was undoubtedly ridden with deep social and economic tensions and conflicts, some of which the Cultural Revolution laid bare. Would these tensions themselves have produced anything like the Cultural Revolution without Mao? The New Left admirers of Mao might have had faith that Mao had actually found a new path to modernization that would bypass all the evils of materialistic selfishness and of bureaucracy, but the subsequent course of events proved that the grand old man had no idea of how to implement his apocalyptic vision. The Cultural Revolution does indeed raise theoretical questions about the potency of the Mao cult and the behavior of human beings in extreme situations, but these questions may relate more to depth psychology or philosophic anthropology than to sociopolitical models.

The Modernizations

With the death of Mao, we finally have the emergence of Deng Xiaoping and the period of the "four modernizations." Was this then to be only another episode in the episodic history of the People's Republic or had the country finally entered a steady mainstream of development uninterrupted by the arbitrary caprices of the aged Mao? It is quite clear that the period from the late 1970s to the late 1980s has indeed been entirely different from all previous periods in terms of the decisive turn by the leadership (even the "conservatives") from Mao's anti-economism to a deep commitment to technological and economic development. In fact the "four modernizations" have already had a visible impact and there have been tangible, striking successes in the sphere of economic development. In its decollectivization of agriculture the new regime demonstrated its willingness to support deep institutional change in pursuing its developmental goals. Above all, the new freedom has made it possible for us in the West to come into closer contact with the living reality of Chinese society. We have come to appreciate regional differences, to know a multitude of individuals as living individuals, and even to have direct contact with people from all economic and social backgrounds. Even if the current turn leads back to a regime of silence and uniform standard responses, I trust that we will never again allow ourselves to return to the stereotype of the kingdom of blue ants.

What then of the old party leadership which returned to power after the humiliations of the Cultural Revolution? They certainly did not come back with any desire to witness the demise of party authority. In fact they were firmly convinced that this authority had been illegitimately usurped by the aged Mao, and there is no reason to assume that Deng Xiaoping, a leading policy maker, was any more willing than his elderly colleagues to witness the demise of party authority. When the Democracy Wall movement of 1978–79 raised the dread possibility of imposing institutional limits and controls on the party leadership, Deng promptly proclaimed the "four cardinal principles," which reasserted the unchallengeable authority of the Communist party, meaning primarily its top decision makers. The legitimacy of this authority derived from the fact that the party virtually represented the "people's democratic dictatorship" and was presumably based on the doctrines of Marx, Lenin, and Mao, but as a true pragmatist Deng tended to focus on the idea of party authority itself rather than linger on the presumed doctrinal base on which it rested.

What differentiated Deng from some of his colleagues, however, was that having presumably assured the unassailability of ultimate party authority, he proceeded to pursue the goal of a "wealthy, powerful, and modernized China" with enormous boldness and willingness to take risks. He had no doubt that China would require the talents of the intellectuals and also realized that to win the intellectuals it would be necessary to create an atmosphere that would foster a certain space of freedom and security for all intellectuals, just as it would be necessary to secure for the people as a whole a certain sense of immediate improvement in their material lives. He was indeed quite prepared to go forward with Bukharin's motto, "Enrich yourselves," for the population as a whole. He seems to have genuinely appreciated the need for legality in the economic sphere and even in some areas of civil law. He also seems to have been prepared to accept the decentralization of power in the realm of economic life, perhaps on the tacit assumption that such power could always be reclaimed by the center if necessary. Finally, in his own mind he may have drawn a distinction between the extension of individual freedom in the economic and cultural spheres and the call for "bourgeois democracy" as a challenge to the decision-making power of those on top. He often paid lip service to the need for "political reform" and even seemed prepared for minor dabblings with the political structure, but he never seemed really serious in this area. On the question of cultural and ideological control he seemed to vacillate occasionally when his more cautious colleagues urged him to combat "bourgeois spiritual pollution." Yet in the end his pragmatism may have led him to feel that "ideas in people's heads" were not important enough to permit a diversion of energies from the tasks of modernization.

In retrospect, it may have been precisely his pragmatic bent that led him to underestimate the depth of alienation created in the young by the Cultural Revolution. The extent of this alienation was made plain to me from conversations in 1981 with former Red Guards who had witnessed both the Cultural Revolution and the Democracy

Wall movements of 1978–79. It became clear that although they had felt betrayed and tricked by the aged Mao, many had nevertheless also absorbed the message of Mao's systematic desanctification of the party bureaucracy. Even though they seemed to respond with gratitude to the new policies of "liberalization," some did not refrain from raising questions about the legitimacy of Leninist authority itself, and Deng responded at the time with predictable anger as well as with the promulgation of the "four cardinal principles." It is nevertheless clear that this older generation of youth and older intellectuals had managed to transmit its rejection of the Leninist mystique to a younger student generation.

⚋⚌

One can only speculate on why the same Deng, who with his four principles had clearly tried to fence off the question of highest party authority as forbidden territory, continued with occasional vacillation to support bold policies of intellectual liberalization. Perhaps he was convinced that the spectacular successes of the four modernizations in the late 1970s and early 1980s had won the support of the masses, thus isolating the narrow stratum of intellectuals and students. Perhaps he was also confident that as modernization proceeded the students themselves would be caught up in the practical tasks of modernization and the pursuit of their own careers. While it seems to be part of the current American creed that the concern for "enriching oneself" and ardor for democratic principles go hand in hand, Deng may have thought otherwise. Even the remarkable permissiveness and openness that has prevailed in literature, philosophy, and legal and political thought may have reflected a pragmatic disdain for the practical importance of abstract theories. This freedom helped to foster a congenial atmosphere.

Most recently, China's economic development, despite its successes, has entered a time of troubles, and one need not deny that economic grievances, ubiquitous corruption, and disappointed expectations have played a part in the discontents of students and intellectuals. In fact, economic grievances and political discontents seem to be totally entwined. The economic development of China has not evolved simply from "public, planned economy" to "private market economy." Among the most aggressive entrepreneurs of the new China (some are involved with the world economy) are former cadres and relatives of cadres and even military men, who use their political leverage to launch new enterprises. These enterprises, while operating in the market, are not really part of any sharply demarcated private sector. In the eyes of intellectuals who live in the grossly underfunded educational-cultural sector, these new "bureaucratic capitalists" represent a source of gross corruption, inequity, and hypocrisy. Many of these students and intellectuals who claim to be ardent supporters of the "free enterprise" system find the combination of unbridled political power with the avid pursuit of private wealth unacceptable. Here, their attitudes resonate with a long tradition of Confucian moralism. At the same time, these attitudes make them deeply appreciative of that aspect of Western constitutional democracy that maintains that the corruption of the political elite can only be tamed by subjugating their power to constitutional control. Contrary to the usual facile assertions that Chinese cannot understand democracy, some of the Chinese students I know understand these notions quite clearly. This does not, of course, mean that the students in Tiananmen Square had any idea of how to realize such democracy within the present framework of power.

The discussion of democracy in the Chinese intellectual media has grown in strength since the beginning of the year. Meanwhile, China's economic problems have not abated. Even the students and intellectuals do not believe that all the problems are simply due to corruption, but there has been an equal lack of faith that the highest decision makers possess any higher wisdom in these matters. It is also important to note that 1989 marks the seventieth anniversary of the famous student uprising of May 4, 1919—an event that many were now prepared to interpret in a way entirely hostile to the official interpretation. A very common view of May 4, 1919 is that what seemed like a promising turn to "democracy and enlightenment" in the May 4th movement was derailed by the false promise of Marxism-Leninism. One thus had reason to expect trouble as May 4, 1989 approached.

All of this taken together with calls for the release of the Democratic Wall hero Wei Jingsheng, the prolonged occupation of the sacred site Tiananmen, and the insulting challenges to the top leadership no doubt began to loom in Deng's eyes as an unacceptable threat to the principle of party transcendence, which he had never for a moment abandoned. His speech of April 26, which we received very late, establishes all the premises for the crackdown of June 4. The preservation of supreme party authority and prestige, we are told, is an imperative that transcends all foreign and domestic opinion and that may even involve bloodshed. It is not a question of whether students can topple the government. China, unlike Poland, does not have to contend with the Catholic church and Solidarity—only with a group of students and intellectuals "who can be dealt with."

If the premises for the crackdown were present, at least in Deng's mind, on April 26, one may ask why the final act did not occur until June 4. There were, of course, large parts of the government and party establishment that obviously did not share his premises, including the vacillating Zhao Ziyang. Deng and his elderly cohorts clearly mistrusted the "deliberative" bodies of the government and party. There was already the hint in the April 26th statement that in the end the army might have to play a crucial role. Despite Deng's statements of April 26, many seriously doubted whether a disdain for "foreign opinion" would be compatible with an "open door" policy. Yet as May moved on there were further, even greater, challenges to the four principles. It appeared that most of the urban masses were prepared to express solidarity with the students, and after the declaration of martial law it even became evident that there were signs of softness in the armed forces.

From the point of view of Deng and his aged colleagues the entire mystique of party authority was endangered. Could the students have been handled otherwise? No doubt this was possible. The Gorbachev of 1989 might have handled it differently. In the universe of Deng Xiaoping, however, whose entire life is coterminous with the history of the Chinese Communist party, the decision to preserve the notion of party authority at whatever cost was a thoroughly pragmatic decision. The alternative, in his view, was anarchy.

Were the "China watchers" incapable of predicting the crackdown? In fact the possibility was widely discussed but tended to be regarded as unlikely because of its presumed prohibitive costs. During the last ten years, the "rational-development model" has again become ever more plausible. Many have been able to observe on the spot the results of new policies in agriculture, industry, culture, and in China's increasing involvement with the world economy and foreign societies. While many have been critical, even pessimistic, about many policies and while it is by no means clear that anyone (including foreign experts) has easy solutions for China's problems of modernization, the notion that the priority of the emphasis on modernization was now "irreversible" was almost implied by the rational development model. Within this context, Deng's "four principles" seemed to have less and less relevance.

It may indeed prove true that there are "irreversibilities" in the Chinese scene. The new leadership itself professes to believe that its policies of repression are compatible with certain irreversibilities. Deng insists again and again that the policies of "reform and the open door" are entirely compatible with the current stress on the "four principles." What was most questionable, of course, was the notion that the government had irreversibly lost both the coercive power and the will to suppress tendencies that it regarded as threats to its survival. Deng has recently even confessed his own errors in underestimating the need for "ideological and political education." Does he really believe, as Mao presumably did, that his ideology can "transform men's souls"? What he probably does believe is that it can forcibly mute the communication of dangerous ideas and create again at least the appearance of massive consensus.

It is not my contention that the various deep theories and models that we have imposed on China's episodic history in the last forty years had nothing to tell us. The totalitarian aspiration, the aims of economic development, the interplay with the culture of the past, the silent weight of demography, the role of nationalism, the ideology and the concept of the party, and other factors have all entered into the complex drama of the history of contemporary China. Yet, if we must have a "framework," I would precisely recommend the metaphor of an unfolding and unresolved drama rather than that of all-encompassing models or "deep theories" with their claims to provide totalistic, predictive knowledge. If the word "crisis" were not now a watered-down cliché, I would say that in the case of China what we have is a mammoth and sustained cultural-historical crisis involving the interaction between the society and culture of the past and claims of modernity (both of these terms themselves refer to vast and unresolved complexities). It would appear that the Communist revolution by no means ended this crisis and the Chinese (like the rest of us) will continue to grope toward their own solutions.

NOTES

CREDITS

INDEX

Notes

Introduction

1. In consideration of the different periods in which these collected essays were written, both the Wade-Giles and Pinyin systems of transliteration have been for the most part preserved as originally published.

2. These texts offer limited access to the conscious lives of the rural masses, which for the most part were still embedded within the popular culture and religion of the past. Here we owe much to the empirical studies of cultural anthropologists, however much their work may reflect pre-established models.

3. The fact of the indeterminacy of signifiers applies as much to the language of the translator as to the language being translated.

4. See Benjamin Schwartz, Introduction to *Chinese Communism and the Rise of Mao* (Cambridge, Mass.: Harvard University Press, 1951), p. 2.

1. Some Stereotypes in the Periodization of Chinese History

1. They are, of course, transitional in the same sense in which all historic phenomena in all periods are transitional.

2. Chien Po-tsan, "Kuan-yü Chung-kuo li-shih fen-ch'i ti wen-ti" (The Problem of Periodization in Chinese History) in *Tôyôshi Kenkyu* vol. 4, no. 4.

3. *Chung-kuo Li-shih Kai-yao* (Peking, 1956).

4. Ibid., pp. 2–3.

5. This manuscript, subtitled "Rough Draft," was first published by the Marx-Engels Lenin Institute in Moscow in 1939.

6. Ibid., p. 393.

2. A Brief Defense of Political and Intellectual History

1. Claude Lévi-Strauss, "Overture to *le Cru et le Cuit,*" cited in "Structuralism," *Yale French Studies* (October 1966).

2. See M. Freedman, *Lineage Organization in Southeastern China* (London: Athlone Press, 1958).

3. In actuality the theories of history that stress vast impersonal forces do not really ascribe any truly creative role to the masses. The masses simply provide the psychological energy through which the large structures and processes manifest themselves.

4. Frederic Wakeman, *Strangers at the Gate: Social Disorder in South China, 1839–1861* (Berkeley: University of California Press, 1966).

5. Maurice Merleau-Ponty, *Éloge de la philosophie et autres essais* (Paris: Gallimard, 1965), p. 325.

6. See Chapter 9, "History and Dialectic," in Claude Lévi-Strauss, *The Savage Mind,* trans. George Weidenfeld and Nicolson Ltd. (Chicago: University of Chicago Press, 1966).

7. Ibid., p. 247.

8. The question of how far this cosmology had developed in Confucius's time remains a matter of dispute but there is a tendency to interpret the statement in the Analects that *t'ien tao* (the "way of heaven") was one of the matters which the master seldom discussed as a reference to this type of cosmology.

3. The Limits of "Tradition versus Modernity"

1. In all thinking in terms of development models one often finds, even in the same author, a constant oscillation between a descriptive-determinist approach and a prescriptive-projective approach. One speaks of how intellectuals will necessarily behave in terms of the laws of development or how they ought to behave if the project of modernization is to succeed. In the one case the intellectuals are included within the entire impersonal process. In the other, modernization is conceived of as a project and the intellectual and political elites are conceived of as standing outside. They navigate the ship of history.

2. Particularly among students of Japan. Also noticeably in the work of Professor S. N. Eisenstadt.

3. It is interesting to observe that Max Weber, whose concept of "traditional modes of domination" is one source of the prevailing more generalized concept of traditional society, was himself overwhelmingly concerned with the *differences* among the higher civilizations of the past.

4. This leaves open the question of the ulterior purposes of this mastery, which, it seems to me, is left vague in Weber.

5. It is, of course, impossible to say that any of them were new in any absolute sense. They may all have deep roots in Western culture, as Carl Becker insisted. Whether absolutely new or not, there were serious and profound differences in the world visions of Voltaire, Rousseau, Montesquieu, Hume, and the Marquis de Sade.

6. Of course, Marx's concept of modernization incorporates the moral conflict element of class struggle.

7. Here again, the term "classical Chinese" covers a complex history of stylistic conflicts—conflicts in which the transitional generations continued to participate.

8. We are here speaking, of course, of the creative minority.

9. But not all. The scholar Wang Kuo-wei was very soon to turn away from the preoccupation with national power to his more fundamental concern with perennial problems of the human condition. Significantly he was greatly attracted to Schopenhauer.

10. *Yü Wai-chiao pao chu-jen lun chiao-yü shu* (Letter to the editor of *Wai-chiao pao* on education) cited in my *In Search of Wealth and Power: Yen Fu and the West* (Cambridge, Mass.: Harvard University Press, 1964), p. 49.

11. This does not necessarily have optimistic implications. It may not be the best elements of both cultures that are compatible.

12. See Schwartz, *In Search of Wealth and Power*.

13. We may loosely call this the "May 4th Generation" if we include both the older vanguard figures such as Ch'en Tu-hsiu, Li Ta-chao, Hu Shih, and so forth, as well as the student generation of 1919.

14. In Chinese terms he must himself be classed as an intellectual or marginal intellectual. He is not a peasant leader in the Zapata sense.

5. Review of *Law in Imperial China*

1. Derk Bodde and Clarence Morris, *Law in Imperial China: Exemplified by 190 Ch'ing Dynasty Cases, translated from the Hsing-an hui-lan* (Cambridge, Mass.: Harvard University Press, 1967), p. 150.

2. Ibid., p. 28.

3. Lanzetta v. New Jersey, 306 U.S. 451 (1938). See pp. 530–533 in Bodde and Morris.

4. State v. Provenzano 34 N. J. 318, 169 A.2d 135 (1961). See pp. 521–522 in Bodde and Morris.

5. Bodde and Morris, p. 161.

6. Social Role and Sociologism in China

1. Steven Lukes, *Individualism* (New York: Harper and Row, 1973).

2. Ibid., p. 127.

3. It is by no means my intention in these remarks to defend all the modes of "methodological individualism" which Lukes attacks.

4. Lukes, *Individualism*, pp. 156–157.

5. Perhaps the Chinese counterpart of this kind of absolutist sociologism is the kind of cosmico-socio-historic determinism we find in Wang Ch'ung or Shao Yung.

6. Lukes, *Individualism*, p. 157.

7. Ibid., p. 149.

8. Ibid., p. 151.

9. Ibid., p. 171.

10. I would suggest that Lukes confuses Kierkegaard's Christian existentialism with Sartre's non-Christian existentialism.

11. Herbert Fingarette, *Confucius: The Secular as Sacred* (New York: Harper and Row, 1972).

7. On the Absence of Reductionism in Chinese Thought

1. While reductionism as here defined may have been one of the essential ingredients of the scientific revolution in the West, the problem is more specific and manageable than the hazier problem of the absence of "science."

2. Some may suggest the simple word "materialism" for what is here called reductionism. In fact, the word materialism has come to be used in Western thought in many non-reductionist ways. This has considerably complicated the problem of its application to Chinese thought.

3. W. W. Jaeger, *Theology of the Early Greek Philosophers* (London: Oxford University Press, 1947).

4. F. M. Cornford, *From Religion to Philosophy* (New York: Harper & Bros., 1957).

5. For example, his explanation of heat as a "matter which is compressed and condensed while cold is a matter which is fine and 'relaxed.'" See Geoffrey Stephen Kirk and John Earle Raven, *The Pre-Socratic Philosophers* (Cambridge: Cambridge University Press, 1960), p. 148.

6. R. Collingwood, *The Idea of Nature* (London: Oxford University Press, 1967), p. 51.

7. See also Kirk and Raven, *Pre-Socratic Philosophers*, p. 404.

8. See Joseph Needham, *Science and Civilization in China* (Cambridge: Cambridge University Press, 1956), vol. 2, p. 30.

9. The Hebrew word for "breath" has the same soulish qualities which it has in so many other cultures.

10. For example, see the symposium *Beyond Reductionism*, eds. Arthur Koestler and J. R. Smythies (Boston: Beacon Press, 1968).

11. There is strong reason to believe that the two are by no means mutually exclusive in Chinese thought.

12. Jen-min Chu-pan she, *Tu Kuo-hsiang wen chi* (Peking, 1962).

13. See Ch'en Meng-chia, *Wu-hsing chieh chi-yuan* (The origins of the five elements) in Ku Chieh-kang, *Wu te chung-shih shuo-hsia ti cheng-chih ho li-shih* (Hong Kong: Lung-men, 1970), appendix pp. 29–32.

14. Ibid., p. 46.

15. See Kuan Feng, *Ch'un ch'iu che-hsüeh shih lun-chi* (A collection of essays on the history of philosophy in the Spring and Autumn Period) (Peking: People's Press, 1963), pp. 274–377.

16. See Kurita Naomi, *Jôdai shina no Tenseki no mietaru [ki] no kannen* (The

concept of *ch'i* as seen in ancient Chinese texts) in *Chûgoku Jôdai shisô no kenkyu* (Tokyo: Iwanami).

17. *Hsün-tzu chi-chieh* (Collected essays of Hsün-tzu with commentaries) in Chu-tzu chi-ch'eng (Peking: Zhonghua, 1957), vol. 2, p. 205.

18. Ibid., p. 206.

19. Heaven is, to be sure, divested of most anthropomorphic attributes.

20. Wang Ch'ung, *Lun Heng* (Discourses and Evaluations), Tzu-jan pien in *Chu tzu Chi-ch'eng* vol. 7 (1954), p. 17.

21. Mou Tsung-san in Chapter 1 of his *Ts'ai hsing yü hsüan-li* (Natural talents and metaphysical thinking) (Hong Kong: People's Press, 1963).

22. That is, language concerning a creator or a creative process.

23. A. C. Graham, "China, Europe and the Origins of Modern Science" in *Chinese Science, Explorations of an Ancient Tradition,* eds. Shigeru Nakayama and Nathan Sivin (Cambridge, Mass.: MIT Press, 1973), p. 57. It is somewhat puzzling that Needham uses the passage in Lieh-tzu concerning the robot as an illustration of the "philosophy of organism" (see *Science and Civilization in China,* vol. 2, p. 53). The story could be cited as evidence for a non-"organismic" strand in Chinese thought.

24. See William Theodore DeBary, "Individualism and Humanitarianism in Late Ming Thought" in his edited *Self and Society in Ming Thought* (New York: Columbia University Press, 1970).

25. The term is a misnomer in that it was a culture widely shared by the ruling classes.

9. The Primacy of the Political Order in East Asian Societies

1. I use the sociological term "political order" (roughly in the manner of using the terms economic order or religious order) so as to avoid some of the endless controversies which surround the term "state." Some might be inclined to assert that a full-fledged state emerges in China with the rise of the centralized bureaucratic empire in 221 B.C. Yet some of the characteristics of the political order discussed in this essay seem to have already been present well before the rise of the Ch'in empire.

2. The Western word "political" is, of course, laden with semantic pitfalls. Hannah Arendt would certainly not apply the word to the administrative side of government in which officials simply issue orders to "passive" inferiors. Politics, a word which derives from the ancient *polis*, should refer only to the active participation of more or less equal citizens in the active life of political decision-making. Yet even her idealized Athens related to the colonies of the Athenian empire as an administrator. Moreover, in modern usage the term applies to the administrative quite as much as to the deliberative aspects of government. Functions such as the military and police, taxation, and "public works" are all treated in political science. Even in our most ancient Chinese texts, *zheng* involved these functions as well as others.

10. Hierarchy, Status, and Authority in Chinese Culture

1. Thomas A. Metzger, "The Definition of Self, the Group, the Cosmos, and Knowledge in Chou Thought: Some Comments on Professor Schwartz's Study," *The American Asian Review*, vol. 4, no. 2 (Summer 1986), pp. 68–116.

2. Due to limits of time and space I shall mainly discuss what has been loosely defined as Confucianism although that some of the major contending schools of thought also fully accepted the necessity of hierarchy, status, and authority as aspects of social organization.

11. Review of *Disputers of the Tao*

1. A. C. Graham, *Disputers of the Tao: Philosophic Argument in Ancient China* (New York: Open Court, 1989).

2. It may be argued that there are aspects of technical mathematical logic in logical positivism and the writings of Quine which are inaccessible to non-professionals. This is not true of Ryle and Austin.

3. H. Fingarette, *Confucius: The Secular as Sacred* (New York: Harper Torchbooks, 1972).

4. *Philosophy of Language,* ed. J. R. Searle (London: Oxford University Press, 1971), p. 14.

5. Ibid., p. 23.

6. Graham mentions this term only in its connection to Mohist utilitarianism (p. 145).

7. Fingarette, *Confucius: The Secular as Sacred,* p. 21.

8. Ibid., p. 78.

9. I am somewhat inclined to distinguish between the two.

13. The Reign of Virtue

1. Regis Debray, *Revolution in the Revolution? Armed Struggle and Political Struggle in Latin America,* trans. Bobby Ortis (New York: Grove Press, 1967), p. 78.

2. Ibid., p. 101.

3. Ibid., p. 104.

4. Ibid., p. 102.

5. Ibid., p. 125.

6. Ibid., p. 105.

7. See for instance "Gel'bras o stanovlenii voenno-burokraticeskoi diktatury v Kitae" (On the establishment of a military bureaucratic dictatorship in China), *Narody Asii i Afriki,* no. 1, 1968.

8. New China News Agency (NCNA) Service in English, May 14, 1975, Foreign Broadcast Information Service (FBIS) vol. 1, no. 95.

9. See *Joint Publications Research Service* (JPRS), no. 44,204, January 31, 1968, *passim.*

10. "The CCP—Orphan of Mao's Storm," cited in the Hong Kong Consulate publication *Current Scene*, vol. 6, no. 4.

11. One may speculate that some of the "ultra-leftists" may have conceived of doing away with the party entirely.

12. *Hung Ch'i* (Red Flag), no. 1 (July 11, 1967).

13. Cited in Ernst Cassirer's *Philosophy of the Enlightenment* (Boston: Beacon Press, 1955), p. 154.

14. "The Social Contract," Book II, Chapter 3, *The Social Contract: Essays by Locke, Hume, and Rousseau, with an Introduction by Sir Ernest Baker* (London: Oxford University Press, 1953), p. 274.

15. To Robespierre the word "party" was a bad word. There ought to be no "parties" within the sovereign people. The Marxist conception of class struggle, however, when added to the notion that parties represented classes, provided a much firmer foundation for the concept of a party.

16. See particularly *One Step Forward, Two Steps Backward.*

17. In the ideal society of the past, the ethical initiative had been taken by single individuals, the sage-rulers Yao, Shun, and Yü.

18. *The Book of Mencius*, Part I, Chapter 17 in *The Chinese Classics*, Vol. 2, trans. James Legge (Hong Kong: Hong Kong University Press, 1960), p. 419.

19. *The Social Contract*, Book II, Chapter 6, p. 289.

20. And even he should not rule. "When Lycurgus gave laws to his country he began by abdicating his royal power." Ibid., p. 293.

21. Although here too we find ambiguities. Ernest Barker points out that in spite of his emphasis on law, Rousseau "felt in his bones that the nation made the law and not the law the nation." Ibid., p. xxxix.

14. A Personal View of Some Thoughts of Mao Tse-tung

1. John Dewey, *Reconstruction in Philosophy* (New York: Mentor Books, 1949), pp. 84–85.

2. Mao Tse-tung, "Rectify the Party's Style of Work," *Selected Works of Mao Tse-tung* (Peking: Foreign Languages Press, 1960), p. 40.

3. Ibid., p. 41.

4. If one considers the whole history of the People's Republic, one finds much less commitment than in earlier Soviet history to the application of Marxist-Leninist universal truth to natural science (in the manner of Engels), although one occasionally finds references in Cultural Revolutionary literature and in the writings of Mao to the application of "On Contradictions" to particle physics.

5. See particularly Avineri Shlomo, *The Social and Political Thought of Karl Marx* (Cambridge: Cambridge University Press, 1970), pp. 239–249.

6. Franz Schurmann has pointed out that the Great Leap Forward was actu-

ally preceded by a rectification movement directed against regionalist tendencies within the party. *Ideology and Organization in Communist China* (Berkeley: University of California Press, 1966), pp. 215–216.

7. Mao has occasionally invoked the Marxist notion of the dissolution of the state, but his notion of the permanent revolution with its ongoing struggles and contradictions would suggest that the need for a social vanguard will continue into the distant future.

8. Departmentalism is a tendency to identify with particular vested interests whether these be geographic (village, province) or functional (the bureau or department).

9. The argument about the "middling" type relates to a conflict about literary policy in the early 1960s. Shao Ch'üan-lin, a literary bureaucrat, pressed the view that literature should deal with men as they are—complex mixtures of good and evil. See Merle Goldman, "Party Policies toward the Intellectuals," in *Party Leadership and Revolutionary Power in China*, ed. John W. Lewis (Cambridge: Cambridge University Press, 1970).

15. The Rousseau Strain in the Contemporary World

1. See Jean Starobinski, *La Transparence et l'obstacle* (Paris: Gallimard, 1971).

2. Rousseau, "Fragments sur le luxe, le commerce et les arts" in *Oeuvres complètes de Jean-Jacques Rousseau,* ed. Bernard Gagnebin and Marcel Raymond, 4 vols. (Paris: Gallimard, 1959–1969, Bibliothèque de la Pléiade), vol. 3, p. 95.

3. Starobinski, *La Transparence et l'obstacle,* p. 341.

4. *The Social Contract: Essays by Locke, Hume, and Rousseau, with an Introduction by Sir Ernest Baker* (London: Oxford University Press, 1953), p. 254.

5. Ibid., p. 289.

6. *Jean-Jacques Rousseau: First and Second Discourses,* ed. Roger D. Masters (New York: St. Martin's Press, 1964), p. 162.

7. *Social Contract,* p. 291.

8. Ibid., p. 293.

9. Ibid., p. 298.

10. Ibid., p. 295.

11. See Bertrand Jouvenel, "Rousseau, The Pessimistic Evolutionist," *Yale French Studies,* 28 (1961–1962): 83–96.

12. *Social Contract,* p. 293.

13. J. Habermas, *Theory and Practice* (Boston: Beacon Press, 1974), p. 106.

14. Judith Shklar, *Men and Citizens. A Case Study of Rousseau's Social Theory* (Cambridge: Cambridge University Press, 1969), p. 216.

15. Benjamin Schwartz, "The Reign of Virtue: Some Broad Perspectives on

Leader and Party in the Cultural Revolution," *China Quarterly* (July-September 1968).

16. Upheaval in China

1. Lao Chu, "The People's Communes Making Progress," *Hung Ch'i* (February 1964).

17. On Filial Piety and Revolution

1. Richard H. Solomon, *Mao's Revolution and the Chinese Political Culture* (Berkeley: University of California Press, 1971).
2. Ibid., p. 28. Yet the question of the extent to which the traditional political order was "Confucian," and what this means precisely, is a question hotly debated among scholars.
3. Ibid., p. 29.
4. Ibid., p. 30. To the extent that Oedipus is a political parable in Freud, it does not provide an explanation of "individual autonomy," but explains the origins of repressive authority as a necessary ingredient of any high culture. To Freud, who never studied China, repressive authority seemed to be at the heart of all civilizations.
5. Ibid., p. 37.
6. It has often been pointed out in the American context that those who embody these "individualistic" virtues are often highly conformist in their moral and intellectual outlooks.
7. Solomon, p. 516.
8. One might think after reading Solomon that the *Classic of Filial Piety* is the most sacred text of China. Although it is important, it is not included within the canon of the Five Classics.
9. Solomon, p. 261.
10. It might be pointed out that Solomon reads back into the Hundred Flowers campaign and into the Great Leap Forward the kind of conflict between Mao and the party bureaucracy which only fully emerged in the Cultural Revolution. Indeed, during the Great Leap Forward, Mao still deeply believed that the party would be the instrument of his will. It was only after 1960 that Mao became fully convinced that the other party leaders represented "bourgeois revisionism" because of his differences with them on substantive issues.

Credits

Index

117, 118, 147, 149; in Analects, 152; and orthodoxy, 119

te, 146

Technology, 219–220, 224, 225, 233; material, 209; social, 208–209

Ten Commandments, 76

Teng Hsiao-p'ing. *See* Deng Xiaoping

Teng Ssu-yü, 5

Teng T'o, 240

Thailand, 160

Thales, 83

Theory *vs.* fact, 102–104

Third world, 158–159, 164, 165, 166, 238, 244

"Thought of Mao Tse-tung," 15, 182–183, 186, 189–207, 237, 240, 243

Three Dynasties, 132

Tiananmen Square, 257, 266–267

t'ien tao, 87, 91

Tito, 11, 12

Tokugawa Bakufu, 121

Totalitarianism, 116–117, 118, 124, 132, 133, 165, 259, 260, 261, 268; and modernization, 4; theories of, 3–4

Toulmin, Stephen, 194

Tradition, 7, 15, 16, 45, 46, 47, 125; and modernity, 45, 47–64, 225

Transcendence, age of, 65–68

Trotsky, 60, 197, 198

tsao-hua, 94

tsao-wu-che, 94

Tsou Yen, 87, 91

Tu Kuo-hsiang, 88

Tung Chung-shu, 82, 89, 91

Turgot, 177, 212, 219

United States: and China, 2, 157, 158, 206, 233, 236, 244, 263; and Vietnam, 163

Universal kingship, 66, 114–115, 128, 129, 168

Upanishads, 65, 67

Vedas, 67

Vietnam, 99, 155, 163, 166, 168; and China, 114, 158, 160, 161, 164, 233, 236, 237, 238

Voltaire, 52, 73, 177, 210, 212, 217

Wakeman, Frederick, 33

Wallerstein, Immanuel, 100, 112

Wang Chieh, 234

Wang Ch'ung, 91, 92, 93, 96

Wang Fu-chih, 89, 90, 91

Wang Kuo-wei, 55

Wang Yang-ming, 16, 21, 48, 82, 95, 96

War, guerrilla, 154, 158

Warring States, 87, 115

Wars of national liberation, 154, 155, 157, 158, 163

Weber, Max, 57, 109, 126, 188, 249; and area studies, 106; on bureaucracy, 50, 203; concept of capitalism, 110–111; concept of rationalization, 51, 66, 123, 137, 261; on Protestant ethic, 136, 183, 190, 211

wei, 115, 128

Wei Jingsheng, 266

Wei-chin period, 43

West, the, 46, 50, 57, 63, 95, 108; and Chinese thought, 58, 60, 64; culture of, 99, 112, 153, 244, 246, 254; ethical discourse in, 148; feudalism of, 121; individual autonomy in, 78–79, 80; and inequalities of power, 135–137; legal order in, 116; liberalism in, 61; revolution in, 59

Western Chou dynasty, 24

Whitehead, Alfred N., 45

Whorf, Benjamin, 105

Wittfogel, Karl August, 3, 20, 119, 260; *Oriental Despotism,* 97

Wittgenstein, Ludwig, 140, 145

World Federation of Trade Unions (WFTU), 155

The World of Thought in Ancient China (Schwartz), 17, 126, 150

World War I, 15

World War II, 1, 2, 10, 11, 98

wu, 90, 94

Wu Han, 237, 238–239, 240

wu hsing, 88, 89

wu wei, 93, 94, 151

Yang Ch'uan, 88

Yang Chu (Yang Zhu), 115

Yao, 185

Yenan, 9, 190, 191, 193, 194, 229, 232, 233, 238, 260

Yen Fu, 55, 57, 58, 191

yin/yang, 94

Yü, 185